Table Of Contents

Introduction

Welcome!

You are in for an eye-opening experience that may just knock you out of your socks.

This little journey with me is going to, if not shake you to your core, at least disturb you. Maybe even upset you. It certainly will snap you out of any complacency you may be in regarding your life.

When we're done here...when you're done reading this and listening to what I have to say, I am certain that you will never see the world the same ever again, and your life will change forever one way or another.

One of two things will happen.

Either you will awaken. And for perhaps the first time in your life, you will see things with a clarity and perspective that you could not have thought possible before you purchased my book.

Or, you will become a virulent enemy of my ideas, possibly despise me for them personally, and even take action to prevent me from spreading my message.

Either way, after understanding what I have to say to you, you will no longer be able to sit on the fence; you will have to make a clear choice of major impact in your life, consciously or subconsciously, about who you are, what you hold to be of value, and how you are going to behave from this point on.

I am not here to make you my friend. I am here to shake you up.

I make no apologies about it. That is my intent.

I am about Freedom and Individual Liberty. I am who I am and make apologies to no one for what I know to be true. And my job is to do my best to influence how you think.

Here is what I promise you are going to learn in this book:

First, you're going to learn about wealth:

- The fundamentals of wealth;
- What wealth is;
- Where it comes from;
- The awesome power of wealth; and, most importantly...
- Why your production, possession, and use of wealth is so crucial to you being a happy fulfilled human being.

As necessary context to the positive message that I have to give you, you will next learn about the greatest con and greatest lie ever perpetrated on we unsuspecting citizens— we hard-working innocent mortals out merely to provide for ourselves and our families—all the while being screwed and tattooed by those we literally entrust to protect us. If you remain ignorant of what is happening to our country, you remain part of the problem and things will only get worse for you, your kids, and your grand kids.

I will then teach you Twelve 'Secrets' of Wealth that in light of what you have learned about the Great Con and the Great Lie will just blow you away and probably make you first madder than hell, and then very hopeful about the future.

Next, using what you've already learned, you're going to learn how to get and keep that crucial 'abundance mentality' that many of the so-called personal development gurus talk about so much.

...and as part of that mentality, you'll learn how to defeat the negative influences in your life that you allow to rob you of your freedom and liberty. You will learn to not only utterly defeat those people and ideas that you have let keep you from being wealthy beyond your imagination, but as a secondary consequence of you gaining your freedom, you will in the same stroke be fighting for the rest of us as well...just as people like me are already fighting for you.

You will learn a personal code of conduct that will set your mind free, and give you the fortitude to unapologetically fight for what you want out of your life.

You will learn how to create and adopt your own awesome and inspiring vision of a possible world that will bring you wealth and happiness, and keep you in peace and harmony with your fellow man. The Vision you create will motivate you to literally crusade for your own personal welfare and of those you love and hold dear.

Finally, I will provide you with the steps of a personal plan of action for you to follow in your daily life. A plan that guides you, based on what you learn here in my book, on HOW to change in order to become happy, wealthy, and prosperous. It is one thing to know WHAT to do, but more important to know HOW to do what you have to do.

In summary, here is what you will learn from this book:

- The Fundamentals of Wealth;
- The Great Con and The Great Lie;
- How to get and keep that crucial 'Abundance Mentality';
- Twelve Secrets of Wealth;
- A Personal Code of Conduct;
- How to Create and Adopt your own Unique, Inspiring Grand Vision for your Life; and
- A Personal Plan of Action.

That's the roadmap of where we're going, broken down by section of this book. That's our roadmap to take you from where you currently are, in your utterly blind and confused state of affairs (only moderately kidding), to a place where the world and your place in it with other people makes perfect sense....certainly more sense than where you may be now.

That's my roadmap to take you to a world where there are no contradictions, no confusion, and where you will be convinced beyond doubt that unlimited possibilities abound for YOU, to whatever extent that you want them.

I will take you from a place where you may be experiencing a lack of happiness, a lack of wealth, a lack of an inspiring cause that drives your life — all possibly stemming from feelings of guilt, or from confusions and fears of what it would mean for you to be wealthy, and even resentment towards wealth...

...To a place where you happily produce, happily trade what you happily produce with others in harmony to mutual benefit, where your fellow man is not your enemy competing for the same limited supply of happiness out there, where your fellow man's gain is not your loss but your gain, and where peace and prosperity for every human on the plant is the norm, NOT the exception!

But before we delve into the meat of my message, let me say a couple of things.

First, you may ask who I am and why did I write this book? In answer, I'm just a regular Joe who's had questions from a young age and observed the world that I lived in, did some heavy duty questioning, reading, cogitating and soul searching, and went after answers that made simple common sense. You can learn more about me at the end of this book. I am not important. This book is not about me. The only thing that is important is that you benefit from internalizing my message.

So why did I write this book?

I wrote this book because it disturbs me greatly that the seemingly endless suffering of individual human beings all over the world goes on unabated...and that it doesn't have to be! It doesn't have to be like this! Living as a mortal being in a harsh physical world is hard enough and there is no good reason for all of the man-made suffering that is taking place throughout the world.

I absolutely refuse to accept that suffering, misery and premature death on such a grand scale as has existed throughout history has to be!

We CAN be better than this.

The issue that drives me is the role of wealth in human welfare and happiness. The role of wealth in YOUR welfare... your individual welfare and that of all of the other people like you and me out there.

You see, your psychological and physical welfare depends on producing wealth...on YOU producing wealth.

On you producing.

On you being productive.

Your psychological and physical welfare depends upon you consciously and emphatically not living the life of a parasite by sucking the blood from others who do produce wealth, while you contribute nothing or contribute less than what you are fully capable of.

Your own personal welfare depends, here, now, as you live, upon your ability and willingness to produce material stuff, which ultimately depends upon your personal world views and beliefs that either promote or destroy that ability in yourself, in your countrymen, and through your example, in your fellow world-citizens.

I feel that I have gained useful perspectives on life from a long school of hard knocks that are bound to be useful to others, who like me, are just putting one foot in front of the other in pursuit of a better life.

I have personally seen and felt the suffering both in my own life and in the lives of those around me that is caused by confusions and ignorance about the role of wealth.

I've also seen the joys and happiness that a healthy abundance mentality manifests in people's lives, and even the material wealth that it can lead to.

Essentially I feel that I can no longer in good conscience keep my discoveries to myself and thus I wrote this book as a first step to try to shake things up.

I simply have arrived at the point in my life that I can no longer remain silent and have written this book as a means to guide people who are searching for something more, from a place of lack and ambivalence about their lives to a place of empowerment, change, happiness in the present, and a much brighter future.

In a nutshell what motivates me is what this symbol still represents to me: the last great bastion of freedom in the world and the ideas that underlie the fundamental idea of freedom – of individual human liberty:

The second issue that I want to bring up before we start is that there are no real 'secrets' out there. What I have to say to you has been around for centuries... it's just that, odds are, nobody has ever compiled these ideas into one spot and explained them like I am about to do for you.

Does that surprise you?

No secrets?

There is nothing new under the sun, folks! The things I am about to teach you men have known since early times. Just nobody ever told YOU, at least not in any coherent manner, until now. Nobody ever put it together for you in a concise nutshell until now.

The truth is THERE ARE NO SECRETS to living a happy and fulfilled life!

There are just things you know, things you think you know but are mistaken about, and things you don't yet have any clue about.

Just like many people may not be savvy when it comes to investing, there is a tremendous amount of innocent ignorance out there regarding really basic, first-grade-level human nature, and why understanding and promoting the freedom to BE human at the most fundamental level is so crucial to your health and happiness.

There is no mystery to understanding the universe, or to understanding human nature and behavior, or to building wealth. And the really good news is that there are no secrets to being happy!

However, although these ideas have been espoused by the greatest minds throughout history, they may remain a secret to you, until now.

So come with me into that raucous, contentious, awe-inspiring arena of ideas and let's see if I can't stir up your soul and make you feel like fighting for your dreams again.

And for this little journey into ideas, I ask for a commitment up front.

Please stick with me and stay focused when you read this book and listen to my video presentations and check out the links. Expend the mental effort it takes to grow. You're a human being and you are supposed to grow your mind! Like any living thing, if you are not growing, you are dying, and this is especially true for us humans as the only living things that have a choice in the matter.

So don't take it lightly...read and listen when you have quiet time to focus your mind without distractions. It's going to take you many hours to go through this material the first time, so just commit to it now.

Take the time to consume the information in the links. They are there not because I am lazy. They are there because so many great minds have come before and instead of regurgitating their ideas or quoting them at-length excessively, you can simply get it directly from the horse's mouth into your brain without me standing in between.

My main job here is to provide a roadmap, context, and structure.

Also, I intentionally do not dumb down how I write. I strive to elevate my ability to communicate. You should too. I am imperfect and make mistakes, but I am what I am. If you don't understand something, don't be a lazy bum. Go look it up! Go do some additional research.

Commit to Growth!

If you can commit to doing this, I promise that you will not be disappointed.

If you can commit to doing this, I promise you will learn something of tremendous value to you.

Also, consume this book piecemeal. One chapter at a time.

Read a chapter and take a long break, then come back and read another.

The reason I say this is because much of the subject matter will be new to you. Much of the subject matter requires thinking at a level you are most likely not used to doing. Thus, it's best to expose yourself to it in manageable pieces so that your brain can cogitate on things subconsciously and chew on them for a bit before you go back for another bite.

Finally, THERE IS A REASON YOU PURCHASED MY BOOK. Odds are there is a pain in your life — an unsatisfied, unanswered, mystifying need that you have — and it has something to do with making your life matter. Of making your mark, of making a difference in the world before you die. If you want your life to matter, if you want to know why you are here and why you feel unfulfilled and even fearful or anxious about your life, heed what I have to say.

Make the mental effort it takes to grow!

To quote a famous powerful quote by T. S. Elliot,

> "We shall not cease from exploration, and the end of all our exploring will be to arrive where we started and know the place for the first time."

And with that let us begin….

Prologue

After years of thinking and cogitating on the ideas of great men and women who have come before, I have come to the conclusion that the key issue for all of us here on this little blue marble is happiness.

Brilliant right?

Yes, I understand that on the surface of it, this is almost ridiculously obvious. We all want to be happy. But what is not obvious for most of us is understanding, and more importantly internalizing, HOW to become and remain happy in spite of all the trials of life that we have to deal with day to day.

How to GET happy and STAY happy.

Some people are blessed and seem to be naturally good at it. For whatever reason: good genes, great upbringing and happy early life, or through just plain good luck, they seem to be naturally happy in their lives. If that is you, count your blessings, and if you have a generous soul, go share what you know.

Some of us have gone through maybe more than our share of crap and have to work at it a little harder.

Some of us have to work at it a lot harder...or at least it has seemed this way.

That's just life. We get knocked down and feel beat up by chance events in life. That's the way it is.

The key is to know HOW to become and remain happy in spite of what life throws at you. The actual steps. What you have to do and how you actually go about doing it. Knowing that if you do X and Y and Z then you will be happy...or at least in the grand order of things be a hell of a lot more likely to be happier than you were before.

If I can truly provide that for you, would it be of value? Would it be useful to you? Would it not be worth whatever you spent for this book?

Of course it would. It would be worth countless times what you paid for this little manuscript.

I have a basic view of living: If you are a good person with a good soul, what you truly require for your life will follow and happiness and joy will be yours. So be a good person with a great soul and be unafraid.

The challenge is HOW do you go about being a good person with a great soul, and be unafraid?

I am going to approach this from a bit of a different angle than most, but my approach is all part of "eating the elephant" called human happiness, personal fulfillment, and self-actualization.

From a very general point of view, one important

requirement for being happy that is bantered about so much these days is to be continuously grateful, to relish and cherish the simple things in life: loved ones, sunsets, health...having a simple place of beauty for you to go to recharge and re-center yourself as the base of your happiness.

True enough. I believe gratitude and beauty are necessary.

But being grateful is not enough. It is not a "sufficient condition" to being happy. Being grateful implies and originates in a certain outlook on life...a certain world view, where one is, at least intuitively and subconsciously, in tune with human nature and in consonance with the world around you.

You can be grateful for what you have in your life, and even momentarily happy, but by our nature – if we are healthy – we are normally not content...or certainly not content for very long. By our nature, even the simplest, least ambitious among us seeks more, yearns for more, desires more in order to continue to feel personally fulfilled. Human beings need variety, newness, and growth.

In how to deal with this yearning part of our nature lies the key to happiness.

This doesn't mean that we will automatically seek more of what is good for us. Oftentimes we do the opposite. I'm sure you can think of several instances where you have sought things that were detrimental to your mental or physical well-being. After all, you are human with all of your human frailties.

Although healthy human beings are still teleological creatures..."goal-oriented" creatures, we must actively consciously work to seek more of what is good for us, more of what is life-promoting. But once started, and once we are successful at consciously achieving what is good for us, the more we work to achieve more of what is good. Being creatures of habit, we will tend to always seek more.

I postulate that because of this, to be truly happy we must always, always, pursue a big dream that is unique to each of us and be productive in the pursuit of that dream, no matter how simple that dream may be for you or how difficult or easy it is for you to reach it.

So in this sense, I want to introduce this syllogism into your head as a start to rewiring your brain:

Your mental and physical welfare is the source of your happiness.

Being productive is the source of your mental and physical welfare.

Thus, you being productive is the source of your happiness.

This may sound like a stretch to you so follow me here.

The healthy physical state of your body and the healthy

psychological state of your mind is the source of your happiness because you ARE the emotions and feelings that you experience on a consistent basis, and your mental and physical state dictate how you feel.

I recall one of Tony Robbins quotes that made a profound impact on me:

"Your life is what you feel!"

I don't think he originated that thought, but it was how he said it that hit me.

He essentially said that the quality of your life is the quality of the emotions you experience on an on-going consistent basis. And if you can grasp this you are well on your way to understanding what you are going to learn.

Being productive (the process of creating material values) and producing wealth (material values), including **understanding and internalizing why you must be productive and hold the values and taking the rational actions that these imply**, is the source of your physical and psychological welfare.

Why? Because, as Dr. Leonard Peikoff puts it, for any healthy person, being productive is your central purpose in life (emphasis is mine):

> "Productiveness is not only a necessary element of a good life, it is the good life's central purpose....a central purpose is the long-range claimant on a man's time, energy, and resources. All his other goals, however worthwhile, are

secondary and must be integrated to this purpose. The others are to be pursued only when such pursuit complements the primary, rather than detracting from it....

There is only one purpose that can serve as the integrating standard of a man's life: productive work. The activity of productive work...incorporates into a man's daily routine the values and virtues of a proper existence. **It thus establishes his spiritual base**, the fundamentals that are the precondition of all other concerns: the right relationship to thought, to reality, to values. A man doing productive work is a man exercising his faculty of thought in the task of perceiving reality and achieving values. Such an activity is...inherently long-range: each phase of creative work endeavor makes possible the next, without limit. The producer moves through his days not in random circles, but in a straight line...motion from goal to farther goal, each leading to the next and to a single growing sum."

Nothing can replace productive work in this function... neither social relationships or recreational pursuits can replace it. Social relationships are an important value, but only within the appropriate context. First, a man must be committed to the development of his mind and must achieve the right relationship to reality. Then, as a form of reward, he can properly enjoy people (those who also achieve such a relationship and who share his values). **First he must be pursuing a productive purpose. Only then, as a complement to such pursuit, is he fit for love, parties, or a social life.**

You producing wealth (and by extension and association

selling wealth, servicing wealth, even just using wealth) by being productive is the source of your happiness because, as your central purpose, it is the long-range claimant on your time, energy, and resources which requires the values and actions of a proper existence... The necessity to "be productive" originates in what you choose as your core values. Producing, being productive, requires the values and actions necessary to live in a sound physical and psychological state of being. Being productive requires the core and derivative values and actions necessary to be happy and fulfilled.

You acting as a rational, integrated mind-body being, producing wealth in order to make your own life better, to increase your own enjoyment including of those that you love and cherish, is the source of true happiness.

Again...

As a healthy, rational, human being, you valuing things and acting to achieve the things you value—that is, producing for the sake of your own life, your own enjoyment—is the source of true happiness.

A corollary formulation to my syllogism above is this:

> *Because productivity IS the pursuit of material values, the pursuit of material values is the source of your happiness.*
>
> *Your values, both core and derivative, including material values, depend upon your world view, your mental outlook on*

life.

Thus, your happiness depends upon your world view and mental outlook on life – your mindset.

Producing wealth is the material manifestation of pursuing your mindset-dependent core values out in the physical world.

Thus, Happiness is living in accordance with your mindset-dependent core values.

This is what this book is all about.

Living your life in the pursuit of your values.

Living your life AS the pursuit of your values.

Life, living, and being productive is both value and virtue. We pursue values in order to Live; we do not live in order to pursue values.

Regardless of what you believe to be the ultimate source of human nature, the fact remains that to be happy you require the pursuit of values that promote your life, and by extension and association the lives of those you love and cherish.

This book is all about understanding these words and internalizing what they mean as a guiding creed by which to live your life. To rationally LIVE your life is to BE happy and fulfilled, unfettered by irrational nagging misgivings, disillusions, disappointments, anxieties, guilt, and fears.

I am about driving home the vital role of wealth, and the implied tenet of being productive, in elevating human welfare, YOUR individual welfare, beginning now, today, and by effect, the welfare of every man, woman and child that lives now or ever will live.

I am all about you understanding the fundamentals of wealth and the incredible productive power that YOU possess to change your life and the lives of the ones you love, and, incidentally, along with everyone else out there producing in their own way, the lives throughout the rest of the world.

Many of those I speak to tell me that they've never heard this before....

That's because we have all been conditioned to subconsciously hold a relatively negative mental outlook and world view, and thus to hold faulty and conflicting values that fail to guide, and actually mis-guide our daily actions.

This may sound like a strange approach to you because we've all been sold a bill of goods. So I ask you to accept this need for personal productivity for now and the rest of this book will explain in detail my position.

You see, we've been sold a way of looking at the world that defeats the very "sense-of-life" that is normally innate within us that would naturally compel us to create better lives for ourselves and the ones we love.

We've been cheated. We've been lied to. We've been conned.

We've been conditioned.

We've been conditioned NOT to think the way of individual liberty.

And the consequences of this conditioning are earth-shaking and totally perverse.

I almost feel a need to apologize for what follows, but to get my point across you MUST understand why we are where we are, in what I can best describe as a dysfunctional society.

For decades, while we as citizens of this country have been busting our asses to build an American dream for ourselves, politicians and their puppet masters have sold us a line of crap (bull-doogy as my daughter would say), a way of economic life...a social system, a faulty world-view, that is absolutely contrary and diametrically opposed to our very core nature as human beings. One that literally destroys our innate optimistic sense-of-life.

They have sold us (and we have accepted) a way of economic life that is the very source of the evils that continually rape this country: evils ranging from embarrassing unemployment to the ridiculously huge prison population; from the never-ending war on drugs to the never-ending war on poverty; from immigration problems to ever-increasing racial tensions; from the throngs of welfare recipients to the throngs of unwed teenage moms to the legions of divorcees; from the Vietnam War, Somalia, Iraq, Afghanistan, Syria, and Ukraine to the NSA, CIA, DEA, TSA, from Common Core to your own local militarized police department...to mention but a few.

The state of affairs that we currently have in this country is now only a small step or two removed from the absolute horrors of the implementation of the ideas of the Hitlers, Stalins, Mao Tse-Tungs, Pol Pots, Kim Jung Ils, and all other 'successful' dictators of the world—the anointed ones of that ultra-special cadre of "them that know"...them that see.

Aside from natural disasters over which man historically has had no control, my contention is that the tremendous amount of human suffering and death that has occurred since man has recorded his history is the result of small groups of men seeking to control the lives of all other men, pretty much because they think they know a better way for other men to live.

When all that was ever needed was for men to leave other men alone in freedom to pursue their lives in mutual respect and harmony.

In a word, some men always want to control how others live in a society, for reasons of religious beliefs or political ideals, but always for ideas.

I do not apologize that this sounds simplistic. It is accurate.

Pleasant? No.

Simple? Yes.

Let's take a walk back into history for a moment or two. Take a look around at this website:

20th Century Deaths from Major Wars, Oppressions, and Atrocities

Now let me recap it for you. Here are the military and civilian deaths, by major dictators, resulting wars, and other social upheavals that occurred during the 20th century (1900-2000):

Deaths Greater than 5 Million

Congo Free State (1886-1908):   **8,000,000**

First World War (1914-1918):   **15,000,000**

Russian Civil War (1917-1922):   **9,000,000**

Soviet Union, Stalin's regime   **20,000,000**
(1924-1953):

Second World War (1939-45):   **66,000,000**

People's Republic of China, Mao   **40,000,000**
Zedong's regime (1949-1975):

Deaths Between 1 and 5 Million

Mexican Revolution (1910-1920):   **1,000,000**

1st Chinese Civil War, Nationalist   **5,000,000**
Era (1928-1937):

Post-War Expulsion of Germans from East Europe (1945-1947):	**2,100,000**
2nd Chinese Civil War (1945-1949):	**2,500,000**
Korean War (1950-53):	**3,000,000**
North Korea Communist Regime (1948 et seq.):	**3,000,000**
Rwanda and Burundi (1959-1995):	**1,350,000**
Second Indochina War (1960-1975):	**4,200,000**
Ethiopia (1962-1992):	**2,000,000**
Nigeria (1966-1970):	**1,000,000**
Bangladesh (1971):	**1,250,000**
Cambodia, Khmer Rouge (1975-1978):	**1,650,000**
Afghanistan (1979-2001):	**1,800,000**
Sudan (1983-2005):	**1,900,000**
Kinshasa Congo (1998 et seq.):	**3,800,000**

...Are you getting the picture?

I won't keep the list going...you can read the website yourself. But if you total all such deaths in the 20th century, the best approximation of total dead is 203 million, with an upper estimated limit of close to 260 million people.

To help put this number in context here are some death tolls from other things you might normally perceive as injustices such as smoking, racism, disease, etc.

Other Death Tolls

Smallpox in the 20th Century:	300 million
Smoking (1930-1999):	71 million
Influenza Pandemic (1918-1919):	20 million +
AIDS (1981-1998):	11.7 million
Murders Worldwide (1900-1999):	8.5 million
Natural Disasters (2oth Century):	3.5 million
Natural Disasters (since 1000 A.D.):	15 million
Racism (U.S. 1900 – 1970):	3.3 million

So, 203 million people in the 20th Century alone.

Then add another 500,000 for the 21st Century to-date.

Then add another 80 million for the 19th century and another 15 million for the 18th century from approximately the time of the formation of the ideals embodied in the US Constitution and the Bill of Rights (for reasons that will be clear later).

In all, we arrive at a close approximation of 300 million, with an upper estimate of 360 million dead human beings.

THREE HUNDRED MILLION HUMAN BEINGS wiped out in the last 300+ years.

NOT because of natural death, but ultimately because of ideas anathema to, of ideas opposed to and even destructive of, human welfare and happiness.

That's the equivalent of the combined present-day populations of Los Angeles basin and New York City wiped out eleven times over. Seventeen times just for the LA basin alone.

...the equivalent of wiping out the entire population of southern California thirteen times!

...The entire present day population of the United States— wiped out.

Standing shoulder to shoulder, that's a line of people stretching around the earth over 4 ½ times at the equator!

... That's three thousand full 100,000-fan football stadiums— wiped out.

These people died from direct military action, outright wholesale slaughter, and directly-related disease or starvation. They died unimaginably horrible, brutish, painful deaths. Certainly some sizable percentage of these were children; if a mere 1%, that's 3,000,000 children forever deprived not only of pure innocence and happiness of childhood, but of any chance at a long and prosperous contributing life.

Ultimately all died because of the competing beliefs and ideas of one group of men against another as to the nature of man and how man should live with other men.

I am sorry to be morbid here, but you simply MUST understand that ideas do matter!

These were people like you and me with real lives and families. Can you not imagine that these people to one degree or another had real hopes and aspirations of possibly living good and happy and prosperous lives to whatever extent that was possible in their day and age?

Do you not think that only some very small percentage of these people were outright war mongers?

All because some men wanted to control how others live.

Now listen to me here: Those same desires to control others burn bright in the breasts of a lot of evil people who are alive and well and active today in attempting to control how each of us lives, now, in our own contemporary society.

Do you get the hint that what I have to say to you is deadly serious?

What we have as a social system is NOT what we have been told we have, and this is a very, very bad thing and becoming worse by the day.

We have been told we are capitalist. That we live in a capitalist society. That what we have is capitalism. And that because of the supposed problems that capitalism causes because of alleged inherent flaws of capitalism, capitalism is a very bad thing.

Folks, what we have is NOT capitalism. **The world has not yet seen Capitalism!**

What we have for a society is a disaster managed by men who if not simply misguided by their ignorance must be horrifically evil, and who are driving us all into an abyss.

But the great news, the AWESOME news, is that it doesn't have to be this way!

....and, incredibly, tragically, certainly for the last century or two, it never had to be this way! The pain and agony and untold suffering of tens of millions of innocent men, women, and children just in the more recent past literally never had to happen!

Thankfully, there is still time to change things.

There IS a way out of this mess. In fact, it's the ONLY way out of this mess.

And no, I am not talking about God coming down from the heavens and smiting evildoers. And I am certainly not talking about religion or faith in an angelic afterlife. Both have been around for the duration of all the mass killing from the time man first walked the earth to the present....and NOTHING has changed. One or another version of "God" or "State" has been the very source of most of the suffering and death through all the centuries past! If you want to say that God is the source of what I am about to tell you in the pages below, fine. But that God has to be one that gave man the power to create peace and happiness and prosperity on his own, and who has told us in his very act of creating us: "Fix your own damned problems that you created by denying and attempting to destroy the very nature I have given you! Until you do, you deserve the suffering you experience."

I told you at the beginning above that you will either hate what I have to say, or it will resonate and you will come of the dark. You will make a choice: either I am full of bull-doogy, or there is tremendous merit in what I say.

There IS a realistic and simple way out that we humans can create that literally benefits everyone living and anyone who will ever live again. There is a way for us as Men to create an incredibly beautiful garden on this rock where you and your loved ones and their loved ones will prosper and partake of all of the wonderful goodness and utter joy that is possible.

But for you to prosper and benefit those you care about, and as a secondary consequence literally save the world...you have to change.

YOU have to change. You have to change NOW. And for you to change, you have to look at the world a whole different way.

And to do that often takes a tremendous amount of courage.

"For evil to be powerless, good men must be unafraid."

CHAPTER ONE

What Nobody Ever Taught You about Money, Stuff, and Happiness

The 'Secret' to Life and Living Well

"True happiness comes from deeds done well, the zest of creating things new"

-Antoine de Saint-Exupery

"If you want to live a happy life, tie it to a goal, not people or things"

-Albert Einstein

"The man who will use his skill and constructive imagination to see how much he can give for a dollar, instead of how little he can give for a dollar, is bound to succeed"

-Henry Ford

What Is Wealth?

To start our journey I want to spend some time talking about wealth. This all may sound formal and esoteric and too "economic" at first, but it is crucial that you understand the nature of wealth if you want to live a happy and fulfilled life in harmony with your fellow man.

If you want to live a happy life, acknowledge and value the importance of wealth...

So what is Wealth?

Very simply, wealth is material values made by man—it is physical goods.

Wealth is the physical products out there that were made by us humans, both products made for immediate consumption like cars and macaroni and cheese dinners, and products made for the purpose of making more products, like tractors and assembly lines.

It is all of the man-made physical stuff that you or anyone else possesses that satisfies our very human needs and wants.

It is your clothing; it is your house and all of the physical things in your house; it is the landscaping around your house, the plumbing and sewer lines under your house; the power and communication lines running into your house; it is your car, your computers, TVs, cell phones, wristwatches, eyeglasses, Google glasses, and Apple Watches.

Wealth is buildings and roads, bridges and tunnels; the power plants and power distribution systems that send electricity virtually everywhere; wealth is the water and the water system that brings water to you, and the sewer systems that take away your waste; it is the all of the produce, meat, dairy and prepackaged products in your grocery store; it is all of the medicines and medical technology.

Wealth is the Hoover Dam, the space station, and the Large Hadron Collider. Wealth is gardens, and parks, and to the extent modified or rearranged or made accessible by man, national parks and monuments, waterways, beachfronts and boardwalks.

From the time of early man, wealth has progressed from holes scraped out of the ground, grass huts, spears, fire-making materials, bone and shell jewelry, and animal skins to the wheel, swords, to gunpowder and muskets, horse-drawn plows and buggies, and flint-lock rifles, to light bulbs, refrigeration, automobiles, black and white TVs, microwave ovens, MRI machines, space rockets and satellites, tanks and cruise missiles, graphene, and the latest physical manifestations of any recent high- or low-technology you care to name.

Contrarily, a rock or a stretch of land or a plant is not wealth until a man values it and controls it for the purpose of meeting a human need.

Wealth is NOT money (more on this later). Nor is it stocks, bonds, or any other similar intangible asset; at most these are all claims to wealth. And while actual wealth may decay and become dilapidated or worn out or obsolete, it has none of the potentially evaporative characteristics of these mere claims.

Wealth is material goods made by man.

Ok, so what?

Life Without Wealth

So what!?

Without wealth you cannot live. You cannot exist. You would not be here.

Without producing, without being productive, you cannot be happy.

Wealth is as vital to your existence as a living human being as the air you breathe. Without wealth you would live a short, brutish life if you make it through birth at all, and then you would quickly die. Whether you were born in the first century or last week, the extent of your life without wealth would be the first few moments or hours or maybe even days after you leave your mother's womb, after which time you would simply starve or succumb to disease or the elements and perish, all in a state of terrible physical pain.

Are you getting this?

To live at all while you are young you must have access to wealth and be supported by the wealth of your parents. To live a happy and fulfilling life as an adult, you must create, possess, and use a far greater amount of wealth than that required merely to subsist as an infant or child.

And that's just to survive as a healthy human being. To the extent you really want to enjoy your life, you require vastly more amounts of wealth in your life.

My position is that to be truly happy and fulfilled as an adult you must produce...meaning: you must create wealth directly, or sell, or service, or in a domestic capacity, use the wealth of others.

The world revolves around the production and use of wealth. You cannot escape it.

No matter what your political affiliation, you cannot escape the fact that your very life depends on the existence, possession, and use of wealth, and that all other things being equal, the greater the degree of wealth that you create, possess and use, the longer, healthier and happier you will live.

If you are a mentally balanced person, almost intuitively grasp that the production, ownership, and use of wealth is the means to living a full life in happiness, here, now, in the physical world where you have no choice but to reside.

Do you doubt what I say? Ever heard of Maslow's Hierarchy of needs? Take a look....

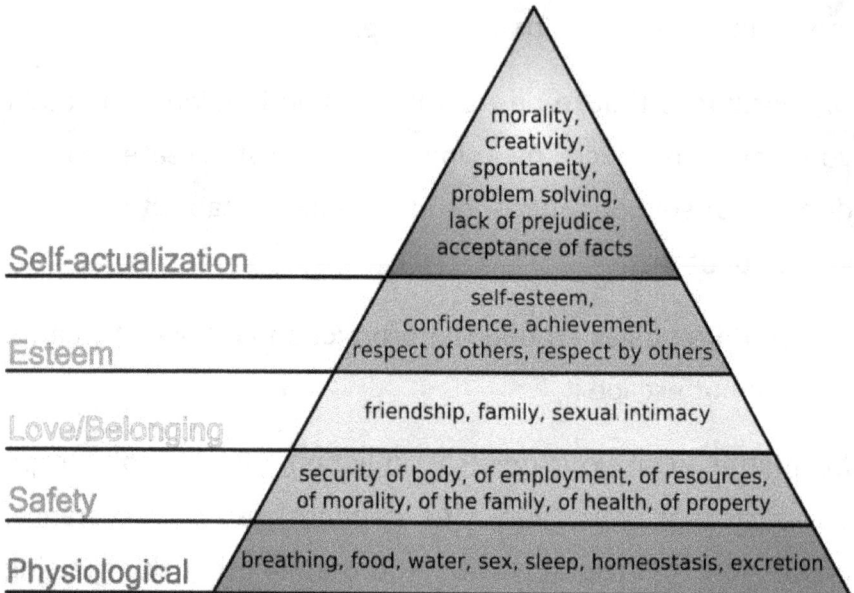

Maslow's hierarchy of needs pyramid with levels from bottom to top: Physiological (breathing, food, water, sex, sleep, homeostasis, excretion); Safety (security of body, of employment, of resources, of morality, of the family, of health, of property); Love/Belonging (friendship, family, sexual intimacy); Esteem (self-esteem, confidence, achievement, respect of others, respect by others); Self-actualization (morality, creativity, spontaneity, problem solving, lack of prejudice, acceptance of facts).

Maslow basically says that basic survival needs always trump high level needs if they are not satisfied first. If you think about it, your need for wealth would appear to be the most critical in the satisfaction of physiological and safety needs than for love, esteem or self-actualization needs. After all, without your life and safety, nothing else matters, right? Well, you would be correct, but only when you are living at that bare level of existence where your very life hangs in the balance.

My contention is that as you satisfy more basic needs, the higher level needs awaken and your need to satisfy them predominates, each in their turn (safety, love, esteem, then self-actualization). But at each stage the ownership and use of wealth is as vital to your well-being at that stage of existence as it was back when you were starving and looking for someplace to spend the night out of the cold.

And I stipulate that your higher level needs are better fulfilled the higher the degree of wealth employed at that level in terms of quality and quantity of wealth.

For example, of course you can have friendship and love when you are poor and possess little in terms of material possessions, but can you deny, that other things being equal (the basis and quality of your friendship or love remains unchanged) the more wealth that you and your friends possess, the far greater is the range and intensity of experiences you can both enjoy? Are you not far more likely to enjoy traveling throughout the Caribbean with your family and friends than sitting huddled around a smoky open dung-fire in a one-room cardboard and plywood shack in shanty town?

It really does not take much imagination to understand that ALL of your needs ultimately depend upon the ownership or use of wealth, and the more wealth employed in the satisfaction of any level of Maslow's needs, the richer your experiences, the fuller your life, and the happier you are likely to be.

Ok, the world is happier with wealth than without, but, you say to yourself consciously or subconsciously, "I can simply mooch off others who produce...that way I will have access to and use all the wealth that I personally need to live comfortably and enjoyably...why should I make the effort to produce? Let someone else do it."

Because you cannot be happy if you do not produce, and your level of enjoyment of what life you do experience would always, necessarily, be limited. You can fake it, you can cheat and steal and parasite your way through life, but when you're alone with yourself and turn your thoughts inward, and genuinely face yourself with intellectual honesty, you are nothing but fear and an empty shell skating on the thin ice of an emotional breakdown till death takes you. You are NOT happy. You are not even a man or woman anymore. What happiness you experience is shallow and meaningless. By stealing from those who do produce, you actively work to destroy their desire to produce and ultimately you and/or your progeny will be left holding the bag.

But I'm not talking to the career parasites out there. They cannot see. They are essentially dumbed-down dead-enders. Nor am I talking to the elites of the world. They are all human beings that I and others like me cannot reach. I am speaking to those who have some remnant of manhood left in them and who know in their core that things are not right with the world and that there must be a better way...

If you are not happy with your life, odds are it's because you do not focus your mind and you are not productive because you hold confusions, uncertainties, and guilt about wealth.

You fear the inability to create wealth for yourself in your life, and thus create self-imposed limitations on your happiness and ability to fully enjoy your life. You may even resent wealth and those who are productive and do have it, for no other insane reason than that they do. You may be living as an unwitting parasite without fully understanding what you are.

The best definition of man, man the species, that I have found, is "the rational animal." However.....man, in this day and age, in practical everyday life, has become the unhappy irrational animal, because he has forgotten or never learned what it means to be MAN. He has forgotten how to demand, and to fight if necessary, to be left alone to BE a man, with the greater part of a real man's character being that of the producer.

Is this too strong for you? Too "intellectual?"

Buck up.

Learn.

Grow.

Where Does Wealth Come From?

Survival-Thrive Motive

Wealth comes from the productive genius of the individual mind or the collaboration of individual minds in the reshaping of the physical world around us into material, physical values that serve us in the maintenance, extension, and enjoyment of our lives.

Wealth comes from the creative genius of the minds of individual men. Wealth is created by individuals to satisfy purely selfish individualistic needs.

In this respect we are not like lower level animals (unlike a lot of nut jobs out there I do not equate the value of the life of my daughter to that of a bacterium, a lizard, a monkey, or a dolphin).

Animals, as creatures confined to the perceptual level of awareness, automatically respond to stimulus in their environments; they automatically act in response to stimulus in the only way that their nature allows them. They are hungry? They chase and kill other animals or eat grass. That's the extent of their mental process. They just DO in response to their simple nature. There is no thinking or choosing about it.

Man is different in that because he has an advanced conceptual consciousness, his unique level of awareness, he must first decide to react to stimulus, and he must choose how he reacts...he must choose what he wants and then discover what he must do to get what he wants. And to do what he wants, he must act out there in the physical world, and to act in the physical world to accomplish what he wants, he must create wealth.

You cannot escape this.

No matter what manner of magical, mystical utopia you can imagine, somebody somewhere has to create the material values that make your little utopia possible.

Even the caveman had to rearrange the physical world around him just to have the simple wealth of clothing, of a cave or hut, of a fire, and some means of bringing down wild game or collecting wild edibles.

The only difference between the material needs of a caveman and yours is that the technological progress that men have created over the centuries has enabled us to satisfy our needs far better. Men building on the ideas of previous men has resulted in a higher standard of living that permits you the elevated comforts of a life that the caveman most happily would have accepted and enjoyed if he had only been capable of producing them.

You must grasp something here as an inherent part of the

fundamental nature of man and natural order of the universe. And that is that man is meant to be productive... and when he is left alone, guess what? He produces and he produces like he is possessed.

The Individuality of Wealth

To repeat, wealth comes from the creative genius of the minds of <u>individual</u> men. Wealth is created by individuals to satisfy purely selfish individualistic needs.

Wealth comes from people like you and me.

Wealth ultimately comes from ideas and the guiding, directing intelligence of a single man's mind that directs his actions in forming, reforming, shaping, rearranging, and molding the physical world around him to turn into reality, to make real, to create a physical manifestation of, to create a product from, that which previously only existed as an idea.

Don't ever get sucked in to the nonsense about the 'collective mind' or 'society' or government agencies, or even companies creating wealth. As a physics professor of mine used to say, "That's a bunch of hooey." All wealth, the creation of all physical products, must first be undertaken by individual minds. Always and everywhere; there are no exceptions! Individual men may collaborate and do so to an extreme extent in industrialized societies, but every aspect of the conceptualization, design, and production process of a product can only take place in an individual mind. Men may think alike and from communication hold the same ideas and concepts and take similar and synergistic action, but always, and necessarily, the formulation of those ideas and concepts, and the taking of action MUST be formulated by and taken by individuals, no matter how complex the process or product.

Groups and tribes and governments and "collectives" do not create wealth.

This is the way things are.

A man is a man. You are a separate and distinct beast motivated by your own survival. You are not a physically integrated cog in some imaginary collective machine.

Think with me for a minute here....and this is critically important for later...

If you go outside, pick a wildflower and give it to your child, that wildflower has become wealth in the form of a gift to satisfy your purely selfish individual human need for giving—giving a gift to your child for the sole purpose of the emotional high that you receive from seeing the child enjoy her gift. In this simple form of wealth, YOU conceptualized the use of the flower and YOU took the action to turn that flower into wealth. Your mind-generated intent and physical action created the wealth character of an otherwise useless object.

We may not actually think this way consciously, but this is in fact what we do.

The process is no different for the creation of more complex wealth like, for example, a turbine in a hydroelectric power plant. You may be the first to conceptualize a new widget for a turbine to make it run more efficiently, or whatever. You may then communicate this to an associate so that he understands it as exactly as you do. But the fact is that your mind created the idea of the improvement, and in-turn, the associate also had to form the concept of the widget on his own by learning from you. He may in turn add to or modify the concept to make it better, and he does so being the originator, the creator, of that modification.

It's even more so for actually producing the gizmo and turning it from an idea to a concrete physical thing in reality: whatever individual men or women are involved in the production process, they must take actions to produce the gizmo individually...either they all take the same actions and run the same machines in a parallel production process where several components are produced side-by-side at the same time, or they all take different specialized actions in a linear production process that produces only one component at a time.

They cannot physically all drive the same screw at the same time.

Something as physically complex as taking three men to the moon was a massive 'collective' effort, but only in the sense that it was a collection and sequence in time of the thoughts and physical actions of a whole bunch of individual scientists, engineers, manufacturers, suppliers, administrators, etc., etc.

This applies to any human endeavor you care to think about. **Nothing happens collectively. Everything happens individually. Individuals experience...groups, associations, companies, or tribes do not. This is super critical to understand because producing IS a purely individual thing!**

Thinking, valuing, and acting on those thoughts and values is INDIVIDUAL. Individuals think. Individuals value. Individuals act. Individuals LIVE. Contrary to pronunciations of our politicians, that's the way it is.

By god, as the individual guiding directing intelligence of your business, you DID build that!

Ok, so wealth comes from individuals and the collaboration of individuals. So what? How does one actually get 'rich'? How do I actually acquire wealth? How do I get wealthy? How do I amass the bounty in material goods that I want for my life?

Well, you have taken the first step in respecting what wealth IS and where it comes from.

How Do People Get Wealthy?

Want some great news?

Whether you are a business-owner or businessman, or a wage-earning employee, provided you are left free to do so, you can get flat out stone wealthy; whatever wealth means to you...whatever amount of wealth is important to you.

I'll break it down both ways... but ultimately the path is the same.

From the business owner's perspective: Driven by the desire to produce and the motivation to profit (ultimately by the desire to live well) businessmen get wealthy by selling a quality product or service that consumers want for more money than it costs to make the product or service, then SAVING more of that money than they consume, INVESTING those savings in their own business or through the businesses of others, and REPEATING the process!

From the wage-earner's perspective: Driven by desire to produce (ultimately by the desire to live well), employees get wealthy by producing and providing value to the businessman, trading their time and labor in earning a wage, SAVING more of that wage than they consume, and then INVESTING through the businesses of businessmen, possibly earning a higher-paying job (or becoming a business owner themselves), and repeating the process.

Here are some words of wisdom from Rick Rule of Sprott Asset Management, when queried on some of the characteristics he felt would lead to becoming rich (my editorial comments):

> *"Not focusing on becoming rich is one. Focusing on delivering value. You gain utility by providing utility. Simply put, if you make rich people richer, they will make sure that you get rich.* (If you improve the lives of a lot of people who are not necessarily rich, you still become rich.) *So I think [it's] doing something that you love that adds value to other people, so that your work isn't work. It's something that you can't help but do.*
>
> *People look at me and tell me I'm an extraordinarily hard worker. The truth is in a conventional sense, that is with regards to my vocation as an obligation, I've never worked a day in my life. I've only had fun.*
>
> *I have expended a hell of a lot of energy having fun and I've made stupendous sums of money, but it has to do with the fact that I really like what I'm doing. So it's very easy to add utility for others because it's like playing for me.*
>
> *The second thing is that particularly earlier in your career, you must be thrifty. You can't be a capitalist if you don't have capital and if what you want out of money is bass boats or fancy clothes or vacations, you're doomed to being upper middle class at best.*
>
> *If what you want with money is to make money, as opposed to spend money, what you learn is that compounding*

interest is truly the eighth wonder of the world, but you can't enjoy compounding interest if you don't have any principal.

So to become rich, one must save and one must save absolutely ruthlessly, absolutely ruthlessly. One must save every paycheck. One can't defer savings. One can defer and must defer spending but you cannot when you're early in life defer savings."

Folks it is literally that simple!

Part of my message to you is that anyone who can think can get wealthy to whatever degree they are capable. And what ultimately determines your ability to acquire wealth is the value that you provide to the world....that is, your contribution.

There is no metaphysical reason that you cannot be wealthy to your heart's desire! What I mean by this is that there is no reason, out there in the physical universe as any matter of natural law in the natural cause and effect nature of things that this cannot happen for you or anyone who has the ability to think and act and who is left free to do so.

However, what CAN stop you, other than the completely acceptable uncontrollable random misfortunate occurrences of the physical universe, assuming that you have the desire, is the intentional interference of other men acting on anti-human ideas....principally those in government.

Another key ingredient to getting wealthy is to stop doing stuff with your money that keeps you in relative poverty.

Study this graph:

The rich hold assets, the poor have debt
Household wealth by percentile (% gross assets)

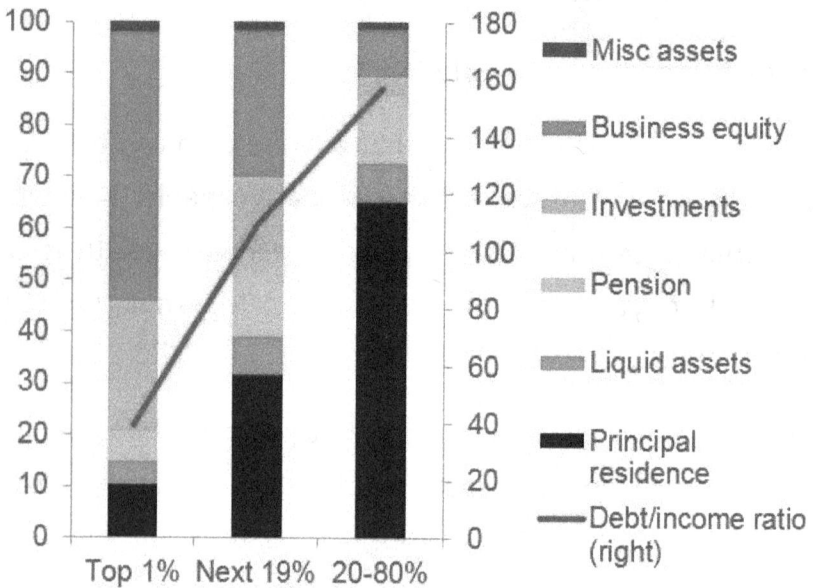

Source: Recent trends in household wealth in the United States, E.N.Wolff, Levy Economics Institute, March 2010.

Do the things that rich people do with their money and stop following the crowd and keeping up with the Joneses!

I will spend much more time on exactly how getting wealthy is done and how "making money" and "getting wealthy" is possible, and what interferes with you getting wealthy, in a minute or two so hang in there with me while we lay some more foundation...

Why Should I Care?

Ask yourself: "Ok, even if I accept what you say about the vital role of wealth and how to get wealthy, why should I care? I get the point, wealth is important. Ok. Sure… But what if I don't want to BE wealthy? What if I don't care if anyone else gets wealthy or not…. And what if I actually think some people are way TOO wealthy and need to be cut down a notch or two or ten? Why should I care one more iota about what you have to say about it?"

In a word, because if you don't, then you are actively intentionally working to add to the pain and suffering in the world by detracting from those who do care, and in my opinion you are no kind of Man.

Getting that off my chest, logically there are four main reasons that you should care—not only should you care enough to read on and finish this book, but start to fight in whatever way you can to promote and protect a truly capitalist society.

Here are the four reasons which I will address in greater detail below:

1. Lack, principally a lack of wealth, is a major source of unhappiness in most people's lives; odds are that you are not satisfied with your life because of a lack of wealth, and all that this implies;

(Take note...and all that this implies including your psychological makeup...more on this later)

2. 'Being wealthy" is relative. Relative in the sense of being purely selfish. You're crazy if you give a flying flip what anyone else possesses except as a possible source of additional inspiration-motivation. Much animosity towards wealth and the rich stems from feelings of not being 'good enough' to produce what somebody else has. You should care about building wealth in your own life because we are talking about YOUR life, and only your life, about what YOU want and need for YOUR happiness and welfare, irrespective of the needs or wants or desires of any of the other 7 billion people on the planet!

3. You can't get wealthy in a vacuum. The production of wealth, and thus the sheer availability of it, and thus your ability to acquire or create it and use it for your benefit, whatever your desired level of benefit is, doesn't happen automatically. In fact, if certain attitudes towards wealth persist in society as they to today, what wealth does exist will simply go away. You cannot escape that your long-term creation, accumulation of and retention of wealth, YOUR personal welfare, VITALLY DEPENDS upon what you and your

fellow man thinks and does.

Which leads us to the most important reason...

4. Being wealthy is a mindset, and getting wealthy and living with wealth is a journey. Producing wealth IS living. Living IS producing. The quality of your experiences, and thus your on-going emotional health which are largely determined by your physical comfort, IS your life! The quality of your life depends upon your acquisition and use of wealth, whatever the level or quality that YOU desire.

Let me address each of these below in more detail.

First, Purpose is All.

All other things being equal, meaning all other lesser needs in your life's hierarchy of needs being relatively squared away, like many of us, you are probably not feeling fulfilled in your life because you have no Cause. You have no central purpose. What I mean is that you either do not have wealth, or do not have your desired level of wealth, because you are ambivalent about it, or even fear it and hate it because of the confusions and faulty values that you hold about what wealth and the creation of wealth means.

And you are likely not even conscious that you feel this way.

Because of these personal failings regarding wealth and its value to your life, you are not motivated to be productive. You don't produce. You don't seek to create value. You have no cause. You have no reason to produce. You have no driving reason to produce beyond maybe the immediate satisfaction of mundane daily needs through a J.O.B. that you likely hate...

You are afraid to try. There is too much uncertainty for you.

You currently may not possess the ability to get up in the morning with an internal fire that burns in you and drives you to happily and eagerly attack the day and blow through all obstacles on your way to your goals and dreams.

But you see, that drive, that burning, that need to pursue a purpose, is the natural state of a man. Not fear and loathing and uncertainty and anxiety and pain and lack. No! That burning in your soul is what is natural...that craving to be something. To be somebody. For YOU to be somebody. To matter. For your own personal, totally selfish reasons...for the literal health of your soul, to BE something...to

CREATE something, and to call it your own, and to feel a tremendous amount of heart-swelling pride that YOU created it! Whether you be a housewife or a gazillionaire real estate mogul, the need is the same.

Some out there know exactly what I am talking about. Some get it and are already out there fighting the good fight. Some already know what it means to swing for the fences.

Some may be beaten down and suffering, but their soul still screams: I AM! I LIVE! MY LIFE MATTERS! I DESERVE TO BE HAPPY AND I AM WILLING TO DO WHATEVER IT TAKES FOR AS LONG AS IT TAKES TO MAKE A LIFE THAT I DESERVE AND THAT I AM PROUD OF!

And then, some have secretly given up doing anything truly meaningful with their lives. Someone somewhere along the way may have stolen this from them (hint: it wasn't guys like me).

The good news is that, if you never had it, you can find it. You can discover it. If you had it at one time and lost it, you can get it back. It's easier than you think.

Is this stuff making sense to you?

Second, wealth is relative.

Assuming that you understand and have a healthy desire of wealth for yourself, your desired level of wealth is as unique to you as your fingerprints. No one else on the planet desires the things that you want, certainly not in the order, location, timeframe, or most importantly, for the reasons that you want. You should not give one iota of care as to the desired level of wealth of anyone else on the planet! They are not YOU, and the creation of your wealth only involves others to the extent that their productivity undertaken for their perfectly selfish reasons necessarily enhances yours.

To the extent you actually partner with others outright, then their productive abilities directly affect and contribute to your level of wealth. However, your desires for wealth are YOUR desires, and no one else's. A favorite philosopher of mine said something to the effect that "An independent man is as alone in a crowd as on a desert island." Independence is a primary human virtue. Be an independent man. Don't link your desires and expectations and successes to those of others! Don't measure your dreams and goals and aspirations and successes by those of others—except purely as a source of inspiration.

Now, your desired level of wealth is still wealth. And all of the vitality and importance to wealth that I mentioned earlier still applies with respect to YOUR life...the only one that matters to you.

Whatever degree of wealth you desire to accumulate is as critical to your existence as mine is to mine. If your true desire is only to possess the 'low-budget accommodations of a monk' (ala Mother Teresa), then likely their possession is as convenient and helpful, as burden-relieving, or as relaxing to your life as my possessions are to mine. And their lack is as much of a source of cause for your actions as my lack is to mine. If I truly want something that I lack, I get out and find a way to get it.

If you are mentally sound, you will do the same.

Third, you can't do it alone.

Although exceedingly independent, no productive man is an island. Your material welfare and happiness depends upon the life-promoting motivation and productive abilities of your fellow man and the willingness of your fellow men to voluntarily trade with you and with each other to mutual benefit. You need other men in a social atmosphere that is conducive to each individual man being free to be as productive as he is capable.

You can't easily accumulate wealth, and you certainly won't keep wealth, in a society whose population is largely laden with ideas that are fundamentally opposed to the individual production of wealth and individual productivity—as time goes on in such a society, there is literally less and less wealth to BE accumulated!

Fourth, being wealthy is a mindset and getting wealthy is a journey.

I have touched on this previously and this is the principal focus of this book.

As someone once said, "you don't trade being poor for being rich; you trade being poor for being on the road to being rich."

There is a ton of wisdom in that.

Getting wealthy is 10% the mechanics of business and investing, and 90% mental. Maybe even 5%-95%. The 95% is Mindset. The 95% is the mindset of the producer. The 95% is the mindset of the independent man.

Getting wealthy has everything to do with how you look at the world and what is possible.

Getting wealthy, whatever your desired level of wealth is, depends upon your desire to provide value to others and upon your ability and willingness to produce through the pursuit of your central purpose, which of course depends on the values you hold, which in turn depends upon how you think and what you think about, which in turn depends upon your fundamental view of the world, and your basic philosophical premise about life—how you see the world, part of which being how you think you should best live with those around you.

And equally as important, it depends on the desire to provide value and the ability and willingness to produce by everyone else in society, and thus upon their world view and values. Again, you can't easily accumulate or retain wealth in a society whose population is largely laden with ideas that are fundamentally opposed to the individual production of wealth and individual productivity!

If there is one message that I can get you to hold in the core of your being as the summary of my effort with you, it is this:

Champion The Producer. Do Not Take The Producer And The Existence Of Wealth For Granted

Neither exists automatically.

Respect and honor the producer! VALUE the man or woman who produces. VALUE the man or woman who seeks to contribute to the world out of pure self-interest, out of personal gain—who seeks to profit, because it is through their selfish desire that each of us benefits.

The sheer amount of wealth produced in the world since the advent of western man is stupendous. But, the productive man of the western world has not always existed–he has existed for as long as he has been free to exist; he will produce and continue to improve and advance the world only as long as he is FREE to produce.

And not only must wealth be constantly produced to advance human welfare and make life in the future easier, longer, and more enjoyable, but because physical stuff wears out, it must be continuously replaced just to stay at the level of well-being where we currently are today so that we can progress!

Think about it: In order for you to just maintain the level of life that you have today, SOMEBODY has to produce the replacement clothes, cars, electronic gizmos, food and shelter that you consume—the more you drive your car or your golf balls, the faster they wear out and have to be replaced for you to go on happily consuming at your current level of enjoyment—somebody somewhere has to keep making all this stuff.

Now, let me expound on mindset further because I want you to understand what is at stake here before I get into the detailed meat of my message in subsequent chapters

Life Ain't No Cakewalk.

Look, the world is a beautiful place, but it's an objectively dangerous place. There are a multitude of things outside your front door that can kill you. Life can be short and brutish or long and blissful, and it's really up to you which one you are most likely to manifest for your life.

Meaning, you have to consciously choose to consistently do the things that give you the greatest chance at succeeding at the maintenance, extension, and thorough enjoyment of your life.

There is no other way.

The bitch of it is that even if you do all the right things and live as a good person, there are absolutely no guarantees that you will ever succeed at your most impassioned heart-felt dreams, live a long happy and fulfilled life, or never die suffering horribly from some terrible mishap or disease. And that's not even talking about the lives of the ones you love. It does not even matter if you were born with the proverbial silver spoon in your mouth, or acquired tremendous riches along the way. Nobody gets out alive, and there are no guarantees. THERE ARE NO GUARANTEES.

...but the producer couldn't care less.

Building wealth is a journey fraught with perils and evils along the way, but the man with a producer's mindset easily faces any perils presented purely by chance by a benevolent universe, and does not take setbacks or failure seriously.

You live in a physical world. You have no choice about this. The world is a tough place for any animal (recall that the real animal world is where animals eat other animals alive), so be thankful you're the kind of animal that can choose to rearrange the physical world around you to reduce the risks you face and improve the odds of success for making your life better. You're the only animal that can.

Check out the wisdom of Steve Jobs...

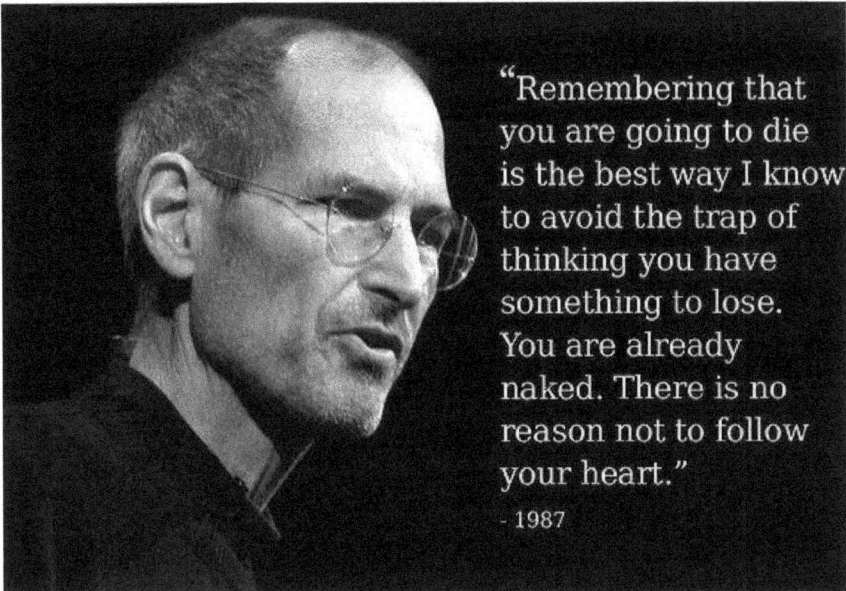

"Remembering that you are going to die is the best way I know to avoid the trap of thinking you have something to lose. You are already naked. There is no reason not to follow your heart."
- 1987

Listen to me: Whatever you believe about an afterlife...you are stuck in the here and now on this planet, with a daily, even moment-to-moment choice to make...

You must choose to 1) give up, do nothing and die; 2) live like some ascetic monk in a cave with a cot, one legged stool, and moldy crusts of bread for sustenance, intent on 'denying thyself' for the sole insane purpose of self-inflicted suffering as your cardinal value (or the modern equivalent of this); or

3) think and act as a MAN who desires to make his life easier and more enjoyable for the sole purpose of getting as much joy and happiness as you can muster for your life during your brief stay here, regardless of the dangers and uncertainty.

I first heard this from a gentleman named Neil Askew many, many moons ago: There aren't but two things that you have to do in life...die and live until you die. Everything else that you say you have to do you made up. Everything else that you say that you have to do is optional.

You don't even have to pay taxes...you can choose to be hounded by the IRS and even go to jail.

But you have to live.

And you have to live until you die.

I don't know about you, but if I'm going to make stuff up about how to live, I'm going to work to make my life and the lives of those I care about more comfortable, longer, and happier....to hell with the odds.

I hate to risk overusing this phrase, but you can't escape this. These are your choices and these are the choices every single one of us has to make consciously or subconsciously. And you make the choice in every waking moment in how you live your life from moment to moment. Some of us are on autopilot and choices are made for us as the winds of life buffet us hither and yon, but once you become aware, then the starkness of the choices slaps you in the face.

You have to choose whether you focus your brain and consciously (and then subconsciously) DESIRE and WORK to live as well as you can to improve your odds in the world, or choose to drift in an un-focused, almost mindless state, accept what crumbs of subsistence come your way via some boring J.O.B., and even worse, while awaiting your death, condemn those who 'have' because they have, or equally abhorrently, actively work to destroy the productive man and the wealth of the world, all the while sucking what lifeblood you can from your host while you kill him.

Or, you can simply give up and kill yourself.

These are your choices.

I am dead serious here.

There aren't but two kinds of people in the world folks: producers and parasites. Which one do you choose to be in this beautiful, yet uncertain and dangerous world? The man who, regardless of its dangers and uncertainties, sees the world as primarily a beautiful and benevolent place and aspires to success and happiness in spite of the odds and the dangers and the uncertainties? Or the hopeless, defeated, world-fearing, man-hating, self-loathing dolt who sees the world as a place of torment to be tolerated until he can be finally freed of his earthly suffering through death?

If you're not choosing to live like a MAN and revel in all that you can create and enjoy in the world while you live, including sharing your bounty with others and reveling in their success, you're by default choosing a long slow death as an unfulfilled, unhappy, miserable, envious, pitiful blood-sucking dead-beat full of excuses.

Note that the operable word here is choose.

For the producer, for the MAN, the world is a place of inspiration, hope, magnificence, and abundance.

To the parasite, it's a place of discomfort, hate, disease, horror, anxiety, terror, fear, pain, suffering and death.

It's the exact same world. Which world view do you choose?

The universe will manifest whichever one you ask for. You can be certain of this.

It happens all the time...

Money v. Happiness

Money does not buy happiness. I believe this is true.

Do not confuse what I have been trying to tell you in any way with the pursuit of money.

I believe that if you pursue money, you will be disappointed.

If you are pursuing money, your values are messed up.

So why talk about producing as the source of happiness? At

the root of it, isn't it all just about money?

NO!

Life is not about money. A good life is not at all about money. A good life is emphatically NOT about money. There is no end to the examples of people who have tons of money but are miserable, profoundly unhappy human beings.

Life is about being productive. Living is about doing something with your life. Living IS the doing of something that matters to you.

The key to productivity leading to happiness is that you have to be productive at something that is uniquely you. At something that matters to you. At something that burns within YOU.

We have all heard the saying "do what you love and you'll never work a day in your life." This is very accurate.

Think about what Rick Rule said above.

For you to feel fulfilled in the central purpose of your life, you have to produce at something that you absolutely love and cannot imagine living your life without. Anything else is a stepping stone, or worse, a distraction or an excuse. And if you pursue anything else for any great length of time, you are going to become disillusioned.

And by fulfilled, I don't mean kinda-sorta content in a way that you really can't explain...at least until something better comes along—I mean downright utterly joyous and thrilled that you actually get to do this for your life!!...whatever this is for you...whether it's being a mommy or janitor or a real estate mogul.

Would it not be insanely cool to feel this way on a consistent basis?

There is no good reason that you can't.

You see, we all have an innate need to find that central purpose that is unique to us that drives us to get up in the morning, get out there, and slug it out against whatever obstacles come our way in order to realize our dreams.

Fundamentally we all have the one master governing purpose of maintaining, extending and enjoying our lives, but each of us needs to find our central productive purpose that integrates all of our dreams, goals and aspirations, as the means to maintaining, extending and enjoying our lives.

Makes sense?

So part of the producer's mindset that I have been talking about comes from the process of searching for, discovering, and developing within yourself a clear, concise central productive purpose for your life towards which you can devote the vast majority of your time, energy and other resources to making a reality.

When it comes from within you; once YOU have taken that

self-imposed walk in the desert in search of who you are, the resulting unstoppable convictions that you give birth to are the engine that will propel you to do whatever it takes to achieve your purpose, to LIVE your purpose, no matter what trials and tribulations come your way. …Even though there are no guarantees and even though the world is still a dangerous place.

I like to think of actor Will Smith's quote to the effect that the difference between him and other actors who were trying to make it in show business was that he was "willing to die on a treadmill" for what he wanted—in order to manifest his central productive purpose of becoming an awesome world-renown actor.

THIS is the producer's mindset! THIS is where the juice of life comes from: manifesting your central purpose of becoming an awesome (fill in the blank). THIS is why you should care.

So How Do I Get Wealthy

Hah! The $64,000 question! I'm going to give you a little insight on this now, but you have to read on to get the full measure. We can only eat the elephant one bite at a time, and you can't bite the ear and the tail at the same time.

Above I outlined the overall practical steps to get wealthy, the process you have to go through whether you're a businessman or employee. However, as I have been alluding to, something else is essential for you to acquire and practice before you even develop the discipline to take these steps.

Again, it's all about attitude and mindset.

In a nutshell, here is what you have to do before you even start trying to make and save money as businessman or employee:

Get right with reality.

Clear your head. STOP thinking wealth is for somebody else! Stop thinking small. Dump the garbage that has been thrown your way since childhood. KILL the negative influences in your life. SEE the world as the incredibly beautiful place of abundance that WILL manifest for you what you desire if you only WILL.

Some are farther along this path than others...but whatever your place, changing your head requires vigilance and effort until it becomes habit.

Get a new perspective on life and the world.

For things to change, YOU have to change. (We will spend considerably more time on mindset and changing your head in later chapters).

Identify what you value. Be absolutely CLEAR on what you hold dear and will not compromise on. Hint: those things that elevate the physical and psychological health of a man are proper values; those which do not are not (more on values later too).

DO WHAT YOU LOVE and never work a day in your life.

Do not chase money; if you do, you're bound to suffer and lose. I can personally attest to this.

I like Steve Jobs in this respect. Steve once explained that his "passion has been to build an enduring company where people were motivated to make great products. Everything else was secondary." Including money. Here is an excerpt from an interview for the PBS documentary Triumph of the Nerds:

> *"I was worth about over a million dollars when I was 23 and over 10 million dollars when I was 24, and over 100 million dollars when I was 25 and it wasn't that important because I never did it for the money." Jobs life testifies to the fact that the reason genuine profit-seekers get out of bed in the morning is because they love creating things:*

they love producing new products, improving old ones, finding better ways to do things, building a business into something great, and making a fortune in the process. They are at heart producers. Jobs said it well. As he told the Stanford graduating class of 2005, "I'm convinced that the only thing that kept me going was that I loved what I did. You've got to find what you love. And that is as true for your work as it is for your lovers. Your work is going to fill a large part of your life, and the only way to be truly satisfied is to do what you believe is great work. And the only way to do great work is to love what you do."

Above all, be Pro-Freedom. Be Pro-Capitalist. Set meaningful financial goals. Save money and invest. ...and Never Ever Quit.

REMEMBER THIS: The fastest way to get rich in life is to solve other people's problems.

There are TONS of sources of information out there on how to go about conditioning yourself to take action, and the kinds of actions you need to take. Here are a couple (I have no affiliation with, nor do I make money off any business that you might do with these folks):

Tony Robbins. The Elevation Group. Robert Kyosaki. Richard Matthews. Fabian Calvo.

There is nothing new under the sun here kids! The stuff you've got to do to condition yourself for success has been around since western man has walked the earth. For you to condition yourself, the first step is you have to want it...Bad. For you to want it bad, you have to convince yourself of the rightness of creating a joyous world for yourself in freedom.

If you want something badly enough, nothing in the natural order of things can stop you.

Yet, there is STILL something even more important and more fundamental than these things I just talked about that precedes you taking action to condition yourself for success, and even precedes you becoming motivated in the first place. I have been alluding to it all along. And that is HOW do you become motivated and STAY motivated to take action? HOW do you convince yourself? Can you identify it? If you can't, hang in there because it's critical to your success, and I will spend a lot more time on this below.

That's The Good News. Now For The Bad

OK, we've spent some time learning about how it's man's nature to be productive in order to be happy.

And we will spend much more time on the nature of man and a proper mindset before we are done.

But now it's important that we talk about a major factor that's been limiting all of us in our pursuit of happiness...the limiting social system that we live in, the degradation of our productive spirit, and the resulting limit on our material prosperity and happiness. In a word: being under the control of other men for no reason other than their desire to control us for personal gain at our expense.

It's the phenomenon of our unwitting voluntary subservience to those I call the TTK (them-that-know, or them-that-see).

Before we get into this subject in the next chapter, I want to state that I do not like devolving into a conversation that, because of the subject matter, is inherently negative.

But we must.

We cannot ignore it because to ignore it means to go through life wearing blinders to the literal evil that lurks not in the shadows, but flaunts itself right out in the open in its conspiracy to destroy our ability to be happy.

For you to fully grasp the criticality to your personal welfare of you being free and to live in a society that is truly free, you must understand what is NOT free and how things came to be not free.

So focus on learning here and be objective about what I will tell you. As with all such things, you must make the effort and do your own research. Also, a man does not let these things depress him; he merely accepts them as evils that need to be destroyed, and that need to be dealt with until they can be destroyed—all while still living one's life in happiness.

Look. Mine is a message of hope, of a rational belief in oneself stemming from certitude and conviction about one's place and role and ability in the world.

Mine is not that of the parasite which is the false hope

spouted by the likes of an Obama. With false hope, we get what we've had, not just for the past 7 years, but for the past thirty or forty: economic chaos and dependency, an extremely polarized citizenry, and rampant racism and hatred.

Real hope, the truly empowering feeling that comes from the rational expectation and reasonable confidence that something expected will happen, results come from purpose-driven action. And as long as there lies even a smoldering ember of a yearning to be free in the souls of the majority of men, then I am very hopeful and optimistic that our world can be turned around. I am absolutely certain that with real leadership based on individual liberty as the guiding principle, the average Joe and Jane will rise up and end the insanity that reigns.

Yet, even with the actions of others who seek to control us and the battle that rages against these people, we are still reasonably free in the United States, and thus can STILL achieve our dreams, albeit harder than it needs to be....but we risk losing our cherished freedom by default if we are not aware, and once aware, do not act to defeat these people—these TTK.

If you have not been exposed to it before, the content below might take a little more effort to understand, but I promise we will end our journey on a very powerfully positive note!

(For now, I suggest taking a break from this material and coming back after a long rest)

CHAPTER TWO

The Greatest Fraud Ever Perpetrated on the American People

Betrayed by Them That Know, be they innocently misguided or just plain evil.

"Perhaps the sentiments contained in the following pages, are not yet sufficiently fashionable to procure them general favor; a long habit of not thinking a thing wrong, gives it a superficial appearance of being a thing right, and raises at first a formidable outcry in defense of custom. But the tumult soon subsides. Time makes more converts than reason."

—Thomas Paine

"Sometimes I wonder whether the world is being run by smart people who are putting us on or by imbeciles who really mean it."

—Mark Twain

You and I, your parents, and all of your family and friends have been lied to.

We have been conned.

Defrauded.

Outright and grievously.

We have been conned for a long, long time and on a massive scale, by a long line of politicians and by those who put those politicians in office and who buy their votes.

Elitism and mass control of citizens by TTK is the predominant characteristic of the 20th and 21st centuries. And it has never been more pervasive and active than it is today. In modern times (19th century to today) the elites, TTK, sincerely believe that you're too stupid or otherwise incapable of seeing what's really good for you...that the great masses of the unwashed are not capable of learning useful knowledge and thus of making the proper decisions as to what you need and want in your life; that you cannot provide for your own material welfare, and if you are so capable, you are too ignorant to restrain yourself; that you not only cannot be trusted to take care of the planet; that you cannot properly raise your children without their help; and that you do not show enough respect for the plight of your fellow man.

They think that our "capitalist" system is fraught with too many flaws and built-in dysfunctions that hurt the poor and underprivileged; that the business cycle of booms and busts inherent in "capitalism" causes the inevitable perpetuation of poverty, economic losses and upheavals for the middle-class, and that they alone have the intelligence and foresight to save us from these inherent evils of our society, if only we give up our freedom in exchange for their blessings and protection.

But in a free society, even a marginally free society such as what we have in the United States, TTK cannot win you over on the battle field of ideas with explicitly stated anti-freedom bromides and propaganda. Although there are a growing number of vocal and ideologically violent advocates for abolishing your liberties in favor of TTK one-world plans and policies, for the most part they dare not come right out and state that what they want is to gradually turn us into serfs under a new world order.

Still, as marginal as they sound, some elites and sundry highbrow academics openly advocate radical policies and solutions to our plight. Even for a dramatic forced reduction in the world's population in order to achieve their objectives in hopes of desensitizing large portions of the population, however ineffectual their effort is.

So theirs by necessity is a method of insidious incrementalism...a long slow tedious march in changing how individuals view the world and man's role in it, a piece-meal breakdown and destruction of the old true-to-man values and the inculcation of new faulty and evil values by persuading us to deny our own nature.

As to the Great Lie and the Great Con?

There has been an insidious attempt throughout the decades by those on the collectivist-altruist end of the ideological spectrum to get you to accept that it is flat out wrong for you to live for the sake of your own happiness—that there is something mentally imbalanced in you that you would want to do so.

TTK tell us that the only proper mode of living is as a servant to others (altruism) without concern for yourself, that you can't truly own anything because it belongs to all of us based on our need (collectivism), that the community, the church, or the tribe, and ultimately the state, are the only legitimate authorities, and that their proper role is to direct you how to live your life....and to 're-educate' you if you refuse.

It used to be that in the U.S. only the really radical out-of-touch nut jobs would come right out and tell you that you owe your allegiance and obedience to the elite and that you owe the fruits of your efforts, literally your life, to your neighbor, to the inner-city youth, to the homeless, to the ever-needing bum walking the streets, to the planet, or to the hereafter.

But now these former man-hating, life-hating 60's-era nuts jobs are the actual individuals running the federal government and much of the state and local governments.

They are entrenched on both sides of the aisle, Republicrats, Demicans, and many conservatives alike, who all with their own brand and marketing tilt are clamoring for more dependency on government, centralized control over your actions, and the commensurate destruction of individual liberty. Every single government program has the effect, if not the outright intent, to make more and more of us dependent upon handouts from and control by the government, and by extension under the thumb of TTK.

And it's all based on them propagating, and you and I accepting, an altruist-collectivist man-is-inept view of the world. And in order for TTK to sell us this world-view, you and I had to accept some major lies about life and reality, and we had to be unwitting victims of a major-league confidence game that has spanned now over a full century.

Today, this confidence game is principally targeted at the young and the relatively poor, uneducated, and ill-informed because if they can influence enmasse a generation or two or three of radicals for socialism, their fight is won.

Have you not noticed how TTK and their politicians pander to the lowest common denominator, the most ignorant and needy among us? How they promote the mass unlawful immigration of the neediest people?

The Great Lie

From the time we were in elementary school and could begin to grasp events around us and form causative explanations for the things we saw, there have been messages bombarding us throughout society intended to reduce the human mind, YOUR mind, into a subservient mindset...into a fearful way of thinking.

TTK seek a docile state of mind in a large portion of the population where one learns to perceive one's plight in life as naturally precarious and pain-filled; where one learns to perceive the world as a malevolent place where you cannot trust other men, and where men consume each other as bitter rivals as the natural order of things; where you huddle in terror of the latest advertised dangers and disease that lurk in every corner of the globe.

TTK want most of us in a state of mind where we subconsciously hide in fear and self-pity, live our lives of 'quiet desperation' and in constant need of someone's assistance, aid, and comfort. A state of mind where we will readily and eagerly forgo our very liberties in exchange for TTK providing some small piece of 'security' and 'peace', however fleetingly and precariously they provide it—with you having no real concern for whatever controls TTK choose to impose on you in order for you to receive their protections.

To you and me as relatively educated and productive people,

this seems ludicrous as we are not nearly as susceptible to their messages and machinations as their demographic of choice...so keep in mind who they are targeting. This is not to say of course, that there are not so-called 'highly-educated" people outside of their preferred demographic who also buy into the lie... Merely look at the majority of Hollywood types and tenured professors!

So what is the Great Lie?

The Great Lie they tell you is three-part:

1) That you are wrong and <u>evil</u> to live for yourself, that 'selfishness' is evil, that you are right and good to live for the sake of others without concern for your own needs; that your happiness and fulfillment in life can only come from denying your nature as a human being and by literally sacrificing your hopes, dreams, aspirations, your productivity, to those you do not know and whom have not earned it; and

2) That independence and individual liberty are a farce. They are unworkable. They want you to think that a great population of free, independent, sovereign individuals doing their own thing can only lead to chaos, tremendous inequality, destruction of the planet, and profound worldwide poverty, unemployment, and unhappiness. That capitalism as a social system and the capitalists who steal from you the fruits of your labors

are the epitomes of evil and all that is wrong with the world.

3) That only those who truly understand how the world works, who truly understand your needs of security and peace, can save you from worldly calamities that would otherwise befall you.

Although the names and the faces and the particular group affiliations of these people have changed over the decades, their bottom-line core message, the punch-line implied in their lies, is unchanged: "Your only realistic chance at happiness is to let us control your life, and if you will not willingly submit, we will make you submit—initially through all of our behind-the-scenes political machinations, through laws favorable to us as passed by the ignorant 'democratic' majority, then by executive order when lawmaking no longer works, and then ultimately through outright physical force. You will submit or you will perish, and you will live a troubled life until you perish. The State is supreme. As proxies to the State, society, your fellow man, and the planet are supreme. You as an individual human being are subordinate to these. You are expendable. The State is all; you are nothing.

Think I am being extreme? One only needs to look into the recent history of the USSR, China and other dictatorships.

So Why? Why is this?

Why in the modern era would men seek to control other men so?

Am I talking a bunch of hyperbole here?

Fear-mongering maybe?

Do the names of Hitler, Stalin, and Mao conjure up any nice memories or positive associations for you?

Their Goal

Their goal IS a "New World Order."

That's what they actually call it in today's jargon.

Call it one world government. Call it Utopia. Call it Nirvana. Progressivism. Call it a giraffe on a pogo stick. It doesn't matter what you call it. Hitler tried to create it with the chosen Aryan race where all individuals were only of value in subservience to the race as embodied in the Fatherland, run of course by an Arian TTK. Lenin, Stalin and gang attempted to create it, calling it the USSR and its satellite countries, by praising the proletariat in their noble self-sacrifice for the good of the collective. Mao tried it on a large scale too with the Great Leap Forward and all his wonderful fervent communist idealism of the Cultural Revolution.

Look it up!

Americans today are woefully ignorant of the lessons of history. Go back to the Prologue above and read again the source of the largest mass genocides in history and let it sink in.

Whatever they call it today, I call their program The Great Lie.

Some degree of The Great Lie has existed in virtually every corner of the planet, and now it faces you today, here in what once was the beckoning beacon and last bastion of individual liberty in the world, the United States of America. The ONLY difference between TTK at work today in the US, the EU and what's left of the other "western" nations, and those dear leaders who have gone before, is that present-day TTK think that the likes of Hitler, Stalin, and Mao went at it too quickly and forcefully, were too isolated and disunited without a sufficient "coalition of the willing", and produced results that were far too chaotic and bloody for the world wide masses to willingly accept.

Haven't you heard? Present day TTK have a kinder, gentler approach.

In the next chapter I will get in depth as to the psychological reasons for why TTK want what they want, and why we are willing to accept it, but what matters here in this chapter is that you are introduced to it and are made aware that TTK are working tirelessly to make it reality. I want you to you face it squarely and realize that you have to do a gut-check, even some intensive soul searching, and make a personal choice about it because it affects your ability to be happy.

It most certainly affects even the possibility of happiness for your kids and grandkids.

If ever there was a human crisis, a crisis facing the very existence of humankind as predominantly fulfilled and happy living beings, then the climax of that crisis is upon us now. This is not the time to sit on the fence and remain ambivalent about today's social issues.

Still think I'm maybe a conspiracy nut or a fear monger?

This isn't me making this stuff up! Here are a few of the more infamous TTK villains in their own words:

Political unification in some sort of world government will be required... Even though... any radical eugenic policy will be for many years politically and psychologically impossible, it will be important for UNESCO to see that the eugenic problem is examined with the greatest care, and that the public mind is informed of the issues at stake so that much that now is unthinkable may at least become thinkable.

-Julian Huxley,
First Director of UNESCO

"The real truth of the matter is, as you and I know, that a financial element in the large centers has owned the government of the U.S. since the days of Andrew Jackson."

I do not pretend that birth control is the only way in which population can be kept from increasing... War... has hitherto been disappointing in this respect, but perhaps bacteriological war may prove more effective. If a Black Death could be spread throughout the world once in every generation survivors could procreate freely without making the world too full... The state of affairs might be somewhat unpleasant, but what of that? Really high-minded people are indifferent to happiness, especially other people's... There are three ways of securing a society that shall be stable as regards population. The first is that of birth control, the second that of infanticide or really destructive wars, and the third that of general misery except for a powerful minority...

War has been throughout history, the chief source of social cohesion by providing an external necessity for a society to accept political rule.

> -Bertrand Russell, 20th Century Philosopher

"Let me control a peoples currency and I care not who makes their laws."

> -Meyer Nathaniel Rothschild

"We are grateful to the Washington Post, The New York Times, Time Magazine and other great publications whose directors have attended our meetings and respected their promises of discretion for almost forty years. It would have been impossible for us to develop our plan for the world if we had been subjected to the lights of publicity during those years. But, the world is now more sophisticated and prepared to march towards a world government. The supranational sovereignty of an intellectual elite and world bankers is surely preferable to the national auto-determination practiced in past centuries."

"We are on the verge of a global transformation. All we need is the right major crisis and the nations will accept the New World Order."

"Some even believe we (the Rockefeller family) are part of a secret cabal working against the best interests of the United States, characterizing my family and me as 'internationalists' and of conspiring with others around the world to build a

more integrated global political and economic structure – one world, if you will. If that's the charge, I stand guilty, and I am proud of it."

- David Rockefeller

Whatever the price of the Chinese Revolution, it has obviously succeeded not only in producing more efficient and dedicated administration, but also in fostering high morale and community of purpose. The social experiment in China under Chairman Mao's leadership is one of the most important and successful in human history.

- David Rockefeller, 1973

"Today, America would be outraged if U.N. troops entered Los Angeles to restore order. Tomorrow they will be grateful! This is especially true if they were told that there were an outside threat from beyond, whether real or promulgated, that threatened our very existence. It is then that all peoples of the world will plead to deliver them from this evil. The one thing every man fears is the unknown. When presented with this scenario, individual rights will be willingly relinquished for the guarantee of their well-being granted to them by the World Government."

-Dr. Henry Kissinger

"I just wonder what it would be like to be reincarnated in an animal whose species had been so reduced in numbers than it was in danger of extinction. What would be its feelings toward the human species whose population explosion had denied it somewhere to exist... I must confess that I am tempted to ask

for reincarnation as a particularly deadly virus."

-Prince Philip

"A total world population of 250-300 million people, a 95% decline from present levels, would be ideal."

-Ted Turner

"This [man's "remaking the earth by degrees"] makes what is happening no less tragic for those of us who value wildness for its own sake, not for what value it confers upon mankind. I, for one, cannot wish upon either my children or the rest of Earth's biota a tame planet, be it monstrous or – however unlikely – benign. McKibben is a biocentrist, and so am I. We are not interested in the utility of a particular species or free-flowing river, or ecosystem, to mankind. They have intrinsic value, more value – to me – than another human body, or a billion of them. Human happiness, and certainly human fecundity, are not as important as a wild and healthy planet. I know social scientists who remind me that people are part of nature, but it isn't true. Somewhere along the line-at about a billion years ago, maybe half that – we quit the contract and became a cancer. We have become a plague upon ourselves and upon the Earth. It is cosmically unlikely that the developed world will choose to end its orgy of fossil-energy consumption, and the Third World its suicidal consumption of landscape. Until such time as Homo sapiens should decide to rejoin nature, some of us can only hope for the right virus to come along"

-David M. Graber*

Research biologist with the National Park Service, in his prominently featured Los Angeles Times book review of Bill McKibben's The End of Nature.

Want more proof of this attempt to control? Just Google 'New World Order', "population control" or any number of related terms, and start researching it yourself. It's all out there in text, images and video. You have to sort the wheat from the chaff because there are real loonies out there who go beyond reason when it comes to evaluating what is happening, but there is enough to convince you of its presence.

Folks, to any rational person who is aware it is INSANE what TTK seek to achieve! It is preposterous and outrageous!

It is also becoming reality.

Go read Saul Alinsky's 1971 Rules for Radicals.

Folks, this clown directly influenced the mad statist "community organizer" in the White House and all the other socialist radicals of the 1960s and 1970s. He has influenced the Hillary Clintons (she did her college thesis on his writings) and the Bernie Sanders and the Nancy Pelosi's, and most of your average liberal politician and media pundits.

> *"The organizer's first job is to create the issues or problems,' and 'organizations must be based on many issues.' The organizer 'must first rub raw the resentments of the people of the community; fan the latent hostilities of many of the people to the point of overt expression. He*

must search out controversy and issues, rather than avoid them, for unless there is controversy people are not concerned enough to act. . . . An organizer must stir up dissatisfaction and discontent.'"

"An organizer working in and for an open society is in an ideological dilemma to begin with, he does not have a fixed truth -- truth to him is relative and changing; everything to him is relative and changing.... To the extent that he is free from the shackles of dogma, he can respond to the realities of the widely different situations....

And

"A Marxist begins with his prime truth that all evils are caused by the exploitation of the proletariat by the capitalists. From this he logically proceeds to the revolution to end capitalism, then into the third stage of reorganization into a new social order of the dictatorship of the proletariat, and finally the last stage -- the political paradise of communism."

And

"The tenth rule of the ethics of rules and means is that you do what you can with what you have and clothe it in moral arguments. ...the essence of Lenin's speeches during this period was "They have the guns and therefore we are for peace and for reformation through the ballot. When we have the guns then it will be through the bullet." And it was.

And

"I have on occasion remarked that I felt confident that I could persuade a millionaire on a Friday to subsidize a revolution for Saturday out of which he would make a huge profit on Sunday even though he was certain to be executed on Monday."

These people are dead serious about their collectivist ambitions and it is becoming reality by default because most men are not aware of it and if they ARE aware of it, they do not know how to fight it, much less defeat it.

And the crucial thing to understand is that these TTK handmaidens they think they are right. That theirs is the way, if only they, the TTK are left alone to pursue their course and structure the world for the rest of us. Do not kid yourself... they will do whatever they have to do to gain power.

Choose: The "political paradise of communism" or individual liberty.

Their Purpose. Their Mission.

Short of outright genocide of whole segments of the population (which would be highly unpopular and hence is not mainstream thinking yet), their purpose is to turn the majority of the population into slaves through the diminution of the individual human spirit.

Does that sound too extreme to you?

Here is the definition of a slave from Merriam Webster's dictionary: "someone who is legally owned by another person and is forced to work for that person without pay; a person who is strongly influenced and controlled by something; a person held in servitude as the chattel of another."

When the produce from the productive genius and effort of your life is not yours to be held by you for your sole benefit, but taken from you to be given to others against your will through outright confiscation (taxes) and through insidious depreciation of your money (manufactured inflation), then you are a slave.

The nicest way one can phrase it is that you are an indentured servant who is allowed to keep just enough of the results of your work to keep you motivated just enough to willingly struggle against the controls in order to continue producing, even while you are fully aware that you are propagating the system.

Do you think there might be a reason why you are only required to work through April just to pay your taxes and not through August? The fact that you are forced to give up only 50-75% of your productivity does not mean you are less of a slave...even black slaves of the plantation era were allowed some degree of autonomy and subsistence.

At best, you and I are serfs.

Don't you leave these last paragraphs until you grasp what I am saying.

Read it again.

You are an indentured servant who is allowed to keep just enough of the results of your work to keep you motivated just enough to willingly struggle against the controls in order to continue producing, even while you are fully aware that you are propagating the system.

So WHY do TTK want to enslave and control?

In order for you to understand the magnitude of this crisis, and the seriousness and passion with which they are pursuing their agenda, you must understand why TTK do what they do.

TTK are motivated by 1) power born of Elitism—of errant egoism, and 2) hatred of Man's nature—hatred of his innate productive tendencies—hatred of man's yearning to be independent and free—at bottom, hatred of man's mind.

To understand these motivations you must understand how

TTK see the world and how they view us, the great mass of lowly toiling men.

In the eyes of TTK the world is indeed a beautiful place, except to the extent that the little crass and dirty people like you and me mess it up. They see it as a place where man, at least large populations of us common ignoramuses, is a blight on the earth, and where it is best to limit what natural and man-made beauty exists to the benefit of those who possess the wisdom to truly appreciate beauty, for those who can see, for the self-styled, self-proclaimed elite.

For the "common man" TTK see the world principally a cruel, harsh, and dangerous place. That common man, if left to his own individualistic devices can only cause general worldwide chaos and pain, with fleeting happiness achievable by some limited few but only at the unjust expense of the far greater many. They see the great mass of human beings acting in freedom and independence out of pure self-interested is the literal cause of the world's problems. TTK see that the sheer inequalities in men's talents, if man's actions are left unchecked in a world of limited resources, cause the divisions and arguments among men and thus the chaos and major upheavals of human history.

TTK see that the only solution to the world's misery is universal control by them. All TTK believe that you are not worthy of the liberty that they are because you will abuse it; that you are not capable of acting in freedom and autonomy without destroying or preventing an otherwise achievable utopia; that selfishness and "looking out for No. 1" is the absolute evil because it is uncontrolled. Individual rights sound nice but are not practical and thus not right for the modern world.

Some of the more naïve TTK fervently believe in the quest for "equality" and that the ideal of egalitarianism is absolutely achievable on earth, if only man's evil nature can be altered over time and if not alterable, then at best contained and strictly controlled.

Most TTK secretly do not believe equality is achievable, but that some degree of forced egalitarianism is nevertheless the best means of bringing the masses under control and in line with whatever degree of utopia may be achievable by their wise and true hand.

ALL TTK believe that control of man's actions is necessary and that individuals cannot be left free to do as they wish with their lives without oversight by someone with a clear, even cosmically-inspired vision, especially with the vast populations of the Third World coming online with modern technology.

TTK propagate the idea that a common man's life is a zero-sum game; that because of "limited resources" you can only succeed at the unjust expense of your neighbor and that if left free to do as he wishes your fellow man is necessarily your enemy. When he succeeds in achieving his piece of the so-called American Dream, you are necessarily left with less; there is less available for you. You are being "exploited" and the fruits of your labors are being stolen by your employer, or somehow, by that guy down the street who has a better-paying job and nicer house than you.

TTK sell us the idea that your only safety and security, and certainly your only real shot at happiness in life is not to be attained by being independent and fighting it out there in the cold alone, but to adhere to a group or a tribe...to a collective. Thus, the favorite strategies of TTK are divide-and-conquer, promotion of class warfare, pitting group against group, and positioning government intervention and control as the only rational alternative to the chaos and hatred and resulting widespread misery and unhappiness.

And in the event that modern industrious western man, with his powerfully ingrained yearning to be free, does not subscribe to the idea that unrestrained inequality of ability and talent is bad, then the TTK alternative strategy of choice is to convince you that acting individually out of self-interest is destroying the very planet that your life requires. And that on that count alone you should be ashamed to even think of your personal selfish dreams and aspirations because of the destruction and suffering you wreak on the innocent animals and rocks, which in themselves are intrinsically more valuable than your material happiness.

In either case, they are convinced that there are too many of us on the planet and that we need a healthy virus to come along and eliminate 5 billion people or so, or else we the TTK may have to do the messy job ourselves eventually.

I will expand on TTK motivations and why the great masses of men buy into their hype and propaganda in the next chapter, but now let's talk about what TTK actually need in order to achieve their giraffe on a pogo stick.

The Great Con

In conspiring to gain control of the world, TTK need just two things to achieve their goals in the real world of heretofore predominantly independent, free-thinking, reasoning men. In addition to the legions of mentally-diseased weak and evil minds that have already either consciously or unwittingly adopted the ideology of anti-man altruistic self-immolation, they need:

1.   A compliant majority of the population, and

2.   Lots and Lots of Money

The Great Con Part 1: The Breaking of the American Mind...Sell Us Your Liberty and Join Us in Utopia

A New World Order would have to do away with individuality and in its place create fearful, self-loathing, and hence obedient slaves. Nations and national institutions and governments would remain in some nominal form, and these would even prove useful in the short term, but individuality–independent MIND–has to be destroyed. The self-oriented, selfish activities of a free man living for his own happiness must end, because again nothing but widespread exploitation, inequality, chaos, poverty, misery and unhappiness can result from the aggregate actions of independent sovereign men.

And to destroy the independent mind of a free man, their chief objective is, initially at least, that of changing how the individual mind views the world, its place in it, and its relation to other minds. **Through their Great Lie, their objective is to fundamentally change what men think about how best to achieve whatever happiness is attainable on this rock.**

And the best way to accomplish this is to get men to doubt their ability to even BE happy and secure without the aid of TTK—without the aid of a gifted elite who has been to the summit and by divine intervention, communion with the higher power, or their own glandular excretions and dope-induced visions of grandeur, simply knows what is best for you. **To get men not just to fear standing alone in the big bad world, but that it is actually morally wrong to want to do so.**

And how best to accomplish this?

The weapons of the Great Con protagonists are principally four:

Anti-Man Values. Great Con Tool #1 is the inculcation of faulty anti-man, anti-liberty values. Again, this is principally targeted at the young, the ability-challenged and the ignorant, because if they can influence several generations of radicals for socialism-statism, their fight is won. One only need look into recent history at the hordes of man-hating Cultural Revolution evangelists inspired by the likes of Mao and the resulting horrors of mass extermination.

To this end, knowing that the methods of Mao won't result in the subjugation of the western nations, the enlightened TTK of the west bring us our wonderful modern 'western' educational system which has recently been enhanced to include the statist monstrosity called Common Core.

Propagate the Envious Poor. Another Great Con Tool is to implement policies that actually propagate and enlarge an uneducated poor population because these folks are far more inclined to accept that those who achieve in their lives have somehow done them wrong. It's easier for them to believe that 'the rich' or literally anyone who is better off than them win at their expense; that the game of life is rigged against them, and that the only way that they stand a chance at a decent standard of living is to kneel before and present their grievances to TTK who will then, through moral acts of justice and righting wrongs, forcibly take from the rich and give what they have taken to them, and to open doors that otherwise would remain locked, euphemistically the latest forms of "fairness" or "affirmative action."

One only need to listen to the Marxian exploitation babble and the anti-business rants of our nation's so-called leaders, objectively analyze our immigration policies and our wonderful behavior-modification (tax) code which results in all manner of taxes on the middle class and the rich (including minimum wage legislation), see the explosive growth of hand-out programs, listen to the official pap constantly blaring from government-controlled media, and again, observe our world-class educational system.

Raping Mother Earth and Planet-Wide Catastrophe. Yet another tool of the Great Con is to literally scare an otherwise psychologically healthy man into giving up his rights, his values of freedom, self-sufficiency and productiveness and the American Dream by showing him laughable imaginations of 'concrete proof' that because of his individual selfish actions, the planet is becoming too cold or too hot, that too much plastic is in the landfills, that the spotted three-legged lizard is dying off at a precipitous rate, that ALAR will give you cancer if you eat too many apples, that DDT is destroying the condors, that SARS or MERS or Ebola, created by overpopulation, are soon coming into your home to wipe out your family, and that in general and increasing in magnitude and at exponential rates, all manner of ills that exist in the world do exist because man is too free.

Why is man being free a problem? Because he is the only animal that has a brain that can think and choose his values and if he is left free and unchecked, will continue to alter the physical world to his personal benefit, and cause harm to his fellow man and destroy the planet.

In a word: because man is uncontrolled.

Man, acting on his own individual judgment in accordance with his nature, is a blight on the earth. Man is an aberration in nature and has no constructive role to play in the natural environment of planet earth, but since he IS here, he must be controlled.

His numbers must be reduced, and those that remain must be severely controlled for his own good and the good of his fellow species.

Oh and let's not forget the boogieman as a fourth tool for propagating the Great Con!

Terrorism. Can't get the more educated to feel sorry for his fellow man or the planet? Get them to fear some small insignificant group of religious maniacs (Islamic radicals, Iranian mullahs, ISIS-ISIL, pick your poison) who want to destroy their western way of life! And if these 'terrorists' operating overseas in some distant land do not strike fear in their hearts, let's bring it home and give 'em a real show ala Pearl Harbor and conspire to allow the boogiemen to take down a few skyscrapers in Manhattan. Voila! Out rolls the Patriot Act; FEMA Camps; National Defense Act; Executive Orders ad infinitum; and Fusion Centers. How about the out-of-control NSA, CIA, FBI spying; drones; cell phone tracking; license plate readers, smart thermostats, and the labeling of conservatives, free-thinkers, libertarians, and patriots as domestic terrorists, and on and on and on and on.

Can you not see?

Can you not see the intent to manifest chaos as a means of justifying control behind Rahm Immanuel's words "never let a good crisis go to waste?"

Manufacturing chaos and fear is the oldest trick in their book!

Today, you literally have far more to fear from the gang of thugs called the U.S. Government and entities like the United Nations than you will EVER have to fear from any burglar, criminal street gang, murderer, band of terrorists, or rogue third-world dictators.

I genuinely pity you if you as a thinking adult human being will not open your eyes to the possibility of their tactics. After years of scoffing at it myself, the evidence is undeniable. As the most recent blatant example of contrived crisis, TTK were responsible for the WTC attack, just as they were responsible for the lies about WMDs in Iraq, AIDs, the Gulf of Tonkin Resolution, our entry into WW II and WW I, and on and on.

Honestly, if you cannot be willing to look objectively at the widely published evaluation of physical evidence alone, then I cannot reach you. None are so blind as those who refuse to see. If you doubt all of this because perhaps you are exposed to it for the first time, but are willing to research it on your own, I applaud you in your effort to remain awake.

However, if you are completely unwilling to investigate on your own under the perfectly rational mantra of "Question Authority", stop reading this book now. You have joined the great herd of sheeple and you are happily and stupidly being led to be sheared; I am more than happy to give your money back. ☺

Still here?

Ok, fair enough.

Folks, when I refer to these people as man-haters, I am not flippantly calling names. I mean it literally. Never, ever, ever, doubt that it is man's nature, meaning man's natural desire to be free and independent and individual that they chiefly hate and fear and seek to control. It is man's MIND they seek to control—by stifling it, hand-cuffing it, limiting it, and by the very nature of controlling it, destroying it.

Do not doubt that TTK are terrified of the prospect of the rest of the planet, the so-called Third World consisting of the populations of entire continents, developing the wealth and prosperity and standard of living of the U.S., because of how chaotically and messily it will likely transpire.

In the creation of their own TTK-engineered utopia, they cannot tolerate and will do whatever is necessary to destroy a world of free, independent, sovereign individuals acting in their own best judgment for the sole purpose of the fulfillment and enjoyment of their own lives.

The Great Con Part 2: Funny Money...The More We Make, the Better We Feel

TTK require money, lots and lots of money to control politicians, to place and control other key henchmen and bureaucrats, and to implement their agenda principally through social programs, executive fiat, and war. It costs money to create the propaganda machine that is required to destroy old institutions that protect and promote individuality and liberty which impede their efforts, and to create new institutions to promote their cause. It costs tremendous sums of money to instigate and conduct wars designed to intimidate world leaders and populations into alignment with TTK ideals and bring wealth to those who fund and supply the warring parties.

But in a free market capitalist society there simply is not enough money available for TTK to wage wars and create incredibly wasteful social programs.

Why? At least until the recent past, because no rational person would financially support their plan if they came right out and told us what they wanted to do and demanded immediate compliance. And also because in a truly free market capitalist society with a limited supply of sound money, no one man or any group of men are even remotely capable of amassing the kinds of fortunes needed to realize this kind of control.

And so, because men discovered and successfully used tricks of financial fraud in early civilizations, they resort to mass theft to acquire these fortunes—outright theft from trusting ignorant sheep like you and me, and all who came before us and all who will come after us.

Do not kid yourself. You have been ROBBED. We all have been robbed. Some of us knowingly and complicity, most of us totally oblivious and blind.

I know some of you reading this may be rolling your eyes...'oh man, not another conspiracy theory!'

AT ONE TIME I WAS JUST LIKE YOU.

The information I am introducing you to is all out there in the public domain, it has been all along. It has been thoroughly vetted and all you have to do is be unafraid to look at it. TTK have told us in the past, and are telling us now, exactly what their game is. As the old adage goes, just follow the money. And the money points to a HUGE fraud perpetrated on the American people...all for the financial benefit of TTK, them that own the system.

Remember comedian George Carlin's shtick regarding TTK?

Sure, a lot of hyperbole, but generally he gets it. He was dead serious and people identified with it. People are becoming more aware as time marches on what has been done to them even though for the most part the source and meaning of it all is still somewhat hazy and vague.

....

Now I am going to tell you how they fund their game.

To help me, let me introduce to you Mr. Mike Maloney. For those of you who have not heard of him, in addition to many other endeavors of his in the pursuit of establishing sound money, he put together one hell of a short series of videos on the nature of money and the fiasco of today's U.S. monetary system. I cannot say enough positive things about this guy and what he has done in his attempt to elevate us out of our present course of reversion to the modern equivalent of the Stone Age.

Now listen. You spent your good money on this book, so don't be lazy. Get your money's worth and LISTEN TO THE VIDEOs that I have linked to below. If you only have time for one right now, listen to segment #4 of his multipart series The Hidden Secrets of Money immediately below. I think that once you do, you will feel compelled to complete the series and listen to a lot of what Mike and others like him have to say.

https://youtu.be/iFDe5kUUyT0

Does any of this stir something in you? Is it beginning to wake you up? Does it not at least begin to make you wonder why guys like Mike are saying what they say?

Guys like Mike Maloney are not idiots. They are intelligent, articulate, and a lot closer to sources of information than you and I and they are warning us of the danger with bull horns!

There are many, many others out there. You just have to begin your awakening. For example, try this bit of education from Tyler Durden at Zero-Hedge.

Or this recent post from Jim Rickards.

And David Stockman.

And Peter Schiff.

I generally understood the concepts of the Federal Reserve, Fiat Money, and Fractional Reserve Banking prior to seeing Mike's video, mainly from reading Capitalism, A Treatise on Economics by George Reisman (the full, indexed text of his book is here), The Creature of Jekyll Island, by G. Edward Griffin, and more recently Glenn Beck's entertaining expose' on the banking system below, and David Stockman's The Great Deformation.

https://youtu.be/vB5LK-jihgk

But when I saw Mike's video, I became angry because I finally understood the full magnitude of what has been done to us and our country. And I remain angry. Justifiably so. You are angry too if you understand, whether you're 20 years of age or 80.

Folks it's all out there in thousands of sources as to what the hell has been going on for over a century. If you have not been exposed to this before, you need to muster the courage to face it squarely, open your eyes wide and educate yourself.

I alone cannot do it for you in this brief book.

The U.S. government and governments throughout the world, through the functioning of central banks, simply print money at will. THIS is how they afford to implement their NWO plans and schemes.

They simply create money out of nothing.

Out of NOTHING.

And they charge you and me incredible amounts of money in the form of taxes and inflation...on what they created out of thin air.

TTK create money at will and spend the money on their programs, propaganda, and wars, and as long as they can keep the Ponzi scheme alive, you and I pay for it by outright theft of the fruits of our labors: upfront through taxes, and insidiously out-of-view through inflation, misallocation of capital, loss of productivity, and our resulting progressive impoverishment.

Since 1913 when the United States last created a central bank called the Federal Reserve System, your money has lost at least 98% of its power to buy things.

98%?

This means that the dollar bill has been devalued due to inflation (printing) to the point where it can now buy only 2% of what it used to buy way back the turn of the 20th Century (1900 for the calendar-challenged). The banks and the government literally have STOLEN from the American people 98% of the value of every dollar. As you saw in the video, part of it went to social programs, a huge amount went to wars, and another huge amount went into the pockets of bankers, the already-wealthy, and TTK through asset bubbles (typically the stock and bond markets) and interest payments. The only reason you have not noticed is that it has been a slow, gradual, insipid theft. But theft nonetheless.

Look at the figure below.

Using economic data through 2013, if you're 50, look at what's happened to your ability to purchase all the things that you've needed, and all of the simplest things that you've wanted to enjoy in your lifetime. You've been kicked in the proverbial balls and don't even know because you've suffered a HUGE loss.

What cost you $1 in 1963 now costs you more than $7.60. In other words, $7.60 has the same purchasing power in 2013 as $1 did in 1963. Because of just a little bit of average inflation per year of 4%, you've been kicked with a 660%+ loss of your ability to buy stuff with your own hard-earned money! Another way to look at this is if you had saved $100,000 dollars in 1963, in terms of its ability to buy stuff in comparison to 1963, it's now worth a little over $15,000! This **$85,000** was, in cold hard reality, stolen from you as sure as if you had been robbed by a burglar on the street, and given to the banks and government agencies, and to all of the leeches and speculators who feed off them, all with the full knowledge of those that run your government.

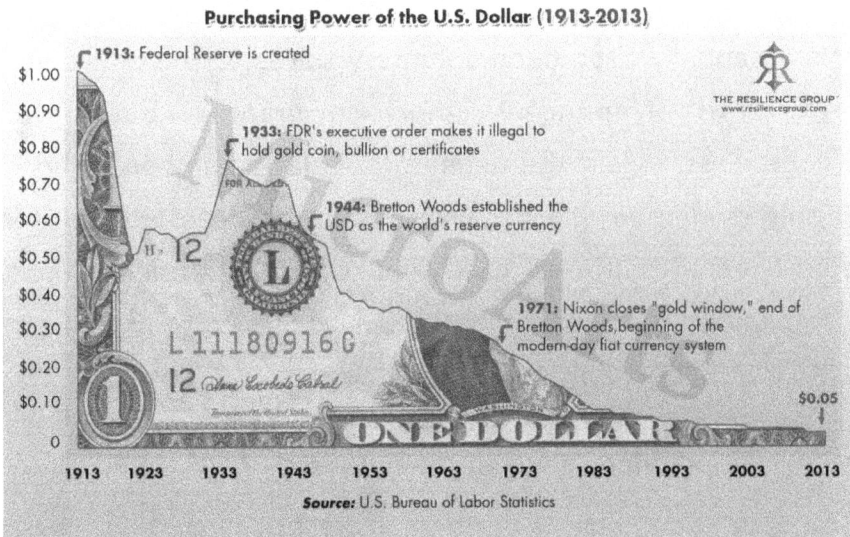

Purchasing Power of the U.S. Dollar (1913-2013)

Source: U.S. Bureau of Labor Statistics

Don't think this is such a big deal for you younger folks?

If you've worked just 20 years thus far in your life, look at what's happened to your ability to purchase in your short lifetime...a whopping 64% loss. This means that what you could buy for $1 in 1993 will now cost you $1.64. You must pay 64% more for the same stuff! And $10,000 you may have saved 20 years ago is now worth about $6,000. $4,000 dollars has been stolen from you without you even seeing it!

STOLEN.

Stolen from me. Stolen from you.

You and I have been the unwitting victim of fraud on a massive scale! And we're not even talking about all the taxes that you have paid on top of these devaluation losses!

We essentially have been voluntary slaves to the banks and TTK. Born of innocent ignorance granted, but slaves nonetheless. Again the definition of slave: someone who is legally owned by another person and is forced to work for that person without pay, and slavery: drudgery, toil, submission to a dominating influence; the state of a person who is a chattel of another.

Watch Mike's video #4 again and let it sink in.

How could you not be angry?

Feel a little abused and lied to? Cheated? Disillusioned?

I understand. You didn't know. I didn't know. Like all good Americans living from the 1930s, 40s, 50s, 60s, 70s and 80s, we trusted our politicians. (Those of you who came of age in the 90s and later have less excuse with the advent of the sheer volume of knowledge freely available on the internet).

But hey! Politicians run by TTK claim that they were just working for your benefit. They meant well after all, right?

Really?

Follow how this works:

Their stated goal (of the Fed in particular) is "price stability" and "full employment." Sure, they would say, along with the drop in the value of your dollar, things will necessarily get more expensive. But hey, you'll still be employed and your paycheck will increase overtime more or less in pace with the prices of everything else, so everything evens out. And in the meanwhile we have protected your money in the bank (hah!). And the really good news is that we as a country produce a lot more per person than ever before so your dollar still kinda buys the same amount of stuff even though it's worth a lot less because there is more to buy! After all, that is our goal....price stability and full employment! And we aim to deliver.

But they were not working for your benefit. While many government bureaucrats were sold that social programs were there to help people, and others were sold that war was necessary to keep the barbarian hordes at bay, the intent of TTK was to work a Ponzi scheme on all of us that permitted them to spend like drunken sailors, while keeping us in voluntary servitude not only to pay the interest due on all of that continuously accumulating debt, but to continue producing in support of the scheme!

Well, here's how it works in the real world where you and I live:

The printing or digital creation of money out of nothing is called inflation. Inflation is nothing more than the increase in the total supply of money in our economy. Inflation is NOT rising prices...generally rising prices throughout the economy are merely a symptom of inflation. The effect of inflation is to reduce the value of each dollar, called 'devaluing the dollar', making the dollar worth less, causing you to have to pay more dollars for any given thing in the form of rising prices, and this of course IS the destruction of purchasing power.

It's very simple to understand: if you have more of something, the value of each unit of what you have becomes worth less.

Let's say you like oranges as they are your favorite food. If you have two oranges in your possession, you value one orange perhaps very highly if they are the only things that you have to eat for the day. You might not even be willing to trade one orange for your friend's ham sandwich even though you have two.

Now, if you have a whole bushel of oranges in your possession, the value you attach to any particular orange is much less than you attached to a single orange previously, and you may very well consider trading three or more oranges for your friend's sandwich now, especially if someone else is offering two or more oranges for the same sandwich.

It's the exact same situation with dollar currency. The more dollars you have, the less importance any one dollar has for you. And the easier it is to bid up the price of what you want in competing with others for the same stuff. The more dollars you have, the easier it is to spend your dollars and the faster you spend them. They are "burning a hole in your pocket" as the saying goes.

As the aggregate rate of spending of money (the so-called velocity of money) by everyone increases in the economy and outpaces the production of goods and services by everyone in the economy, we have a condition where "too many dollars are chasing too few goods", and the prices of the available goods and services necessarily rise. As people spend more money and spend it faster, they necessarily bid up the prices of a limited supply of goods and services that they buy in competing with one another for the same stuff.

Now, knowing that Americans are an industrious people, TTK count on us to continue to produce and create more goods and services, even though our money was becoming worth less over time. We are 'allowed' a certain degree of freedom in order to produce and gain wealth to a limited degree in accordance with their behavior modification code (the internal revenue code and other regulations). What they attempt to do in order to keep milking us in the Grand Ponzi is to keep Gross Domestic Product (GDP), the total supply of goods and services that we produce in our jobs and businesses, increasing in pace with the increase in money supply. In other words, increasing with inflation. That way, prices tend not to increase...voila! "price stability." If TTK bankers increase inflation at 3%, ideally they would want to see us produce more each year to the tune of 3%.

And their interest in maintaining a moderate inflation? They have unlimited money to spend on their plans, and they make a ton of money off of the money they lend to the government through the interest they earn.

If you are still at all confused about this, go back and watch Mike Maloney's videos again.

Printing money to maintain 'price stability" is just a massive scam to milk us and keep the scheme going as long as possible in order to generate the huge amount of funds they need to put their plans into action. Remember the movie, The Matrix? In that movie the machines (the equivalent of today's TTK), used human beings as power sources like batteries. And in order to do so, they had to create a fictitious world where everything is hunky dory, where people go about their daily lives completely unaware that they live in an illusion, and that they are insidiously being used as slaves, as energy sources for the creation of their world.

We live in a similar kind of matrix...a financial-monetary matrix where we are, just like in the movie, individually used as slaves, living blinded to reality in order to generate from us our economic energy.

And here is what will really fry your brain. There is a dirty little secret about this whole fiat money system that they DON'T want you to know that will just blow you away.

Are you ready for it?

You had better be, because it's way too late to go back and take the blue pill!

Here it is:

Without a central bank fractional-reserve system that is capable of creating money out of nothing, in a sound-money (i.e. precious metals based money) free-market truly capitalist economy, your money would actually increase in purchasing power by the day. EVERYONE, without changing their present employment situation, would necessarily become more wealthy by the day because we good hard-working productive Americans would continue producing more and more goods and services of higher and higher quality....AND, are you ready?...the never-ending increase in goods and services would only—could only—be purchasable with the same relatively static amount of money in the economic system, with the result that prices necessarily would <u>decrease</u> over time and your dollar would buy more and more as time went on.

Even with an annual growth in the quantity of silver and gold mined from the earth and converted into money, that increased quantity of money could never keep pace with what a country and world of free citizens could produce in other goods and services.

Without the fiat money system that has enslaved us for the past century, your middle-class wealth now, today, would perhaps be on par with, if not the current billionaires of today, certainly that of multi-millionaires. The poorest today would probably enjoy wealth comparable with someone who today makes $100,000.

Read the last three paragraphs again.

Capitalism, true free-market laissez-faire capitalism, would ensure a never-ending increase in the personal wealth of every man, woman and child who participates in the system.

Folks, if you understand what I just said, then you understand that it is INSANELY OUTRAGEOUS what they have pulled on us!

You don't think this is all by design?

Educate yourself!

The battle has been raging for more than a century.

It's all out there folks. As I said, you just have to be willing to look and listen critically. With a heavy, healthy dose of skepticism of course, but listen and the truth will come out. The truth will set you free as they say...

Even its current perpetrators fully understand what the system is all about! Here's former Fed Chairman Alan Greenspan way back in 1966 before he became a turn-coat and became one of the operators of the machine:

"In the absence of the gold standard, there is no way to protect savings from confiscation through inflation. There is no safe store of value. If there were, the government would have to make its holding illegal, as was done in the case of gold. If everyone decided, for example, to convert all his bank deposits to silver or copper or any other good, and thereafter declined to accept checks as payment for goods, bank deposits would lose their purchasing power and government-created bank credit would be worthless as a claim on goods. The financial policy of the welfare state requires that there be no way for the owners of wealth to protect themselves.

This is the shabby secret of the welfare statists' tirades against gold. Deficit spending is simply a scheme for the confiscation of wealth. Gold stands in the way of this insidious process. It stands as a protector of property rights. If one grasps this, one has no difficulty in understanding the statists' antagonism toward the gold standard."

-*Alan Greenspan,*
Gold and Economic Freedom, 1966.

And, again AFTER he has left the Fed in 2006 after a 19-year tenure as Fed Chairman:

"Fiat money has no place to go but gold."

"Gold is a currency. It is still by all evidences the premier currency where no fiat currency, including the dollar, can match it."

-Alan Greenspan, Council on Foreign Relations, Oct 2014.

Hell, even the progenitor of modern day J.P. Morgan Chase fully understood this on the eve of the creation of the Fed and the IRS in 1913:

"Gold is money. Everything else is credit."

-J. P. Morgan, 1912

Bilderbergers, Illuminati, Tri-Lateral Commissions, Councils of Foreign Relations....Giraffes on pogo sticks...call them whatever you want, there is collusion to control the behavior of free men and you are the victim.

Only now many great intelligent minds of today are saying the Great Ponzi scheme has almost run its course, and a great economic reset is going to occur with a commensurate degree of wailing and gnashing of teeth amongst the unaware sheeple.

Regardless of how long it can continue, there is no conspiracy 'theory' here. There's no need to expose some massive conspiracy theory or cover up. There never has been a secret about what the Fed is and how it operates and who benefits —it's all out in plain view of the public and has been since its formation, right there in the Fed's charter—only you never were told about it. If you've ever heard inklings of it, you may have paid attention briefly, but it didn't feel like it really affected you directly, so you lost interest and went about your daily doings. You became oblivious to the danger just like the people walking the streets in The Matrix.

And if you did care you didn't know where to look or how to fight against it. Today of course we have this magical animal called the internet where TTK can no longer hide in the shadows and their bullshit is being gradually ever-increasingly broadcast and revealed.

The time is now. It is here upon you now and you cannot afford to be careless about this anymore.

You have to decide.

Choose to fight to become and remain a free and sovereign Man and work towards making ours the freest country on earth again, or choose to remain a sheeple and a pawn in the great new world order.

I choose to be a Man.

Join me.

(Take a break. You have absorbed a lot. Let your brain rest)

Current Reality, How We Got Here, Where We're Headed

Environmentalism, Fascism, Socialism, Collectivism...Statism by another name

Reality in America: "Toto, I don't think we're in Kansas anymore."

Now that you have been exposed to the Great Lie and the Great Con, you need to fully understand where we are, how TTK did what they did to us, and where we are possibly headed. To recap, the Great Lie tells us that we are better off denying our very nature as productive beings seeking to make our own lives better, and the Great Con is how TTK sell us the Great Lie and are working to implement their plans.

Only within the context of understanding what a proper society of men should look like can I provide a roadmap to a better future that makes sense to you, and one that you can act upon to build your Life.

So stay with me now. I know this can be disturbing stuff, but I promise we will end on a very, very positive note.

Let us continue....

Today we do not live in a society that is proper to our nature as independent, self-guided productive beings. Therefore, we do not live in a society that is conducive to our welfare and happiness. It is a society that is actually extremely destructive of one's ability to create wealth, abundance and happiness.

It is destructive of our very life.

We live in a society that is a 'geographically isolated mob held together by institutionalized gang-rule'. We are held together, "governed", by a gang that holds as its values whatever will keep the gang in power and control, disguised as competing factions of left and right, with programs innocuously labeled as helping the poor and under-privileged, saving the planet, or fighting the ubiquitous, seemingly never-vanquished whack-a-mole bad buys.

Yet we are told that we live in a capitalist society!

Of course, what we have is emphatically NOT Capitalism.

The world has not yet seen Capitalism.

You must understand this!

Most people in our country do not understand at all what Capitalism is.

Statism and Subjugation of the Individual

What we live in is an elite-controlled State; essentially Statism, a society characterized by the primacy of the Elite with their plans for one-world control, and their control of the population through implementation of the various 'isms' in their arsenal:

- Fascism (government-business partnership where winners and losers are chosen based on how well they tow the party line and contribute to the cause). This is Crony Capitalism;
- Collectivism (redistribution of wealth by the State through taxes and welfare programs all in the name of promoting equality);
- Environmentalism (State sponsored placement of the so-called 'rights' of the planet's rocks or animals above the only true rights of the individual human being); and
- Terrorism (State-instilled fear of boogey-men to convince us to voluntarily exchange liberties for safety and security).

Note that ALL of these ism-tools that TTK use have one thing in common: they depend upon you and I willingly giving up our liberties for the sake of some greater good—for some good 'greater than ourselves'—for some manner of social ideal that is supposedly superior in value and merit to our own individual lives and happiness.

They want us to sacrifice the very best of our lives for the sake of just about anything except our very own happiness.

This one thing they all have in common is called altruism. Webster's defines altruism this way: 1) unselfish regard for or devotion to the welfare of others, and 2) behavior by an animal that is not beneficial to or may be harmful to itself but that benefits others of its species.

Our society today is characterized by the altruistically-motivated subjugation of your Individual Life, Liberty and the Pursuit of Happiness to the needs of the State. That is, to the new-controlled-world-order ideals of TTK...cloaked in the needs of the group such as the inner-city poor and the ever-present 'under-privileged', the needs of the planet, or national security.

Our society is characterized by the limitation of and thus the negation of the right to your life, the hindrance or prevention of taking actions required to maintain, extend, and enjoy your life.

This of course includes the negation of your right to your property, destruction of property security, and the use of force by government to prevent its use as you see fit by government prevention of free trade to mutual benefit with other men abiding by the same values.

I know all this sounds esoteric and formal to you because you may be unaccustomed to the terminology, but there is no other way to say something than to just say it. A thing is what it is. In order to communicate, words mean things, and to be a man you have to call a spade a spade.

So what are the 'benefits' provided by our benefactors in government in exchange for our liberties?

- Mass unemployment (20%+);
- Extreme inequalities in wealth (1% v. 99%);
- Rampant welfare expenditures
- Ever-increasing taxes on consumers and businessmen and ever increasing regulations on the use of private property that destroy the productivity of labor and create regression in real welfare;
- Allowance of illegal immigration and expansion of social programs which causes huge misallocations of capital that could otherwise be used to produce more wealth per capita;
- Perpetual war which also causes huge misallocations of capital;
- Increasing controls and restrictions on what you can do with your property;
- Increasing controls and restrictions on what you can

say;

- Increasing controls and restrictions on where you can go;
- Increasing controls and restrictions on your ability to protect yourself;
- Domestic wars on drugs and the increasingly militarized police state that incarcerates the highest percentage of citizens when compared to any other country...including communist China; and
- Last but not least, among many others, the overall dumbing down and growing dependency of the average Jane and Joe.

Folks, again, this is emphatically NOT capitalism. As I will show later, NONE of this would exist in a purely capitalist society!

These aberrations and distortions are symptoms of a very sick society and they could not happen under Capitalism.

The world has not yet seen capitalism!

So how did it happen? How did they pull it off and how do they keep it going?

As I said before, ultimately it happened because throughout the decades and through all of the changing faces of bad actors at the helm, TTK and their minions have conditioned the majority of people into thinking that to act in accordance with their true nature is evil, and that to act in accordance with controls on their nature, and even to deny their nature, is good.

TTK say that it is necessary and right as a means of justice to penalize anyone who excels or otherwise chooses to exert his independence as a Man.

Why? Again, because according to TTK, men acting freely results in mass inequality, the perpetuation of the poor, overcrowding, overpopulation, over-development, destruction of the plant, and general, world-wide chaos, pestilence, war, and mayhem.

It has come to the point where the vast majority of people don't even know what their true nature is!

Most people cannot comprehend what they have lost because they literally haven't known anything else. The 'normal' IS what TTK have arranged for them over the decades of their lives. They do not know, understand, or expect anything different.

Adoption of a Dark Ages Mentality

People have allowed this to happen to them because they have been dumbed down and conditioned to adopt a Dark Ages mentality: The great mass of individuals out there either consciously or subconsciously believe that their economic ills are caused by an arbitrary power – big business and the rich, or the latest health or environmental scare, or by fear and chaos created by the boogeyman, or that their perceived ills are just due to the nature of the universe...a malevolent universe that is out to squash them like a bug.

All of this of course requires an even bigger arbitrary power to counteract these evils – government, which will act on their behalf to thwart and destroy these threats.

Ultimately, people's adoption of the Dark Ages mentality is at root caused by the existing pervasive antipathy to reason and logic, the correction of which is prevented by the continued propagation of a myopic individual worldview, a near-sighted worldview, of that nasty malevolent universe out there.

And this propagation of a myopic world view includes the fostering of confusion and fear regarding each individual's inability to acquire money and wealth for themselves on their own, and the promotion of an almost maniacal envy-ridden resentment at those who do produce and do succeed.

As an illustration of the modern Dark Ages Mentality, I can't help but include here the classic humorous "Beer Analogy." While cast in the context of taxes, you still get the idea of the general "fairness" that has been bred into most people, including their negative view of the undeserving "rich":

Suppose that every day, ten men go out for a beer and the bill for all ten comes to $100.

If they paid their bill the way we pay our taxes, it would go something like this:

The first four men (the poorest) would pay nothing.

The fifth would pay $1.00

The sixth would pay $3.00

The seventh would pay $7.00

The eighth would pay $12.00

The ninth would pay $18.00

The tenth man (the richest) would pay $59.00

So that's what they decided to do. The men drank in the bar every day and seemed quite happy with the arrangement, until one day the owner threw them a curve.

"Since you are all such good customers," he said, "I'm going

to reduce the cost of your daily beer by $20.00."

Drinks for the ten men now cost just $80.00.

The group still wanted to pay their bill the way we pay our taxes, so the first four men were unaffected. They would still drink for free. But what about the other six men – the paying customers? How could they divide the $20 windfall so that everyone would get their "fair share?"

They realized that $20.00 divided by six is $3.33. But if they subtracted that from everybody's share, then the fifth man and the sixth man would each end up being paid to drink his beer. So, the bar owner suggested that it would be fair to reduce each man's bill by roughly the same amount, and he proceeded to work out the amounts each should pay.

And so:

The fifth man, like the first four, now paid nothing (100% savings).

The sixth now paid $2 instead of $3 (33% savings).

The seventh now paid $5 instead of $7 (28% savings).

The eighth now paid $9 instead of 12 (25% savings).

The ninth now paid $14 instead of $18 (22% savings).

The tenth now paid $49 instead of $59 (16% savings).

Each of the six was better off than before! And the first four continued to drink for free. But once outside the restaurant, the men began to compare their savings.

"I only got a dollar out of the $20" declared the sixth man. He pointed to the tenth man, "But he got $10!"

"Yeah, that's right," shouted the seventh man. "Why should he get $10 back when I got only two? The wealthy get all the breaks!"

"Wait a minute," yelled the first four men in unison. "We didn't I get anything at all. The system exploits the poor!"

The nine men surrounded the tenth and beat him up.

The next night the tenth man didn't show up for drinks, so the nine sat down and had beers without him. But when it came time to pay the bill, they discovered something important. They didn't have enough money between all of them for even half of the bill!

And that, boys and girls, journalists and college professors, is how our tax system works. The people who pay the highest taxes get the most benefit from a tax reduction. Tax them too much, attack them for being wealthy, and they just may not show up anymore. In fact, they might start drinking overseas where the atmosphere is somewhat friendlier.

To paraphrase Thomas Aquinas, for those who understand, no explanation is needed.

For those who do not understand, no explanation is possible.

Methods of the Statist

On all fronts, as part of conditioning a Dark Ages mentality, TTK foster hostility towards producers and wealth creation; they promote **'get-evenism.'** Perceived injustice in observed inequalities in wealth unleashes the incredibly destructive emotion of envy which drives the clamor for "equal outcomes," the goal of **egalitarianism** (an aspect of collectivism), and fosters an environment of tribe warfare—class against class, group against group. "Selfishness" becomes the evil and acting in self-interest by individuals is deemed harmful to others. **Altruism,** sacrificing your happiness to provide for someone else's, is touted as the only proper motive for one's actions.

People succumb to the **zero-sum game mentality**. Here, TTK foster the idea that another's perceived gain is achieved only at their own loss. In order for someone else to win, you must lose. In a zero-sum world, men fear other men: one who is poor fears his fellow man lest his fellow man becomes successful and thus takes advantage of the less fortunate like himself; one who is rich fears his fellow man because the envy and hatred of the less fortunate will threaten his wealth and maybe even his health. Similarly, the product of one's labor is supposedly stolen by the Capitalist, and that slave or subsistence wages, along with child labor, would result if businessmen were not restrained by the do-gooders of government.

All of this of course is just the standard line of bull crap called the Marxian Exploitation Theory that has been solidly and resoundingly refuted time and time again by numerous world-renowned economists, but because of its emotional appeal it still draws a crowd of tremendously ignorant die-hard evangelists.

All of these result in efforts at the redistribution of wealth and thus the actual destruction of wealth.

TTK pander to the great mass of ignoramuses, and work diligently at the dumbing down of the individual mind. They foster dependency and condemn the innate desire to be independent and question ideas that somehow just don't make sense to the normal person. (And, of course, to foster the growth of the great masses of ignoramuses, why not flood the nation with freedom-illiterate welfare seekers from other countries?). (Note: I do not use 'ignoramus' as a derogatory term. Words mean things [ignoramus is defined as a person who does not know much] and it is a term that accurately describes the level of economic literacy of the average Joe out there...certainly of the vast majority of new immigrants.)

We are told that the world is a dangerous place, and only a massive government can ever come close to protecting us from viruses, the boogeyman, and the weather, and that the self-sacrifice of altruism, aided and abetted by the good intentions of government, is one's moral obligation and highest virtue.

So why do people fall for it?

Why are people so willing and ready to give up their liberty?

The Abdication of Reason and Willingness to Think

I want to tell you a story about something that happened to me a few years ago.

I was at a backyard barbecue at an old friend's house who had rented out rooms of his house to students while he had been away. So there were members of the younger crowd at the BBQ. While sipping on my favorite adult beverage at this event, I overheard several of the young men there discussing their plight in college, the expenses of college, the unpleasant need to struggle with working at odd jobs in order to make their way, and so forth. One of the young men was an exchange student from Czechoslovakia, and another was a young American student. Neither could have been more than 19 or 20.

I overheard the foreign student rave about the tremendous benefits to him of state-provided college education in his home country and that the United States should also provide any level of desired education free of charge to the student. He raved on and on about the benefits he receives as a citizen of his socialist utopia back home, and how the student loan trap in the US was just exploitation (which I happen to agree with by the way). And the American student was listening intently and nodding in agreement as to the injustice perpetrated against him by the system—the necessity of paying tuition, and paying for books and room and board—all because he just wanted to better himself. It was unfair he thought and I could tell he was getting angry and upset about having to actually work for something that he wanted.

After their exchange had ceased, I took the young man aside and asked him point blank: "Why is your generation so willing to give up your freedoms...the very liberties that define you as a human being!?"

Stunned, the student respectfully responded to this grey-haired dude that had shown an interest in his welfare that he did not understand. I then asked him in so many words if he wanted to live his life under the control of someone else or if he wanted the freedom to do as he pleased, make his own way in the world, and relish and be proud in what he could accomplish on his own, without owing favors to those who would buy his individuality and independence.

I forgot what else I said to him, but he could see it in my eyes. He instinctively knew what I was getting at. He had not even considered challenging what he had heard from this sniveling excuse for a man from abroad. In an instant, he recognized that he wanted to be free (as any healthy young man would) and definitively stated so in what words he could muster to describe his emotional response to my questions. He clearly recognized the message in my voice and in my meaning. He identified with it as any normal healthy MAN would! I then gave him the website for a favorite economist of mine, Dr. George Reisman, and a few other freedom related sites that catered more humorously and to the younger crowd such as Max Keiser and told him to make the effort to study and learn about what it means to be a free man…

We parted company and I then sat down with my buddy to continue imbibing our adult beverages and relayed to him the story. Later, when the kid was on his way out of the gathering, he came up to me and respectfully thanked me for the conversation and the website reference. He was actually very grateful that I had talked to him.

That is where I left the kid. I hope he turned out well and didn't join some modern version of a hippy commune.

(As an aside, it is very encouraging to me that young men such as he respond to moral leadership. But don't count on our so-called bunch of "leaders!" When was the last time you heard a politician talk fervently and animated about individual liberty like it burned in his soul? Damned sure it ain't Bush I, the Clintons, Bush II, Obama and their gangs of statists…the words freedom and liberty are decidedly NOT in their personal or professional lexicons. Also, this little story is a perfect example of the dearth of leadership out there! Young men and women need to hear the voices of reason ring loudly, clearly and often from whatever promontories, parapets, or soapboxes we can find.)

People like this young wet-behind-the-ears youngster buy into the Great Lie partly because their life's experiences have conditioned into them a deficiency of mental capacity—in the inability or unwillingness to think critically and conceptualize from first principles (e.g. man has a specific kind of nature that requires he take certain kinds of actions to further his life). Their parents have failed them and their teachers have failed them because they are likely ignoramuses in their own right.

Through poor education that has been designed to do so, they suffer from a widespread antipathy towards reason as the very means of their survival, and certainly as their only means of surviving well and prospering in growth and psychological and physical fulfillment and genuine happiness.

Like this kid, many of us have a learned inability to reconcile our plight in life with the true cause and effects nature of reality, and instead we attempt to reason from faulty premises that we have picked up along the way about how life should be. See if this simple syllogism (if A and B, then C) does not ring true for today's simple-minded ignoramus as a guide to their actions:

1.   I am helpless, the world is too big and complex and

unknowable, I am at the mercy of the universe... of events I cannot control, and telling me that I can control my life and that I can live in prosperity through my own effort by pulling myself up by my bootstraps is a lie.

2. Those who have done well did so by pure chance; their wealth is unearned and attained at the expense of guys like me that suffer in struggling to make ends meet.

3. Thus, because I need it and I deserve it, because the universe keeps me from creating it for myself, I demand that those who have done well give up some of what they have to me...and not only that, I also demand they be cut down a notch or two. And if they will not give it to me voluntarily and stop being so selfish, I will petition my gang in government to force them to do it. After all, it is wrong to be so selfish and enjoy life so much while I can't pay my rent, especially when what they have they got by pure chance, or by fraud, or by outright theft from little guys like me.

Can you pick out the faulty underlying premises here? Hint: the world IS knowable including man's nature and his dependence upon reason; wealth is NOT created by chance; one does NOT deserve a living just because one is alive; and selfishness is the Good. (we will deal with this more later, but let me say this now as a heads up: if you want to argue to persuade someone to your way of thinking, identify and attack their fundamental premises: until you can agree on the fundamental premises to argue about with your opponent, you are merely kicking around symptoms of the real problem and you are wasting your time).

People also fall for the Great Lie partly because, again as a learned conditioning, the human mind (on a worldwide scale) struggles with the stark reality that there are no guarantees in life. That death is inevitable and there are no guarantees of happiness.

The world is a tough place, work is difficult, life is short, and there are no guarantees.

This results in perceptual-level resentment that there is even an economic problem that they have to deal with: "Why can't my prosperity be given to me? It is unfair that others do so well and I do so poorly. Wealth and happiness and joy comes to others so easily! Why must I have to struggle to enjoy my life? Why must I have to produce? Why must I have to earn a living? Especially when those that are rich lied, stole, and cheated to get there!"

They accept the Great Lie partly due to the collapse of a work ethic culture and its skate-by-at-others-expense replacement. For the mentally weak (the ignoramus or those who refuse to see) it is easier to be a victim, especially when everything around them tells them that, through no fault of their own, they ARE a victim. Thus, it's easier to condemn the haves and vote themselves freebies.

Listen to this excellent pro-capitalist talk by Yaron Brook; it's a great explanation, at least in part, of how people are conditioned into an anti-capitalist, self-defeating, self-injuring mentality. His main message runs about 48 minutes, with the remainder being excellent Q&A.

He's easy to listen to so stick with it. Go get your favorite drink. It is well worth your time:

Scan To Watch

https://youtu.be/uh8O3rLOppA

I keep harping on this because you have to get it in your head: **TTK and their anti-human minions have conditioned the majority of people to accept an altruistic ethics that teaches that to act in accordance with their true nature as**

beings that must be productive is evil, and that to act in accordance with controls on their nature, and even to deny their nature, is good.

The bottom line is we buy into it for the same reason that you and I do anything... We buy into it for emotional reasons.

But our emotions come from what you and I think, and what and how we think comes from what we hold as values. And values are what drive you to act to obtain those values....those actions you take being called virtues.

Ultimately people give up their liberties because they have forgotten, or have never learned, what it means to live as men. They have never learned or gave up the values and stopped practicing the virtues proper to sustain their life as men.

As serfs, as hapless victims, and as whining parasites, yes. But not as men.

And they do so because no one has stood up to tell them otherwise. They do so because TTK have filled the intellectual void in their being with anti-human "selflessness" crap because no other alternative was ever presented to them.

How do you feel at this point?

Does this bother you at all?

Are you a little anxious and uncertain as to what this means and what you should do?

If you feel these things, it is a good sign that you are still alive.

Take heart. IT IS NOT TOO LATE. It's not too late for me, for you, for our loved ones, for our country, or for the world.

But for things to change, YOU have to change.

It has to start with you.

You have to choose to be a MAN. To THINK like a man. To ACT like a man. To LIVE like a man. And in the process of doing so, present an example that other innocently ignorant time travelers may follow.

Where We Are Headed

The path we are on is unsustainable if we intend to live in freedom—if we esteem individual liberty.

The society we have devolved into is NOT free.

We are headed into another dark ages of sorts, into a new age of feudalism characterized by the localized low-productivity, low standard of living poverty-stricken self-sufficiency reminiscent of the serfs of centuries past.

If we proceed on this path it is only a matter of time before the western nations of the world, heretofore representing the progress of mankind, revert to the misery of the modern era Soviet Union or communist China, or two-bit regimes like Cuba or Venezuela, and along with us all of the other budding industrializing nations of the world.

One has simply to Google "financial collapse" or "2015 collapse" or any variation on the theme to determine for one's self that we are overdue for a financial system collapse that will make 2008 look like a gentle spring rain. I could give you all kinds of sources for these prognostications (listen to Jim Rickards again), but because they are so prevalent these days by so many the greatest financial minds of our times and even government officials, that I would be wasting time here in this book.

Do the research on your own.

But there is reason to take heart. Even in a financial collapse where for example the U.S. dollar goes away as the world's reserve currency and we fall into a major world-wide depression, people will go on living.

Whatever pain, suffering, and gnashing of teeth transpires in the upheaval, people will still have all of the needs depicted in Maslow's hierarchy, and life will go on. Some new monetary system will be set up, hopefully on some manner of precious metals standard that will return governments to fiscal discipline, and life will go on.

Only this time I think there will be a backlash against statism like never before seen, and it will be driven by the great awakening that is taking place, especially among the young.

And to fuel that fire, let's get on to talking about the empowering secrets of wealth that will underlie the backlash.

(Break Time)

CHAPTER THREE

Twelve Secrets of Wealth That Will Open Your Eyes!

(...and make you both madder than hell that no one ever told you AND more hopeful for the future)

Ok, now we are turning the corner on the negative-but-necessary part of my message to you. Now we begin to see glimmers of great expectation and possibilities...

In this section I present to you the solution to the TTK-manufactured path of uncertainty, confusion, fear, anxiety, lack, struggle, suffering and pain.

Remember that I told you earlier that the nature of the problem everyone faces is how to live a long and fulfilling life of happiness and abundance while on this rock? And how your mindset, your mental outlook, your world view is what ultimately will drive you to succeed.

Well, this section and the rest of the book provides insight into what is required to achieve that personal utopia of happiness that is very possible for each of us. What I present in the rest of this book is all about developing that empowering mindset, that empowering world view that you need to succeed.

To get directly to the point, the answer to that problem, the solution to that problem, is Laissez Faire Capitalism.....and all that such a social system implies.

But in order for you to accept Capitalism as the solution to your personal welfare, you must first understand what Capitalism is and what it is not. And to understand what it is, you have to understand some key concepts that I call 'secrets' of wealth.

These are secrets not in the sense that they are new; this stuff has been known for centuries. But they are essentially secrets to those of us who have not been exposed to them before. And understanding them will unlock the mystery for you; they will remove the fog that surrounds us in our daily lives as to the meaning of things, and why things happen the way they do, how things could be different, how you play such a critical role, and **why your active earnest participation in a truly capitalist society is immensely beneficial to you personally.**

Now listen, there is a lot of new material here and lots of new concepts you have not likely been exposed to. So I suggest you read one or two Secrets of Wealth in a sitting, then take a break.

This material is far too important for you to just peruse. I want you awake, fully alert, and refreshed and FOCUSED when you go through these secrets. If you want to get the most out of this, read a little, then take a break and let your brain rest.

You ready?

Here are the 12 'secrets' of wealth:

Secret #1 — You Are Meant to be Productive

The Primacy of the Material World and the Nature of Man

"You Are Good if You Produce. You Are a Saint if You Produce At What You Love"

I have already talked about this, but because it is central to my message, I will harp on it again.

Man's nature is to be productive.

Period.

Your nature is to go out in the physical world and work to create the material values that assist you in the maintenance, extension, and enjoyment of your life.

In the abstract sense, for a man to sustain his very life, he must shape, re-shape, alter, modify, and rearrange the material world around him to 1) provide for his most fundamental needs of food, clothing, and shelter, and 2) upon satisfaction of those most basic of needs, to provide for the fulfillment and extension of his life.

He has to produce or the physical world will kill him.

Sure this may seem intuitive to you, but I want to drive this home because all else regarding your personal welfare and happiness absolutely depends upon you recognizing your essential nature as producer.

This absolutely normal requirement to produce, to rearrange our physical surroundings, lies at the very core of our nature.

Man has to actively engage in the process of production; of producing material values of use to him out of the physical-material world that surrounds him. There is no place else to obtain them.

Even a caveman's existence at the most primitive level relies on his ability to create shelter and clothing to protect him from the elements and food to sustain his body, by taking what is provided by nature and turning those nature-given means into huts, loin clothes, clubs and spears, etc.

At the contemporary level, you and I must still produce at something in order to exchange the values we produce for the other modern values of clothing, homes, transportations, and entertainments that we want.

If we want to live, we have no choice but to produce.

Otherwise, for the primitive as well as the contemporary man alike, we would simply die from exposure, starvation and disease.

Plants and animals automatically pursue the course of life-sustaining and life-generating action inherent in and unique to their nature. The difference between the lower animals and you and me is that we possess reason and by its very nature, volition, the ability to choose: we have to CHOOSE to figure out what to do and to take the actions necessary to sustain and enhance our lives.

We do not come out of the chute equipped with grass-digesting stomachs, or legs fast enough, or with claws or long canines to catch and kill our prey or outrun predators, or even an innate instinct that tells us to eat grass or eat other animals alive. Nor do we come equipped with thick fur or wool body covering to keep us warm. As Yaron Brook stated in his speech above, as a species we're pretty pathetic when it comes to surviving by use of our bodies out there in the physical world.

Sure, like other mammals as our closest comparison, when you are born your purely sensual-level state of nature drives you to suckle your mother's breast. But once you progress into the perceptual and conceptual levels of existence, once you are free of the dependency on your parents, once you can reason, you have no choice but to learn how to survive and prosper using the physical values that you and others produce or, again, you will simply perish and live a miserable life until you do.

Let me close this section with input by Dr. Leonard Peikoff:

> *Productiveness is the process of creating material values, whether goods or services. Such creation is a*

necessity of human survival in any age, whether the values take the form of bearskins, clubs, a pot full of meat, and paintings on the walls of caves; or of skyscrapers, ballet, brain surgery, and a gourmet meal aboard a computerized spaceship; or of the unimaginable luxuries and splendors yet to come.

The other living species, as we have seen, survive by consuming ready-made values. ...From bearskins on up, however, the values required by man's survival must be conceived and then created. For a conceptual being, the only alternative to creativity is parasitism.

The other species survive in essence by adjusting themselves to their background, assuming they have the good fortune to find in nature the things they need. Man survives by adjusting his background to himself. Since he reshapes the given, he does not have to count on good fortune or even the absence of disaster.

Just as there cannot be too much rationality, so there cannot be too much of any of its derivatives, including productiveness. Just as there is no limit to man's need of knowledge and therefore of thought, so there is no limit to man's need of wealth and therefore of creative work. Intellectually, every discovery contributes to human life by enhancing men's grasp of reality. Existentially, every material achievement contributes to human life by making it increasingly secure, prolonged, and/or pleasurable.

There can be no such thing as a man who transcends the need of progress, whether intellectually or material. There is no human life that is "safe enough," "long enough," "knowledgeable enough." "affluent enough," or "enjoyable enough"—not if man's life is the standard of value.

...Productiveness is not only a necessary element of the good life, it is the good life's <u>central purpose</u>.

Secret of Wealth #1: You are supposed to be productive. That is how you are made.

- The best way, the only way, to be happy on this planet and to contribute to the happiness of others, is to produce. And if we want to live well, we have to increase our personal value to the marketplace; we have to contribute more, we have to produce at a higher level;

- Regardless of your view of the origin of man, whether you come from God or by evolution, you were created with a certain specific nature that requires that you rearrange the world around you in order to maintain, extend, and enjoy your own life, which includes by extension and for very personally selfish emotional reasons, the lives of those you love;

- Not only is it necessary that you and I produce, but because it is necessary, because it is part of our nature, it is also morally right. You are moral, you are good, to the extent that you happily produce at a level commensurate with your abilities for the sake of your own welfare. Secondarily your product contributes to the welfare of all, it sets an example that inspires others to do the same, and prevents the rise to power of TTK elitists and statists.

- Those who do not produce to the level of their abilities contribute to parasitism, dependency and a mentality of lack, social malaise and decay, and the general unhappiness that statists feed and thrive upon.

Moral of the Story

You are meant to be productive! Take it to heart. Relish in your nature! Go find what it is that excites you, turn yourself loose, and go forth and PRODUCE! Go BE happy and produce! BE happy by being productive! Don't ever, EVER, give that up for anyone!

As the saying goes, "Do what you love and you'll never work a day in your life!"

Secret #2 — Our Unlimited Need and Desire for Wealth

Man is the measure of all things.

By our very nature, we as a society of rational beings have, in aggregate, an unlimited need and desire for wealth.

Each of us possesses our own unique needs and desires for an improved standard of living, and although each of us is necessarily limited in our immediate needs and desires for additional wealth (we typically don't want a Bentley before we even have the relatively simple locomotive benefit of a Volkswagen), in the aggregate, because we are each unique with different skills, ability and willingness to produce, mankind has an essentially insatiable need and desire for more and better stuff to make our lives healthier, longer, and happier.

The secret of wealth here is this: There is no limit to what material wealth you and I can imagine having in our lives if only we could produce it (or, equivalently, earn enough to purchase it).

Let me quote from Dr. George Reisman. I recommend that you read his entire section on this topic at the link below this excerpt:

> *Man's need for wealth is limitless because he possesses the faculty of reason. The possession of this faculty both*

radically enlarges the scope of man's needs and capacities in comparison with those of any other living entity and, at the same time, makes possible continuous improvement in the satisfaction of his needs and in the exercise of his capacities. Considered abstractly, man's possession of reason gives him the potential for a limitless range of knowledge and awareness and thus for a limitless range of action and experience. Man's mind can grasp the existence both of subatomic particles and of galaxies, and of everything in between. It observes all manner of patterns, and similarities and differences, of which no other form of consciousness is capable. Thus, the potential is created for man to act over a range extending from the subatomic level to the remotest reaches of outer space, and to experience all that his mind enables him to discern and enjoy in the totality of the universe.

Material goods—wealth—are the physical means both of acting in the world (for example, automobiles and airplanes, tools and machines of all kinds) and of enjoying the experiences of which man is capable (for example—in addition to many goods of the preceding category—works of art and sculpture, landscaped grounds and gardens, beautiful homes and furniture). They are the instrumentalities of man's action and objects of his contemplation. The potential of a limitless range of action and experience implies a limitless need for wealth as the means of achieving his potential. **Man needs wealth without limit if he is to fulfill his limitless potential as a rational being in physical reality.** (Emphasis added)

The fact that the need and desire for wealth are limitless does not mean that when people devote themselves to satisfying that need and desire...they go through life with a sense of endless frustration, seeking more than they can ever hope to obtain. The normal man, if he lacks an automobile, does not actively desire a yacht. He actively desires merely an automobile. His desire for a yacht lies dormant until such time as he already has acquired one or more high-quality automobiles. The limitless desire for wealth, in other words, becomes active only step by step. It manifests itself in an active desire for things that are merely one or two steps beyond our reach at the moment. It leads us to exert ourselves and extend our reach. And then, as we succeed, desires previously dormant become active, or totally new desires are formed, and we are led to exert ourselves and extend our reach still further. Thus, the limitless desire for wealth impels us to steadily to advance.

Oriental philosophy and some schools of thought in the contemporary Western world claim that the fact that our desires will always be a step ahead of our possessions shows the futility of our efforts–that instead, we should seek to rid ourselves of our desires and be content forever with some minimum of wealth. Such teachings are utterly mistaken, and their influence helps to account for the stagnation and poverty that exist in the world. They view the excess of our desires over our possessions as a source of discontent and unhappiness. Actually, this excess is the root of our ambitiousness and our rising to meet challenges. It is what impels us to progress, and, as such, is an essential element to our happiness.

(Learn more from Reisman on this, click here)

So we have a virtually unlimited need and desire for wealth, and thus for the ever increasing production of wealth.

In fact, we individuals acting in the pursuit of our own lives in constant pursuit of happiness, have in the aggregate the ability to remake the face of the earth a thousand times over, and if we are left free we will absolutely eventually do so!

Stop and imagine the sheer magnitude of the wealth that needs to be created to satisfy the growing needs and desires of the growing population of the planet.

What does this unlimited need and desire of we humans tell you?

First, it should tell you that there is unlimited opportunity out there for you, as an individual, to satisfy human wants and needs. There is an unlimited opportunity out there for you to get rich.

Secret of Wealth #2: **Because we have an unlimited need and desire for wealth, and because the population of the planet is growing, there are virtual unlimited opportunities out there for you, as an individual, to satisfy human wants and needs, and thus unlimited opportunities for you to become wealthy to your heart's desire.**

Although you as an individual have a limited need and desire for wealth (at this particular point in time the range of focus of your needs goes only so far...), the needs and desires for wealth of all the other people on the planet are in effect unlimited.

Therefore, there is an unlimited opportunity out there for you to contribute and add value to others in doing what you love, because odds are that whatever you are passionate about, there are enough others who feel the same way for you to become stone wealthy.

This is the <u>source</u> of that abundance mentality we continuously hear about...contributing to and servicing an unlimited need in others out there in the marketplace with something you are passionate about.

There is no metaphysical reason out there in the universe, other than self-imposed limits to your own motivation, why you cannot become wealthy to your heart's desire. The ONLY thing that can stop you is the preventive actions of TTK and their minions in government, and they can be defeated in the very act of you demanding that you be left free to produce and become wealthy.

In fact, it is government in its most debilitating forms as created by TTK ideals that causes and perpetuates the world's poor health, poor longevity, and untold misery <u>because</u> it does not permit men to be free, and in the process of being free to solve their own problems through production and trade.

Moral of the Story

Understand that there is TREMENDOUS opportunity out there for whoever is willing to take it and run with it!

The population of the planet, currently at about 7 billion, has doubled since about 1974. According to Wikipedia, the global population will reach eight billion by 2030, and will likely reach around nine billion by 2050. Alternative scenarios for 2050 range from a low of 7.4 billion to a high of more than 10.6 billion. The latest numbers estimate that the population of the planet will be 11 billion by the end of this century.

And what does this tell you? Read again what I said above about remaking the face of the planet!

TTK and their statist brethren cringe and condemn the "population explosion" and actually desire to wipe out a large portion of people that currently live!

Why?

Because they do not believe that the earth can "sustain" an ever-increasing population.

Why?

Because, although they give lip service to the "lack of resources", their real motivation is that they hate the "uncontrolled" productive abilities of free man—they outright despise and hate man for even having this ability and willingness to conquer nature and turn the planet into a garden in his own image—as in each of us uniquely in our own individual manner.

Hopefully by now I am awakening in you a different perspective:

The other thing that this information should hint to you is that although there is an unlimited need and desire for wealth, there is also necessarily a limited capacity to actually create that wealth.

Which brings us to Secret of Wealth #3.

Secret #3 — The Ineradicable Shortage of Labor

The fundamental and essential nature of economic life is this: the need and desire for additional wealth are there and the nature-given means of producing it are there; all that is lacking is the ability of human labor to transform the nature-given (or previously-produced) means of production into additional wealth.

On this foundation, the fundamental economic need of rational beings emerges as the overcoming of the limitations on production imposed by the scarcity of labor. Always, what stands between man and his need for greater wealth is his limited ability to produce wealth—his limited ability and also willingness to perform labor.

-George Reisman

In other words...

Perpetual Mass Unemployment is Bullshit

Because the production of wealth is necessarily a physical enterprise, and the total amount of human labor available for production is limited, it is the mental and physical labor of each of us that is THE single scarce economic factor of production, and the need for continued increase in the production of wealth gives rise to THE essential, fundamental economic problem: how to steadily increase the productivity of our labor in order to satisfy this objective unlimited individual need and desire for wealth.

To drive this point home, I quote again at length from Reisman.

Again, do not be lazy! You bought this book, so make the effort and expend the mental energy it takes to change your head. You bought this book as a solution to how to get and keep an empowering mindset that drives you to build wealth.

Well a big chunk of developing that mindset is knowing the cause and effects of some really basic economic principles regarding being a Producer.

So study the passage and educate yourself. Build the mental foundation that is required for that magic mindset. If you don't have time to focus now, come back later when you do.

Here's George in all his reasoned elocution (emphasis in bold added):

Wealth is the result of human labor. Labor is the means by which man's mind transmits his designs and purposes to matter. It is man's application of his bodily and mental faculties for the purpose of altering matter in form or location and thereby making the matter thus altered serve a further purpose. Matter thus altered by man's labor is a <u>product</u>. Production is the process of thus altering matter. A producer is one who effects such alterations.

The matter which is altered in production, that is, which is the subject of man's labor, can be nature-given, such as a piece of land or ore in the ground, or itself a previously produced product, such as cotton cloth or steel sheet. Always, the performance of human labor is essential to production.

It is important to realize that in a division-of-labor society, the labor applied in production is not limited to manual labor, that is, to labor applied to materials or otherwise in physical operations. In such a society, it embraces much more, such as the labor entailed in founding, organizing, and directing business firms and in providing them with capital. Such labor achieves its effects by operating through the manual labor of others, which renders it more efficient.

*Wealth not only is the product of human labor, but also could be produced in larger quantity if more labor were devoted to its production. Indeed, the application of more labor is the only fundamental requirement for increasing the supply of wealth. This is because more labor is the source of additional equipment and materials, including additional agricultural commodities, and mineral supplies extracted from the ground. Thus, **the scarcity of wealth implies a more fundamental scarcity of labor.***

The fundamental scarcity of labor is manifest in the fact that virtually everyone would like to enjoy an income many times greater than the income he is presently capable of earning. For example, today an average worker may earn on the order of $20,000 per year for working forty hours *per week. If such a worker had it in his power to earn $100,000 per year, he would have no difficulty in finding ways to live up to such an income. Unfortunately, to earn such an income at his present rate of pay, he would have to work more hours than there are in a week. His maximum actual ability to work is obviously vastly less than corresponds to the income he would like to have.*

But this is only another way of saying that the utmost goods and services he is capable of <u>producing</u> are far less than the goods and services he would like to consume. Taken collectively, our desire to be able to spend five or ten times more than we now can afford to spend is an indication that we would like five to ten times more work performed than is now performed. In the present state of technology and productivity of labor (output per unit of labor), this is how much additional labor would need to be performed to produce the larger volume of output we would like to be able to buy.

The only way that earning and spending $100,000 a year instead of $20,000 a year can represent the ability to buy five times more goods is if five times more goods are produced... But in a given state of technology and productivity of labor, this would be possible only if five times as much labor can be performed, which, of course, is itself impossible. People can work themselves to the point of utter exhaustion, and still they cannot produce more than a small fraction of all that it would be useful and desirable for them to produce. Thus, the supply of labor that people can provide falls radically short of the supply *whose products they would like to have.* **Labor is scarce.**

The labor that we implicitly desire to have at our disposal, whether to produce goods for us or to provide us with personal services, is, as I have said, limited only by our imaginations. And yet while nature has provided each of us with an imagination capable of forming desires on a grand scale, it has simultaneously equipped each of us with only two arms to provide for the satisfaction of those desires. Each of us is easily capable of forming desires whose fulfillment requires the labor of multitudes, and yet by the laws of arithmetic, the average member of any society can never obtain more that the labor, or products of the labor, of just one *person. This is so because for each person who exists to consume, there can be no more than one person present to produce. Indeed, when the very young and the sick and infirm are allowed for, who can only be supported by the labor of others, it turns out that for each person who consumes there is, on average, substantially less than the labor of one person available to produce.*

The scarcity of labor is not only fundamental, however. It is also ineradicable.

...Increases in the ability to produce are accompanied by new and additional desires for wealth, which grows out of the very same technological advances that make possible the increases in the ability to produce. The effect of this is that the scarcity of labor is not reduced by increases in the productivity of labor. The scarcity of labor is also not reduced by any increase in the size of the population and

thus the number of people able and willing to work, because the additional members of that population bring with them their own needs and desires for goods and services that are in excess of their ability to add to the supply of goods and services. Furthermore, as the productivity of labor rises and increases the worker's standard of living, the workers tend to acquire a growing desire for leisure. As a result, not only does the desire for wealth grow as the ability to produce it increases, but also the amount of labor the individual is willing to perform decreases. This represents an additional cause of the continuing scarcity of labor.

Thus, the fundamental and essential nature of economic life is this: the need and desire for additional wealth are there and the nature-given means of producing it are there; all that is lacking is the ability of human labor to transform the nature-given means of production into additional wealth.

On this foundation, the fundamental economic need of rational beings emerges as the overcoming of the limitations on production imposed by the scarcity of labor. **Always, what stands between man and his need for greater wealth is his limited ability and also willingness to produce wealth—his limited ability and also willingness to perform labor.** *There is only one solution to this problem. And that is <u>continuously to raise the productivity of labor</u>—that is, continuously to increase the quantity and quality of the goods that can be produced per unit of labor, including the variety of goods. An ineradicable scarcity of labor resulting from a need and desire for labor that are* *always vastly greater than the supply of the labor requires that the productivity of labor be rendered greater and greater. The rise in the productivity of labor is the only conceivable way in which man can obtain the progressively greater amounts of wealth that his rational and progressive nature requires.*

The problem of precisely <u>how continuously to raise the productivity of labor</u>, to make possible an ever increasing production and enjoyment of goods per capita, is what I call <u>the economic problem</u>.

That was quite a reading assignment, but do you get the point?

Secret to Wealth #3: In a free society, mass unemployment and perpetual poverty cannot exist. Because economic life, yours and mine, is characterized by an ineradicable shortage of labor, we will never be able to produce enough to instantly or forever satisfy the ever increasing human needs and wants. So <u>in a free society</u> <u>there is an ongoing</u> <u>unlimited</u> <u>demand for</u> <u>people who are able and willing</u> <u>to work</u>, and virtually anyone who is willing to work will find employment if his wages are free-market driven.

- In a free society, you and I as entrepreneurs, regardless of how productive each of us can become through our own efficiency and/or through the use of machines, will always need the help of multiple others. Also, in a free society we will always have enough people eager and willing to help us contribute;

- In a free society, for those of us who choose to be employees, there will always be an unlimited demand for eager, productive workers until such time as we choose to join the ranks of entrepreneurs;

- Always, there are enough of us to produce enough for each of us to be happy in the present if only we are left free to do so!

- Again, what most inhibits us from producing enough for each of us to be happy in the present are the policies and actions of the one entity that is inherently designed to limit freedom: government.

Moral of the Story

The current state of unemployment and poverty is an insanity in motion. And the anti-freedom fiscal, monetary, and economic policies of government are the direct cause of mass unemployment and poverty and as such, are evil on wheels.

There is no good reason for mass unemployment or poverty!

In a free society, where wages are truly commensurate with one's ability as determined in a free labor market without coercion from government agencies or labor unions, anyone who wants to work will find work and will have an essentially unlimited opportunity to improve himself by expanding his ability to produce at a level commensurate with his ever-increasing skills and degree of personal productivity.

Mass unemployment or poverty cannot exist in a Capitalist society where freedom to be productive is the hallmark of the worthy respectable man.

Which leads us to a second related issue from Secret #3, and that is the role of the increasing the productivity of labor in increasing our ability to produce wealth and be happy.

Secret #4 — The Holy Grail of Productivity

You Win to the Extent that You Contribute and Encourage Others to Contribute

Nothing can be consumed without first being produced. This is certain.

Wealth and your standard of living have nothing to do with money...but have everything to do with what can be purchased with the quantity of money that you have to spend! And the major determinant of what can be purchased with your money is the amount of stuff that has been produced and is available to buy.

Thus your standard of living, your physical welfare, and to a large degree your psychological welfare, directly depends upon what stuff can be produced by all of us in the economy in any given period of time. And what determines that amount of stuff is how many there are of us to produce and how productive each of us is.

As shown in the Secret #3, the single scarce factor in an economy is our labor.

Labor is scarce.

In a free society, we can never get enough of it.

Given our limitless need and desire for wealth, there can never be enough physical or mental labor available to create things. So the only choice we have with what labor there is available at any given time is that this labor must be made more productive.

How much goods and services, how much wealth, can be produced in a given period of time by our available labor is called the productivity of labor (POL).

So your general standard of living depends upon the productivity of each of us in the marketplace. And an increasing or improving standard of living depends upon an ever-increasing POL.

Just by participating in the market with whatever goods or services that you produce, you directly contribute to the mass of goods and services available, and thus to the overall standard of living of each of us.

And for us to continuously improve our personal standard of living through increasing our purchasing power, all each of us has to do is produce more and better quality goods and services! Preferably with something that we enjoy....

But wait! We learned that there is that pesky ineradicable shortage of labor! So how on earth can we all produce more and better quality goods and services?

The answer is simple.

By more efficient and advancing technological progress. These are the beasts that continuously allow each of us to become more productive....to produce more with a given amount of our labor. Both happen because capitalists (entrepreneurs and businessmen) are always interested in finding ways to increase the productivity of labor.

As a simple obvious example, anyone who types the written word is far more efficient with the technological progress embodied in a modern voice-recognition word processor than in a typewriter.

A common example of increasing personal efficiency, is if you hire or partner with someone who has skill sets that you need but don't currently have, or have and don't have time for. Anyone in business does this all the time. This is the origination of "employment."

Secret of Wealth #4: As the aggregate economy-wide POL increases, there are more and higher-quality goods and services out there for you to buy with a given quantity of money in your possession. Thus, the more productive our labor becomes, the more your purchasing power increases, and you can become ever wealthier without even changing

your income.

- Your continuously improving personal material and psychological welfare depends upon the continuous increase in the POL through technological progress and gains in personal efficiency. This is why the latest iPhone is better than the original iPhone.

- But the link between elevating the abstract aggregate POL out there in the economy as a whole and you increasing your own purchasing power in the short term, is that YOU have to contribute a level of productivity or production in your own world, by your own hand with whatever vehicle that drives you, by an amount at least equivalent to what it is you want to purchase—to a level that matches your desired level of consumption, your desired level of wealth—as measured by the amount of money you make.

- As my take on the saying "You don't work, you don't eat!" I add the following: "You eat to the extent that you work." Tell me which is more just and fair: This or the statist maxim of "from each according to his ability to each according to his need"? ...which basically translates into "your neighbor eats (and you starve) to the extent that you produce."

Moral of the Story

Let me illustrate with my own life: I own a modest place on

2.5 acres with an older home and guest house; as I sit on my deck typing these words I stopped to look out and contemplate all that I wish to do to improve my property so that I can enjoy it more.

There are long block walls that need to be built which requires in addition to a mason, the services of a surveyor. There are massive amounts of landscaping to be done to turn my place into the garden spot that I want, both the main house and the guest house need to be thoroughly remodeled, I want to put in a pool and spa, and I want horses which implies the construction of all the infrastructure required for the care and enjoyment of horses.

I also want to acquire, as my next project, a hundred-acre+ ranch in my home state of Colorado.

But I cannot DO these things now even though I intensely desire them. I must first earn enough money to purchase these things; but to earn enough money I have to first produce enough at what I like to do in the world that is the money-equivalent (or more) of the cost of all of these improvements. I have to contribute at least that amount to the world. And to do that, I have to vastly increase my productivity in adding value to other people with my chosen focus of work. I have to contribute to others by servicing the needs and desires of those who want to benefit from what I have to offer. And part of increasing my productivity is to leverage my time, which includes ultimately hiring the labor of other people to help me in my endeavors, in my production.

Of course, as we found in Secret of Wealth #3 above, even with advances in personal efficiency and modern machinery, at any given time there's a fundamental ineradicable scarcity of labor out there....but not to worry! Magic is afoot in our next Secret of Wealth...

Secret #5 — The Magic of the Division of Labor

All the World is a Play, and You May Contribute a Verse

No doubt, you have heard the saying "no man is an island."

The original phrase came from a poem by John Donne (1572 - 1631). In the context of living in a society with other men, it is true that no man is an island. No one can produce all that he needs and desires by his own hand, and ultimately you must rely on the productivity of others both for what you want to acquire and for the help you want to hire to assist you in producing.

If you are a businessman or entrepreneur, you must rely on the productivity of other people for the factors of production and labor that go into making your product or service, principally from other businessmen. As a consumer, you must rely on others, again principally businessmen, for the vast majority of the goods and services that you buy.

Entrepreneurs cannot do everything it takes to make or service a widget; entrepreneurs and businessmen cannot do it alone.

Consumers cannot possibly produce all of life's necessities in their own back yards. Forget about luxuries. Consumers cannot do it alone.

In these instances what we all rely on in order to obtain all the things that we need and desire is others to perform their own self-interested role in the great play called the Division of Labor (DOL).

Understanding the magnitude of what the DOL is and why it benefits you personally, will dramatically affect your world view.

George Reisman again in his statist-killing wisdom (acronyms and emphasis added):

> *Developing and expanding of the division of labor (DOL) is the means of steadily increasing the productivity of labor (POL). The DOL is a social system in which the individual lives by producing, or helping to produce, just one thing or at most a very few things, and is supplied by the labor of others for the far greater part of his needs. The production, the very existence, of wealth vitally depends upon the DOL.*
>
> ***But while human life and well-being depend upon the existence of wealth, and the production of wealth depends upon the DOL, the DOL does not exist or function automatically; it depends upon the laws and institutions a country adopts to govern social interaction.***
>
> *The DOL society is a Capitalist society, which is*

characterized by the pursuit of individual material self-interest under freedom, and rests on a foundation of the cultural influence of reason.

Despite its vital importance, the DOL, as a country's dominant form of productive organization, is a relatively recent phenomenon in history. *It goes back no further than eighteenth century Britain, and it is limited today to little more than the United States, the former British dominions, the countries of Western Europe, and Japan* (and to a very limited extent the BRIC countries). *The dominant form of productive organization in most of the world, the vast interiors of Asia, Africa, and much of Latin America, and everywhere for most of history has been the largely self-sufficient production of farm families and, before that, of tribes of nomads or hunters.*

What makes the study of economics (i.e. Capitalism) necessary and important is the fact that while human life and well-being depend on the production of wealth, and the production of wealth depends on the DOL, the DOL does not exist or function automatically. Its functioning crucially depends on the laws and institutions countries adopt. A country can adopt laws and institutions that make it possible for the DOL to grow and flourish, as the United States did in the late 18th century. Or it can adopts laws and institutions that prevent the DOL from growing and flourishing, as is the case in most of the world today, and as was the case everywhere for most of history. Indeed, a country can adopt laws and institutions that cause the DOL to decline and practically cease to exist. *The leading example of this occurred under the*

Roman Empire in the 3rd and 4th centuries... The result was that the relatively advanced economic system of the ancient world, which had achieved a significant degree of DOL, was replaced by feudalism, an economic system characterized by the self-sufficiency of small territories.

In order for a country to act intelligently in adopting laws and institutions that bear upon economic life, it is clearly necessary that is citizens understand the principles that govern the development and functioning of the DOL. If they do not, then it is only a question of time before that country will adopt more and more destructive laws and institutions, ultimately stopping all further economic progress and causing actual economic decline, with all that this implies about the conditions of human life.

Thus, the importance of defending and promoting capitalism consists in the fact that ultimately not only our entire modern civilization and well-being of its citizens, but the very lives of the great majority of people now living depends upon the existence and functioning of the DOL. And it is the Capitalist who is most responsible for its continued existence and growth.

Secret of Wealth #5: The key to the acquisition, maintenance, and growth of your personal wealth is the ever-increasing productivity of each of us doing our own thing under freedom in a fully functioning uninhibited division of labor economy.

- An ever-increasing productivity of labor under a

free, ever-expanding, and fully-functioning DOL does not happen automatically.

- The laws and institutions that you support directly affect the very existence and functioning of the DOL and thus your ability to acquire the wealth that you desire.

- To support laws and institutions that are anathema to Capitalism is to in-effect cut your own throat—certainly, at least, to tie a figurative ball and chain around your neck while aiding and abetting TTK who will gladly cash in on your willful negligence to further their statist aims.

- If you want to guarantee that your kid's lives will be far superior to yours, then you need to encourage anyone you know to get productive, fight for what they want, and fight for the freedom pursue what they want, including fighting for Capitalism.

Moral of the Story

You can cheat the hangman by accumulating wealth in just about any environment where some degree of production is permitted, but as they say "karma's a bitch." The DOL cannot last without you and me as producers remaining vigilant and fighting for it against those who view freedom as an evil. The existence of wealth does not guarantee its maintenance; that Bentley, Viper, or Volkswagen in your driveway becomes a useless hunk of junk if auto makers go out of business due to an oppressive government that inhibits the functioning of the DOL....of Capitalism.

And to end on a positive note, think about this: If you have an idea that you are passionate about, what better indication is there out there that people will like your idea and pay you money for it than the presence of competition!

The fact that there are already similar products or services on the market that are doing well should tell you that there is room for you to get into the mix and claim your share of the pie. How much of the pie do you want? The question you should be asking yourself is not "Will the competition crush me like a bug?" but "How can I do a better job of marketing a better product or service so I can get a piece of the pie?" And keep in mind that with a free market and fully functioning DOL economy, the pie is an ever-growing pie, so you may only need a very, very, small piece in order to achieve what you want!

Think about the show on CNBC called Shark Tank. If you've watched it regularly you realize how amazing it is that entrepreneurism thrives when people are free, and that people will continue to keep coming up with new ideas—even new themes on old ideas—that make higher quality and more beneficial goods and services for all of us. Goods and services that compete with what is already out there. You also learn from the show that there are always venture capitalists and other investors who are just chomping at the bit to invest in a good idea to beat the competition for the purpose of making money.

Who benefits from all of this competition out there for a piece of an ever-growing pie? Each one of us. THAT is the absolute beauty of the DOL.

Secret #6 — The Power of Purchasing Power

The Primacy of Production and Supply: You Don't Produce? You Don't Eat.

Since we don't live in a barter economy, where for example I give you five chickens for a pair of shoes, we instead trade money for the goods and services that we want to consume.

In actuality, wealth and your standard of living have little to do with how much money you have...but have everything to do with what can be purchased with the quantity of money that you have and want to spend. How much goods and services your money can buy depends on 1) how much of the money you have you are willing to spend and 2) how much stuff there is out there to buy.

This ability and willingness to purchase is called your purchasing power.

Piles of money in a bank somewhere or stuffed in your mattress are just that: piles of money, not purchasing power. Money is a store of the value that you have contributed to the marketplace, but in and of itself, it certainly is not wealth.

If you have $100,000 in cash and the store shelves are bare, you have no purchasing power.

If the store shelves are spilling out onto the floor, and you have no money, you have no purchasing power.

If you have $100,000 in cash and the store shelves are full, but you don't want to buy anything, you still have no purchasing power.

Further, if today $50,000 buys X amount of goods and services out there in the economy, and next year the amount of goods and services doubles, then that same $50,000 will buy twice (2X) the goods and services it did before; the only difference is that on average, the prices of those goods and services will be roughly half what they were the previous year.

In this instance your purchasing power has doubled.

Let's look at the economy as a whole—the economic system in its entirety where all of us consumers and businessmen are buying and selling in the market.

If the total amount of money in the economy stays the same from one year to the next, then the same amount of money would be "chasing" a supply of stuff that is twice as large. If sellers of all of those goods and services want to sell them, on average they will have to drop their prices in order to compete for the same amount of dollars in a world flush with twice as much stuff to buy.

That is the way it works in a truly free society where the quantity of money in all of our pockets and checking accounts does not change—i.e. where banks cannot create money out of thin air like they do under a fiat money reserve banking system (more on this in Secret #8).

If the amount of money out there changing hands in the economy doesn't change from one year to the next, but productivity doubles, average prices have to drop in order to sell the larger supply of goods to the same demand represented by the unchanged money.

Now here's a twist: Just adding more money to the economy (say if the government overnight doubled all of our incomes), prices would in effect have to double. There would be twice as much money chasing the same amount of stuff and buyers like you and I would bid up the price of everything in our attempt to get our share before the supply of whatever it is we are trying to buy runs out. The result being that overall we would be no better off than if the doubling of our incomes had never happened.

Alternatively, if both incomes and the amount of stuff to buy double, prices would stay just about the same on average. If you recall, is exactly what the Fed attempts to accomplish in its goal of "price stability" (but at what cost!).

Does the simple relationship between the amount of stuff produced and the purchasing power of your money make sense to you? If not, read it again. It IS simple so get it in your head.

The key to remember is that in a society where the quantity of money does not significantly change, what drives the purchasing power of your money is the total amount of goods and services available to purchase each year; that is, the supply of goods and services available to <u>sell</u> each year; that is, the total goods and services <u>produced</u> each year; that is, the productivity of labor each year.

What primarily drives the purchasing power of the dollar bills in your pocket is production and supply of goods and services which is determined by the productivity of labor.

What is the lesson here?

Do you hear yet the message that is blaring at you through a bullhorn?

<u>Secret of Wealth #6</u>: **In an economy where the quantity of money does not change significantly from year to year, your purchasing power would increase over time, year after year, without you earning a dime more in income! And the truly awesome thing is that the ever-increasing purchasing power in a fully functioning DOL and ever increasing POL happens**

automatically wherever men are left free to build the DOL!

- Your income is secondary when it comes to purchasing power. What matters is the quantity and quality of goods and services you can buy with one dollar of your money. And, in a stable unchanging money system, the sole factor that determines the quantity and quality of the goods and services you can buy, your purchasing power, is the economy-wide productivity of labor.

- What matters is production and the supply of goods and services, of wealth, NOT money, as the driving factor in anyone's acquisition of personal wealth.

- Necessarily, as the quantity and quality of wealth increases, with the quantity of money remaining relatively the same, prices on average must fall, with the benefit that ALL people, no matter what level of income, are able to purchase more with what money they make.

- In fact, it is the poor who benefit the most from Capitalism...the DOL effect on the POL. Prices are most likely to fall first in housing costs, foodstuffs, and household items that the poor spend a much larger percentage of their income on than those with higher incomes. Conversely, it is the poor who suffer most under any form of statism!

- What matters in an economy is production and not consumption! It is production, not consumption, that is the essential function of an economy oriented to the maximization of the quality of individual human life; thus...

  - Although individual businesses are dependent upon the consumers they serve, from the point of view of the economy as a whole, it is the consumer who is dependent upon the businessman, the capitalist, since businesses are the seller, the source, of everything we as consumers buy and the buyer of what we have to sell, our labor;

  - Consumers are dependent upon Capitalists, not the other way around.

First Corollary to Secret of Wealth #6: Money is not wealth.

Money v. Riches. Money Wages v. Real Wages

The funny money, the green stuff that you have in your pocket, and the funds that you have in your checking, savings or investment accounts...are not wealth.

Wealth is physical stuff...physical goods that man has created.

At best your bits of green paper currency are claims to wealth. They are not wealth in and of themselves.

I talked about this at the beginning of this book.

When one grows rich, what one grows rich of is material goods.

When one has millions of cash dollars, fiat reserve notes, sitting in a bank account somewhere—that alone does not constitute wealth but merely a store of wealth, of pent-up economic energy. Certainly, when one has a pile of green money, one has the immediate potential of being wealthy, but in the strict sense of the term, money in a bank account is not wealth, but merely potential purchasing power for wealth if the owner of the money is ready and willing to purchase material goods. And in this day and age of managed inflation, the purchasing power of money in a bank rapidly declines.

The reason that I point this out is to demonstrate the distinction between the value of the money that you earn, and its real value out there in the marketplace.

I point this out to demonstrate the distinction between money wages and what are called real wages.

Money wages are what you earn. Money wages are the physical dollar bills you get from the ATM and the amount of money shown in your check book or savings account balances.

Real wages are the physical goods or services that you can actually purchase with your money wages...as in buying 'real' stuff. As a simple example, earning $250,000 per year in cold hard cash sounds terrific, right? But not if all you can purchase with the $250,000, due to inflation, are the bare necessities for living.

First Corollary Secret of Wealth: Money is not wealth. It doesn't matter how much money you earn. In terms of getting wealthy, what matters is what you actually BUY with the money you earn. What matters is purchasing power. What matters is real wages.

- You are not wealthy without the material manifestation of the money that you earn. You are not wealthy without physical stuff that you purchased with your money;

- The value of today's fiat money evaporates with the punch of a few keys on a keyboard by the TTK-owned Fed; material goods are durable and remain in existence in the service of your life as wealth long after the money is gone.

- In a fiat money system, what you can buy with your money steadily decreases...you are virtually guaranteed to be used and lose!

- Real wages are determined by production and supply.

- In a sound money system, what you can buy with your money steadily <u>increases</u>; NO government can destroy the value of your money because they simply cannot "print' gold or silver out of thin air like they do with the green stuff you carry around in your pocket!

Second Corollary to Secret of Wealth #6: Your Supply Is Your Demand

Produce Little? Worth Little

I have spoken above about contribution being the source of an abundance mentality, an empowering mindset.

From Leonard Peikoff:

"The economic value of goods and services is (reflected in) their price (this term subsumes all forms of price, including wages, rents, and interest rates); and prices on a free market are determined by the law of supply and demand. Men create products and offer them for sale; this is supply. Other men offer their own products in exchange; this is demand. (The medium of exchange is money.) "Supply" and "demand" therefore, are two perspectives on a single fact: a man's supply is his demand; it is his only means of demanding another man's supply. The market price of a product is determined by the conjunction of two

evaluations, i.e., by the voluntary agreement of sellers and buyers. If sellers decide to charge a thousand dollars for a barrel of flour because they feel "greed," there will be no buyers; if buyers decide to pay only a nickel a barrel because they feel "need," there will be no sellers and no flour. The market price is based not on arbitrary wishes, but on a definite mechanism: it is at once the highest price sellers can command and the lowest price buyers can find."

Second Corollary Secret of Wealth: Your supply is your demand. The monetary value, the price, of what you produce, of what you contribute to the marketplace, of what you have earned by selling your produce to the marketplace, is what enables you to buy goods and services from others in the marketplace.

- The more valuable your contribution as valued by others in the market, the greater is your demand, the greater is your ability to buy from others goods and services that are of higher value.

- Thus, your material welfare, the degree to which you become wealthy, is in direct proportion to the value of your contribution, to the value of what you produce.

Moral of the Story for Secret of Wealth #6

ALWAYS, what matters is production, NOT consumption! Everything else stems from that: the DOL, the necessity for the ever increasing POL, ever-increasing purchasing power, your supply being your demand, and the main thing we have to protect ourselves from: inflation and all of its related symptoms.

What the heck do I mean by "what matters is production not consumption?"

There exists an entire school of thought that drives the idiots in government today that is based the primacy of consuming. The school is called Keynesianism after a dangerously unsound thinker named John Maynard Keynes. It's also referred to by various Austrian economists as Consumptionism.

Its basic premise is that what makes an economy grow is people buying stuff out there. What matters is people having money and then spending the money so as to induce producers to produce the stuff that they want to buy, and thus to thereby, as a primary motivating factor, employ wage earners and buy commodities from other businesses.

This is not an exercise in semantics.

Nor is it like the classic chicken-or-the-egg conundrum. You know—which came first? The chicken or the egg?

In this case it is crystal clear: Production comes first.

Think about this.

Consumers in the act of buying do not design a product or service. Nor do they impart to the producer the idea or design for a product or service. They simply buy a finished product or service that has been pre-created by the businessman. It is always the producer who first looks out on the world, imagines a product or service that will benefit his fellow man, and then proceeds to create the product or service where none existed before. He then takes that product or service to the market to get the consumer's vote or veto. Yes, it is the ultimate consumer who votes "yay" or "nay" on the entrepreneur's creation, but it is ALWAYS the producer who is the first cause of any product or service purchased by the consumer.

And it was this way from the beginning in Adam Smith's early and rude state of society. The producer takes nature given materials, fashions them into a product, and presents that product or service to his fellow hut-dweller for trading. ONLY if the hut-dwelling primitive producer provides a product or service of value to his fellow hut-dweller does he earn raw materials, services or other crude products in trade.

So in the world of Keynesianism, it's theoretically actually good that people don't save heavily and that the government pursues a policy of deficits and inflation to inject money into the economy, into the hands of the people through credit (loans) to "keep the economic engine running" where otherwise people would become sated in their material desires and lose their "propensity to consume." With easy money, governments can induce people to buy when they normally would not.

This is a bunch of hooey.

What matters first and foremost is people producing products and services. From our discussion of purchasing power, **whatever money exists in the economy is more than enough to buy whatever we all produce as long as prices are able to adjust to the level of produced goods and services.** And an ever-increasing purchasing power occurs through producing stuff in a fully functioning DOL with an ever increasing POL.

What matters in creating and acquiring wealth is the production of wealth, NOT the creation and spending of money!

It has been roundly criticized by detractors of freedom, but the analogy rings absolutely true: The rising tide DOES float all boats!

The more that is produced, the lower are prices and the more and better quality of goods and services each of us can afford to buy with what income we earn. Again, money is not wealth. It doesn't matter how much money you earn. In terms of getting wealthy, what matters is what you actually

BUY with the money you earn.

What matters is purchasing power.

What matters is real wages.

What matters is production!

This is the true nature of the so-called "supply-side economics" you have heard that has been so castigated by the statists, only now you see it properly in the context of a free market, in the context of a capitalist society and not the hampered-market-economy-turning-fascist/socialist/ collectivist that we have had now for more than a century where those with the power, those who make the rules, benefit immeasurably more than even the so-called middle-class....certainly more than the poor! (See my discussion again on the Fed above).

Now understanding that production is all that is required for society to progress, what you produce is your demand for other goods and services out there. And your material welfare, the degree to which you become wealthy, is in direct proportion to the value of your contribution, to the value of what you produce. The value of the goods and services that you can acquire is at least equal to the value of your contribution.

What matters is production and supply, NOT money!

The only thing left for you to do is bust your tail in your chosen field of endeavor, and protect yourself from the loss of purchasing power from the TTK inflation machine.

Always mind what inflation does to your ability to accumulate wealth!

Always be aware of current events that shape the value of your money.

Learn to invest in assets that are likely to appreciate in value and avoid holding excessive amounts of cash in your bank account.

Always fight for officials, laws, and policies that favor sound money.

Secret #7 — Profit be Good

Selfishness and the Profit Motive are Good.

"A man's wealth under capitalism depends upon two factors: on his own productive achievement, and on the choice of others to recognize it. Since the system promotes such recognition however, a man's wealth depends in the end only on the exercise of his creative faculty. The more active a mind, within any given field of production, the richer its possessor eventually becomes."

"On one moral issue most statists to not dissemble. They tell us loudly that when they come to power, they will eradicate selfishness."

—Leonard Peikoff

(Enter the Capitalist)

As we have affirmed above, you and I, in the moral pursuit of maintaining, lengthening, and enjoying our own lives, are the rightful beneficiary of the results of our actions, good or bad. And in the context of producing, we are the rightful beneficiary of money profits (or losses) that we generate. You and I are right in acting out of self-interest as a primary motive. As I have demonstrated, it is right, it is natural, and it is profoundly good to be selfish.

And in the world of producing for the market, self-interest is synonymous with the quest for profit...we are driven by the profit motive. It has been said that it is a uniquely American concept to "make money."

So what exactly is "profit?" Why am I making a big stink about profit?

Follow me please…because if you grasp the simplicity of what I am telling you here, your world-outlook will shift dramatically based on this one little "secret" alone.

Profit is defined as the excess of sales revenue over the costs of production.

Profit is no more and no less than this.

It's very simple: when you sell something, the money income from the sale is called sales revenue. The costs that you incurred in making your product or service are costs of production. Sales revenue minus your cost of production is what's left over…this leftover is your profit (or, if a negative number, your loss).

Which begs the question, **how do profits happen? How is it that there is even the possibility of an excess of sales revenue over costs?**

In a nutshell, when you are in business you desire profit when you sell something… you ask your customers to pay you a price for your product or service that is above your costs. If you ask a price that is equal to your costs and your customers pay that price, you "break-even" and you make no money... but you do not lose money either. If you price your stuff below your costs, then you lose money. Profits happen if your sales-revenue-above-cost price is competitive in the marketplace: people are able and willing to pay your asking price for the value you offer.

For example, if you offer your product for $100 and your costs for labor, materials and equipment that went into making your product are $75, and people actually buy your product for $100, you can make $25 per sale in profit all day long if there are enough people able and willing to buy from you and not from your competitors who might offer a comparable product of equal or better quality at a lower price.

So how do profits "happen?"

Profits happen because we ask for them in a free and open market by pricing our products and services above our costs, and because people are able and willing to pay our asking price because they perceive our products or services to be that money-equivalent of added value to their lives.

This is very simple so don't make it more complex than it is. Read this again if you are not clear.

So why am I harping on the origination of profits so much?

Well, there is a really BIG reason I am doing so.

Karl Marx (for the uninitiated, this not Groucho's brother) said profits come about because the greedy capitalist steals unearned money from the workers. And, amazingly, although it has been thoroughly refuted and resoundingly discredited a thousand times over, this notion is still <u>hugely</u> popular and ingrained today among most leftists, among the still-ignorant young, among otherwise intelligent economists, the vast majority of our politicians, and even so-called conservatives, free-thinkers, anarchists, and the like.

Its even held in some manner by libertarians who have not been educated otherwise.

This mentality is part of the "lying-stealing-cheating" image people have of businesspeople so eloquently expressed above by Yaron Brook.

Well, Marx was full of hooey.

Marx was also a dangerously unsound thinker.

It is critical that you understand how simple profits are, and how crucial your understanding of profits is to your personal welfare that you feel right, confident, and unapologetic in your quest for profits and the wealth that you can obtain

and create from profits.

I am beating this horse because I want you to forever be proud that you are a producer, that your creation of value and wealth benefits everyone, and to never, ever, ever, feel less than fully morally justified in your pursuit of profit, in your pursuit of your self-interest, in your pursuit of your life, liberty and happiness, or to ever accept unwarranted criticism about your 'evil profit-seeking' from the masses of ignoramuses whom your productivity benefits immeasurably more than it does you.

The entire last century has been characterized the world over by the literal demonization of businessmen and entrepreneurs to a large degree because of the popularity (indoctrination-conditioning) of what Marx and his progeny teach in this regard. So much so that the average person out there, especially hourly wage employees, holds negative associations to profit-generating business activity.

They hold these false associations to the extent that they openly advocate incredibly destructive laws and policies that inhibit the businessperson from 'getting away with it' without realizing they are shooting themselves in the foot.

An entire block of countries revolted and hundreds of millions of people were sold into what essentially amounts to slavery in the former USSR for 70+ years based principally on this theory!

Not to mention communist China or the host of lesser socialist states.

Governments, intellectuals (and various ideological Hollywood ignoramuses such as Sean Penn and Harry Belafonte) still demand the "worker's paradise" today...the principal example they hold up as a model being the modern disasters of Venezuela (and here) or Cuba (!)

Do the infamous words of a 21st Century so-called 'leader': "If you own a business, you didn't build that!" mean anything to you?

Dr. Reisman:

The leading source of denial of the productive role of businessmen and capitalists and of the hostility to profits and interest is the Marxian exploitation theory. The essential claim of this theory is that all income naturally and rightfully belongs to the wage earners [i.e. employees], but that under capitalism the wage earners receive only bare minimum subsistence, while everything over and above this is expropriated by the capitalist exploiters in the form of profits, interest, and land rent, or, in the terminology of Marx, "surplus-value."

...The conceptual framework of the exploitation theory... assumes that all income due to the performance of labor is wages and that profits are a deduction from what is

naturally wages... This framework is the belief that wages are the original and primary form of income, from which profits and all other nonwage incomes emerge as a deduction with the coming of capitalism and businessmen and capitalists. This framework and its supporting beliefs easily lead to the assertion of the wage earner's right to the whole produce or its full value.

Even our own home-grown Adam Smith ignorantly advocated this disastrous theory, and because of his confused thinking, he can aptly be described as the father of Marxism. In fact, Karl Marx relied on Adam Smith's reasoning. To continue with Reisman:

A... possibly even more astonishing notion that Smith advances... is what I call the primacy-of-wages doctrine. This is the doctrine that in a precapitalist economy—the "early and rude state of society"—in which workers simply produce and sell commodities, and do not buy in order to sell, the incomes the workers receive are wages. Wages are the original income, according to Smith. All income in the precapitalist society is supposed to be wages, and no income is supposed to be profit, according to Smith, because workers are the only recipients of income. At the same time, of course, Smith advances the corollary doctrine that profit emerges only with the coming of capitalism and businessmen and capitalists, and is a deduction from what is naturally and rightfully wages.

The truth of the matter?

...Profits, not wages, are the original and primary form of

income and that precisely because of the work of businessmen and capitalists, wages can rise out of all connection with minimum subsistence—literally without limit.

"Profit" is the excess of receipts from the sale of products over the money costs of producing them—over, it must be repeated, the money costs of producing them.

A "capitalist" is one who buys in order to subsequently sell for a profit. (A capitalist is one who makes productive expenditures.)

"Wages" are money paid in exchange for the performance of labor—not for the products of labor, but for the performance of the labor itself.

On the basis of these definitions [words mean things!], it follows that if there are merely workers producing and selling their products, the money which they receive in the sale of their products is not wages. ...In buying commodities, one does not pay wages, and in selling commodities one does not receive wages. What one pays and receives in the purchase and sale of commodities is not wages but product sales revenues.

Thus, in the precapitalist economy imagined by Smith and Marx, all income recipients in the process of production are workers. But the incomes of those workers are not wages. They are, in fact, profits. Indeed, all income earned in producing products for sale in the precapitalist economy is profit of "surplus-value"; no income earned in producing products for sale in such an economy is wages.

Joe Miller

For not only do the workers of a precapitalist economy earn product sales revenues rather than wages, but also those workers have zero money costs of production to deduct from those sales revenues.

They have zero money costs precisely because they have not acted as capitalists. They have not bought anything in order to make possible their sales revenues, and thus they have no prior outlays of money to deduct as costs from their sales revenues. Having made no productive expenditures, they have no money costs.

Precisely, this last is the situation of the workers in Smith's "early and rude state of society" and under Marx's "simple circulation." Those workers, selling their commodities, not their labor, earn sales revenues, not wages. And precisely because they are not capitalists, and they are not employed by capitalists, there is no buying for the sake of selling, and thus there are no money costs to deduct from those sales revenues.

Smith and Marx are wrong. Wages are not the primary form of income in production. Profits are. In order for wages to exist in the production of commodities for sale, it is first necessary that there be capitalists. The emergence of capitalists does not bring into existence the phenomenon of profit. Profit exists prior to their emergence. The emergence of capitalists brings into existence the phenomena of productive expenditure, wages, and money costs of production.

Do you get this?

If you understand this you are far more intelligent than the throngs of ivy-league economists such as Paul Krugman and his ilk.

This is MAJOR.

This is a HUGE deal!

This is a big deal because as a critical tenet propagated by Marx, Engels and gang, it is a HUGE part of the Great Lie in getting us to believe we are cheated by our employers and those who make huge fortunes in business!

Please do not gloss over this. Make a real attempt to understand it.

You, as a capitalist, bring into existence wages; <u>wages paid to employees cannot exist without you</u>.

> *Accordingly, the profits that exist in a capitalist society are not a deduction from what was originally wages. On the contrary, the wages and the other money costs are a deduction from sales revenues—from what was originally all profit. The effect of capitalism is to create wages and to reduce the relative amount of profits. The more economically capitalistic the economy—the more the buying in order to sell relative to the sales revenues—the higher are wages relative to sales revenues, and the lower are profits relative to sales revenues.*
>
> *Thus, capitalists do not impoverish wage-earners, but*

make it possible for people to be wage earners. For they are responsible not for the phenomenon of profits, but for the phenomenon of wages. They are responsible for the very existence of wages in the production of products for sale.

Without other people existing as capitalists, the only way in which one could survive in connection with the production and sale of products would be by means of producing and selling one's own products, namely, as a profit earner. But to produce and sell one's own products, one would have to own one's own land, and produce or have inherited one's own tools and materials or the money to buy them. Relatively few people could survive in this way. The existence of capitalists makes it possible for people to live by selling their labor rather than attempting to sell the products of their labor. Thus, between wage earners and capitalists there is in fact the closest possible harmony of interests, for capitalists create wages and the ability of people to survive and prosper as wage earners.

And if wage earners want a larger proportion of income in the form of wages and a smaller proportion of income in the form of profits, they should want a higher economic degree of capitalism...

A-fricking-men.

In my fervent, animated, and justifiably anger-toned vociferous opinion, non-capitalists (i.e. employees and non-workers) should be kissing a capitalist's ass in humble gratitude. If we want to progressively improve our lives substantially in our own lifetimes, we should want more, and bigger, and better capitalists...NOT this insanely hamstrung "mixed-economy" or "crony-capitalism" or capitalist-on-a-leash, hell-bent-on-socialism economy that we have today.

Now, with this unambiguously clear understanding of profits and wages in place, what about the very nature of "labor" itself? Isn't "labor" just physical work?

Isn't it just the "blue-collar" person out there who does any real work?

George Reisman:

In a precapitalist economy, the income of labor is profit, and profit is thus obviously a labor income. In a capitalist economy, too, profit is an income earned by labor—by the labor of businessmen and capitalists. ...The labor of businessmen and capitalists (consists of) the creation, coordination, and improvement in efficiency of the division of labor. ...It is labor which supplies the guiding and directing intelligence in production. It must be stressed: guiding and directing intelligence, not muscular exertion, is the essential characteristic of human labor, and the basis for attributing all production to labor. As von Mises says, "What produces the product are not toil and trouble in themselves, but the fact that the toiling is guided by reason."

On this basis, all labor is the "labour of direction." It is because the man directs the tool, that he, and not the tool, produces the product. The tool, whether an ordinary shovel, a steam shovel, dynamite, or an atomic explosive, does not produce, but is the means by which the man who employs it produces...

Guiding and directing intelligence in production is supplied by businessmen and capitalists on a higher level than by wager earners—a circumstance which further reinforces the primary productive status of profits and profit earners over wages and wage earners.

The fact that profits are an income attributable to the labor of businessmen and capitalists, and the further fact that their labor represents the provision of guiding and directing intelligence at the highest level in the production process, requires a radical reinterpretation of the doctrine of labor's right to the whole produce. Namely, that that right is satisfied when first the full product and then the full value of that product comes into the possession of the businessman and capitalist, for they, not the wage earners, are the fundamental producers of products. The employees of the firm are accurately described by the common expression "help." They are the helpers of the businessmen and capitalists in the production of their—the businessmen's and capitalist's—products. It should be obvious that thus understood, the realization of labor's right to the whole produce is exactly what occurs in the everyday operations of a capitalist economy, inasmuch as it is businessmen and capitalists who are the owners first of the products and then of the sales proceeds received in exchange for the products.

By the standard of attibuting results to those who conceive and execute their achievement at the highest level, one must attribute to businessmen and capitalists the entire gross product of their firms and the entire sales receipts for which that product is exchanged.

Do the infamous words of Obamarama "Hey, you didn't build that!" have new meaning for you now? Marxism is alive and well and resides in the hearts and minds of the leaders running our country. Do not kid yourself that they are out to destroy this very fountainhead of wealth—the independent, selfish capitalist.

Folks, this is NOT a word game here. It is not an exercise in semantics.

Words mean things.

A thing is what it is. Profits are NOT wages. A Creator is not an Exploiter! The definitions of sales revenue, costs of production, wages, and profits presented above, along with the related concepts of assets and liabilities, are the entire basis for today's world of double-entry bookkeeping handed down to us by the Europeans since the end of the 13th century! (If you don't believe me, go ask your local accountant-historian).

Now before we move on and close out this Secret, I want to address another major issue that closely relates to selfishness, and profits, and the benefits that business people gain "at the expense of others" through the exercise of their guiding, directing intelligence. I shall again quote Leonard Peikoff here, so bear with:

In a capitalist system, the greater a man's power to think and thereby to satisfy his 'materialistic greed," the greater the benefit he confers on his fellows (although that is not the justification for the system). The less a man's power to satisfy his "greed" or even his needs, the more he depends upon the minds of those above him. This human continuum is what Ayn Rand describes, in a crucial identification, as the pyramid of ability:

"Material products can't be shared, they belong to some ultimate consumer; it is only the value of an idea that can be shared with unlimited numbers of men, making all shares richer at no one's sacrifice or loss, raising the productive capacity of whatever labor they perform. It is the value of his own time that the strong of the intellect transfers to the weak, letting them work on the jobs he discovered [created], while devoting his time to further discoveries [creations]. This is mutual trade to mutual advantage; the interests of the mind are one, no matter what the degree of intelligence, among men who desire to work and don't seek or expect the unearned.

In proportion to the mental energy he spent, the man who creates a new invention receives but a small percentage of his value in terms of material payment, no matter what fortune he makes, no matter what millions he earns. But the man who works as a janitor in the factory producing that invention, receives an enormous payment in proportion to the mental effort that his job requires of him. And the same is true of all men between, on all levels of ambition and ability. The man at the top of the intellectual pyramid contributes the most to all those below him, but gets nothing except his material payment, receiving no intellectual bonus from others to add to the value of his time. The man at the bottom who, left to himself, would starve in his hopeless ineptitude, contributes nothing to those above him, but receives the bonus of all their brains. Such is the nature of the "competition" between the strong and the weak of the intellect. Such is the pattern of "exploitation" for which you have damned the strong."

I know that some of you already in business maybe think this is all nice and esoteric and theoretical... and you initially couldn't care less, <u>but you can't</u>!

Literally, the fate of the entire free world, certainly your personal welfare and the welfare of your heirs, heavily depends on erasing this claptrap from the minds of our fellow citizens in our attempt to live in a free society...in other words, of most of the very employees you have in your business, and the vast majority of the consumers of your products!

<u>Secret of Wealth #7</u>: You as the businessman, the entrepreneur, are the Creator. It is you and you alone who enable others t-o maintain, extend and enjoy their lives both through the creation of products and services, AND in

the creation of wages.

- Selfishness and the Profit Motive are Good; they are profoundly good;

- Because profits are the original source of income, you alone have the right to the fruits of your labor, your profits;

- From your profits you make it possible for the payment of wages and the very living of the great mass of employee-minded people;

- You as a capitalist are the benefactor of those you serve and those you hire; those who earn the least benefit the most in comparison to their contribution;

- Your creation of wages is the very means for wage earners to first of all, LIVE, and secondly, to obtain the tremendous variety of products and services that they need and desire that they could not possibly produce entirely on their own;

- Defend yourself when demonized by the ignorant and the statists: Understand that it is your productive ability that they hate!

- Always BE PROUD of your profession and promote yourself as a committed capitalist;

- NEVER accept criticism for your wealth, your desire for wealth, or your money-making ability;

- Without you the Creator, the Western world would have been overrun by the statist hordes decades ago.

Moral of the Story

In earning money out of self-interest, out of the motive for profit, "making money" is not only profoundly good, but absolutely necessary to your personal welfare as a capitalist-businessman-entrepreneur-human being, and the continued progression of the physical and mental welfare of individual men the world over.

Now, let's get back to talking about the one thing we have been intentionally ignoring in our Secrets of Wealth up to this point, which is such a destructive animal that we can no longer ignore it.

Secret #8 — The Elephant in the Room

Unsound Money and Inflation

In Secret of Wealth #6 you learned about purchasing power. I stated there that in a sound money system, a system where the quantity of money cannot increase significantly from year to year, the natural ever-increasing economy-wide POL will result in an increase in your personal standard of living without you even increasing your income.

In a free society, the natural ever-increasing economy-wide POL will result in a continuous increase in the quantity and quality of the stuff you can buy out there, with the same money you currently earn and spend.

No matter how you slice it, this is awesome!

In a sound money system, your purchasing power would likely increase every year without you earning a dime more!

Now, don't expect TTK to tell you about this.

As to your average run-of-the-mill Keynesian economist on CNBC? Are you kidding?

Of course, the big caveat here is "in a sound money system."

Funny Money

As stated above in Secret #6, if the quantity of money in our economy can be artificially increased without restriction, the absolute indisputable effect is the dilution of your purchasing power. This artificial increase in the currency supply is called inflation.

Rising prices are merely a symptom of inflation and are NOT inflation itself.

And the reason for the dilution of your purchasing power is very simple.

The more you have of something, the less each individual something tends to be worth to you. So in trading that something for any other item that you want to acquire, it will take more of that something than it did before simply because there are more somethings chasing the same quantity of stuff to buy, and sellers of those stuffs ask higher prices because they can obtain higher prices in a high-demand environment.

So the more dollars that there are out there, the less each dollar is worth, and this is reflected in the rising prices of just about everything, especially the everyday stuff we normally buy.

Inflation manifests itself through 'easy credit' from lending institutions to both businesses and consumers, and in obtaining easy credit we tend to feel more affluent, and we tend to desire to spend this additional 'easy' money and so we go out and consume more. After all, that is what we borrowed the money for.

As the quantity of money increases and outpaces the rate at which we as an economy can produce goods and services, there are more and more dollars 'chasing' or being spent on the same relative quantity of stuff to buy; thus in our spending binge we tend to bid up prices in an attempt to get what we need or want.

Think about how this happens. If you are selling or servicing widgets, and you see demand for your widgets going up as evidenced by them flying off the shelves, you think to yourself that you are selling your widgets (or service of widgets) too cheaply, and so you raise your prices.

This is not evil; this is what free men do out of selfishness in response to higher demand.

So what used to cost you $1 last year may now cost you $1.05 or more. Anyone who shops for groceries can see this happening in our present time: sometimes in the form of shrinking product containers or partially-filled existing product containers to offset the effects of inflation in an attempt to keep prices the same. (I first noticed this in buying those little Vienna sausages for camping and hiking trips. One day the sausages were not as tall as they used to be and there was more wiggle room in the container, whereas before it was almost a struggle to free the first sausage so you could get at the rest! Since then I have noticed this phenomena in many products that I routinely buy.)

The cause is inflation. The effect is rising prices and the reduction of the purchasing power of your dollars.

Rising prices is NOT inflation. There are all kinds of reasons prices rise and fall; inflation and deflation are the two that affect virtually everything, and the effects are economy-wide.

The Fed

When you hear the terms Fed Monetary Policy in the news, this is nothing more than the wonder-children at the Federal Reserve attempting to accomplish the Fed's stated mission: to "maintain price stability and control unemployment." We talked about this in Chapter 2 as part of the Great Con....the Great Ponzi.

The Fed folks attempt to do this by creating currency out of nothing in a 'controlled' fashion....not too much or inflation will run away in an "overheated" economy...not too little or people will slow down their borrowing, consuming, and spending of money, which would result in contraction of economic activity, in "recession," and in a commensurate rise in unemployment—potentially to the boiling point of riots in the street and revolution.

Think this is all smoke and mirrors and fear-mongering?

From the Fed itself, The Federal Reserve System, Purposes and Functions:

The Federal Reserve sets the nation's monetary policy to promote the objectives of maximum employment, stable prices, and moderate long-term interest rates.

But get this: They need thoroughly dumbed-down and conditioned citizens to pull off the manipulation of the value of your money...

The statutory goals of maximum employment and stable prices are easier to achieve if the public understands those goals and believes (!) that the Federal Reserve will take effective measures to achieve them. For example, if the Federal Reserve responds to a negative demand shock [i.e. people stop buying stuff] to the economy with an aggressive and transparent easing of policy [aka easy credit], businesses and consumers may believe that these actions will restore the economy to full employment; consequently, they may be less inclined to pull back on spending because of concern that demand may not be strong enough to warrant new business investment or that their job prospects may not warrant the purchase of big-ticket household goods. Similarly, a credible anti-inflation policy will lead businesses and households to expect less wage and price inflation; workers then will not feel the same need to protect themselves by demanding larger wage increases, and businesses will be less aggressive in raising their prices, for fear of losing sales and profits. As a result, inflation will come down more rapidly, in keeping with the policy related slowing in growth of aggressive demand, and will give rise to less slack in production and resource markets than if workers and businesses continue to act as if inflation were not going to slow.

Sounds like an honorable and reasonable goal doesn't it? Sounds like they're looking out for us little guys... Well, they are emphatically NOT looking out for us.

In fact, they come right out and say they are really not much good at accomplishing what they claim they are trying to do:

In practice, monetary policy makers do not have up-to-the-minute information on the state of the economy and prices. Useful information is limited not only by lags in the construction and availability of key data but also by later revisions, which can alter the picture considerably. Therefore, although monetary policy makers (i.e. bankers) will eventually be able to offset the effects that adverse demand shocks have on the economy, it will be some time before the shock is fully recognized and—given the lag between a policy action and the effect of the action on aggregate demand—an even longer time before it is countered. Add to this the uncertainty about how the economy will respond to an easing or tightening of policy of a given magnitude, and it is not hard to see how the economy and prices can depart from a desired path for a period of time.

What?

Are you kidding?

They are politely telling us that their game is not only rigged, but that its impossible to manage and that the cost of doing business under TTK is that "the economy and prices can depart from a desired path for a period of time." Meaning: "we're sorry mister consumer out there, but sometimes you're going to be shafted for periods of time worse than we had planned because managing price stability and unemployment is not an exact science, and besides these are really NOT our primary concerns…making money off your ass IS."

Folks it is a fact of economic life that we are subject to, and are the victims of, what is referred to as a "fiat money" monetary system. Fiat means "by decree." Meaning the green-bits-of-paper currency, the funny money, that they have us using has simply been decreed by them to be so.

And through decades of conditioning, we accept it.

Think about this: the play money used in the game Monopoly can be turned into our day-to-day currency; all the TTK have to do is say it is so.

In this system, called the Federal Reserve System in the United States, banks create currency literally out of nothing, and loan it to you and me through the government and charge us interest to borrow it. Each year, even by the month, and by the day, the purchasing power of the green bits of paper in your pocket and in your checking, savings, and retirement accounts become worth less. Eventually to the point of becoming actually worthless.

Here's another purchasing power graphic:

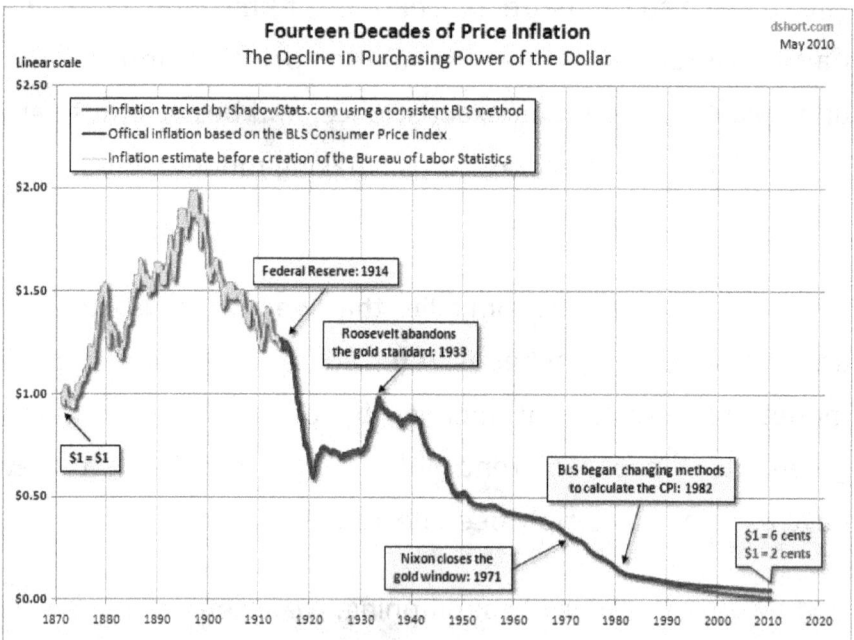

Fourteen Decades of Price Inflation
The Decline in Purchasing Power of the Dollar

dshort.com
May 2010

Linear scale

— Inflation tracked by ShadowStats.com using a consistent BLS method
— Offical inflation based on the BLS Consumer Price Index
····· Inflation estimate before creation of the Bureau of Labor Statistics

Federal Reserve: 1914
Roosevelt abandons the gold standard: 1933
$1 = $1
BLS began changing methods to calculate the CPI: 1982
$1 = 6 cents
$1 = 2 cents
Nixon closes the gold window: 1971

If you need to review in detail again why this is, go back to Secret #6 regarding purchasing power.

And if you want to know the completely fascinating history

behind this curve, go read The Creature of Jekyl Island and The Great Deformation that I alluded to earlier (only be prepared to be shaking your head in disgust and amazement at it all).

In essence, TTK want to get away with being able to continuously create currency out of nothing, lend it to a deficit spending government so they can earn HUGE amounts of interest on it, and grow in wealth entirely disproportionately to what they could ever achieve in a free market with a non-inflating currency.

And I haven't even addressed the reward that speculators get by investing easy money in asset bubbles like the stock market—that's a whole other topic that David Stockman handily addresses, and that you need to become aware of.)

Can you begin to understand why there is a growing discrepancy between the 99% and the 1%? The 99% v. 1% phenomenon could not happen in a true capitalist society!

What they depend upon is that you and I will continue to work our assess off producing in our little corners of the world, enough so that in aggregate, economy-wide, we produce just enough new and better goods and services year after year to keep up with the inflation that they create (as measured by GDP)...thus keeping prices "relatively stable."

And as long as we are allowed to keep producing, we will

keep employing people, thereby keeping unemployment "low" as if the typical 5% unemployment target they pulled out of thin air is anywhere at all acceptable.

If the bankers are at all reasonably successful in 'keeping prices stable and keeping unemployment low', they know that you and I will keep on keeping on because in their minds we have no choice; we have to keep producing if we want to improve our lives. There is no other way for us because we <u>have to</u> create material values out there in the physical world —the place where we have to survive.

We continue to live under the illusion that we are free and in control of our lives, and they will put out whatever propaganda they need to in order to keep us placated so we don't 'pay attention to the man behind the curtain' and revolt. Sure you and I might grumble, demonstrate, form Tea Parties, and change a congressman here or there, but short of heads on sticks nothing in their world changes....they are in absolute heaven, making incredibly easy money hand over fist, laughing their asses off at us the poor donkeys.

We the people?

We the suckers, we the serfs, we the indentured servants, we the slaves.

We work hard in our lives and the entire time they are

robbing us blind.

Mike Maloney is dead on when he calls the system pure evil.

Each day the value of our money drops—a theft from us that is absolutely no different than if they had taken our money and wealth from us at gun point. But by design it is a slow, insidious process that we simply do not notice. And if we are made aware of it, we make little attempt to fully understand it, we cannot identify with it, and we cannot relate it to our daily lives until we see the sausages shrink.

We are left just free enough so we that think we are participating in a free market and can achieve our dreams of becoming wealthy. And many of us, to our incredible credit as producers, still accomplish great things and DO achieve our dreams.

But the cost to us as individuals and to those we love is stupefying.

What is the Cost?

Again, understand that without their fiat money system, our purchasing power would actually increase from year to year. The dollar bills in your pocket could buy MORE next year than this year. Because of the ever-increasing POL of each of us good free citizens, not only would the quantity, quality, and variety of goods and services we could buy increase every year, but prices of nearly everything would tend to drop from year to year!

Imagine if, starting now, this was the case. Without even talking about a dramatic reduction in the regulatory impediments to doing business that would accompany a more-free society, without earning a dime more in income, you would become wealthier...you would have more stuff with the same income that you earn today.

Now imagine if this had been the case since 1900!!

Stop for a moment and imagine the sheer amount of additional wealth that would have been produced over and above what we have today. Can you imagine the impact on the lives of everyone who lived this past century? The effects on the lives of your parents, and their parents?

Not only would poverty NOT be a permanent condition for so many people, but today's "poor" under a sound money system would have a standard of living perhaps comparable to those today who earn a six-figure income in the funny-money system!

The only unemployment that would exist would be those who, for whatever reason, absolutely refused to work for whatever reason.

Life expectancy would have continued to increase faster that it has.

The tremendous suffering from diseases such as cancer may very well have been eliminated 50 years ago!

And I'm not even talking about eliminating the deaths and suffering and the utter destruction of wealth from all of the wars that have been wrought by TTK who have used the fiat central banking system to fund them.

Not to mention that the so-called business cycle of booms and busts would never occur in a sound money system! The Great Depression would never have happened, the multiple recessions since meatheads FDR and Nixon took us off the gold standard in 1933 and again and more completely 1971, would never have happened!

Including the disaster of 2008.

I'm not even accounting for the lost productivity, the lost contributions, the lost joys and happiness, of the hundreds of millions of men and women in the western nations alone who otherwise would have led far more productive and fulfilled lives, but instead have suffered or died as the result of fiat-funded policies.

And then there's the rest of the world!

Can you begin to grasp the magnitude of what has been done

237

to us?

Has it ever occurred to you why there is such a focus out there on maintaining your all-important credit score? Who do you think owns, manages, and manipulates the credit reporting systems?

Who do you think controls the underwriting requirements for mortgages and credit cards?

They WANT us to borrow money...huge sums of money. They just want us to pay it back. Because if we don't, their entire fiat money system begins to crumble and they stop making money off of us. If they stop making money off of us, they stop living the high life, and their wonderful brainchilds of managed political discord and the NWO die a horrible, final, deserved death.

Folks, I am not condemning banking as such; I am condemning the banking system that we currently have. TTK who manage the central banking systems of the world are literal parasites, sucking the life-blood of each of us. They literally skim off the top of our productive ability.

But worse than parasites in nature...these TTK banking parasites suck the blood of their own species!

I need you to fully grasp that this is not Capitalism!

Central banks and fractional reserve banking are not characteristics of a free division of labor society—of a capitalist society.

You should educate yourself and read up on David Stockman, who has been a very outspoken critic of the Federal Reserve with his online website David Stockman's Contra Corner since at least 2010. He does an excellent job of explaining the history of how the Fed came to be and morphed over time since 1913 from a "banker's bank" into the diabolical monstrosity that it is today.

Theoretically, the Fed was supposedly created as a bankers bank, a "lender of last resort" to provide overnight cash, lent on short term at interest rates premium to the market to commercial banks to cover overnight and short-term settlements between banks (but then one has to ask why the income tax also enacted in 1913.)

At the time of the FED's creation, most politicians, out of sheer traditional upbringing on sound money finances, were essentially gold-bugs and adhered strongly to the convertibility of the dollar into gold upon demand by any citizen. Prior to FDR's gold confiscation and dollar devaluation, the dollar was backed by gold and the dollar was convertible to gold at $20 an ounce from 1832 to 1933!

Upon FDR's inauguration, a handful of statist idiots in his

administration kicked gold convertibility in the groin and the deficit creating floodgates of unsound money were opened. The damage was fully consummated in 1971 with Nixon's final and complete default on the gold-based Bretton Woods system that was created in 1944.

The rest is history as they say and we faced traumatic market corrections in the late 1970s, 1998, 2000, 2008, and now the pending granddaddy of them all....the impending worldwide crash and global economic meltdown and reset that many great minds and thinkers are warning about today.

As faith in sound money fled politician's values systems (along with the loss of "individual liberty" and "freedom" from their souls and personal lexicons), Fed policies shifted from banker's bank of emergency lending to banks at a premium, to price stability and full employment, to, as Stockman describes it, "macro-management of Keynesian countercyclical demand management" to offset the supposed boogeyman of Capitalism's inherent flaw of insufficient "aggregate demand.'

Stockman points out that the Fed has actually gotten way too big for its britches and now attempts to macro-manage the entire economy by trying to stimulate their deified "aggregate demand."

And the reason their focus has morphed as it has over the

decades is because, like telling a lie often necessitates telling bigger and bigger lies to cover one's deceit, the inevitable economic distortions and failures that the Fed and Congress have wrought from early interventionist policies have to be plastered over and masked with ever bigger, more intrusive and destructive monetary and fiscal policies.

They do not know what they are doing.

As George Reisman writes, it's as if these people wander in a room filled with banks of computers and machines randomly pushing buttons and flipping switches to see what effect is produced. And if the result is unsatisfactory, they resort to pushing and flipping other buttons and switches to counteract what they have done.

I champion how Stockman comes right out and says that a truly free market has no need for a Fed. As an example:

> *Actually, there is an even more pointed question in the face of still another repudiation embodied in today's GDP release of the "escape velocity" promise that was the basis for $3.5 trillion of fraudulent bond-buying by the Fed over the past six years. Namely, is there any justification for the FOMC's intrusion in the financial markets at all? Does market capitalism really have a death wish and therefore need for an external agency of the state to smooth its cyclical undulations least it tumble down an economic black hole?*

Well, actually, it is all about a wish. That is, the Fed and all other central banks have a power wish; a rank ambition to operate as masters of the financial universe—-unrestrained by either political authority or the discipline of honest free markets.

So motivated, they have bamboozled the political class and the public alike into the false belief that they are the indispensable element—the very mainspring—-of modern economic life. Without their expert ministrations, they claim, we would be faced with a Hobbesian world in which economic life would be poor, nasty, brutish and short.

Not true! On the one hand, market capitalism can function without state management of the business cycle. On the other, it desperately requires honest money and capital markets where savers are rewarded, gamblers disciplined and entrepreneurs are allocated capital for productive investment based on criteria of efficiency and risk-adjusted returns.

Such a world existed before 1914. During the prior 50 years real living standards rose at the highest compound rate for an equivalent duration in recorded history (@4%) —-and without any help from a central bank whatsoever.

There is no reason that benign era could not be revived under Carter Glass' original design of the Fed as a "bankers bank". The latter was given a narrow mandate to operate a passive discount window at which it would liquefy sound collateral at a penalty spread above the free market rate for short-term money.

Under that arrangement, the FOMC [Federal Reserve Open Market Committee] would be abolished and the destructive fraud of massive bond-buying with credits made from nothing would be eliminated.

The Fed would have no need for economists, Keynesian policy apparatchiks or Yellen and her power-drunk band of money printers. A few green eyeshade loan officers randomly picked from the community banks of America could more than adequately perform the task of examining self-liquidating collateral (i.e. loans against finished inventory and receivables) brought to the discount window by true commercial depository lenders.

They do not know what they are doing!

They're making up monetary policy as they go. They're in uncharted waters, flying by the seat of their pants, and literally experimenting with different monetary policies to see 'what works' in the attempt to keep their Ponzi scheme going. Here's Jim Rickards in 2014, another intelligent and well-connected critic of the Fed and the present-day fiscal and monetary madness, in response to a question during an interview:

Don't ever think for a minute that the central bankers know what they're doing. They don't. And that's my own view, but I've heard that recently from a couple central bankers. I recently spent some time with one member of the FOMC, the Federal Open Market Committee, and another member of the Monetary Policy Committee of the Bank of England, which is the equivalent of their FOMC, both policymakers, both central bankers.

And they said the same thing, "We don't know what we're doing. This is a massive experiment. We've never done this before. We try something. If it works, maybe we do a little more; if it doesn't work, we pull it away, and we'll try something else."

And the evidence for this is the Fed has had 15 separate policies in the last five years. If you add it all up, all the forward guidance, all the dates, all the targets, the currency wars, Operation Twist, all the flavors of QE, 15 separate policies in five years, that tells you they don't know what they're doing. They're making it up as they go along.

Does this all make you feel confident that your government is looking out for you?

Does it make you feel like your future is secure?

The coming economic reset and probable Great Depression II , although unavoidable and although it will be painful, certainly for us 99%, is nevertheless a golden opportunity for us to get it right—individually and thus as a society—to lay low the statists, and put more than a few proverbial heads on sticks.

Fortunately, there is a solution to this madness.

The alternative is sound money and a freer society that is the true Capitalist system.

Sound money is something physical that has the following traits making it suitable for use as money:

https://youtu.be/n25w_NeyTrk

Want to see something crazy? Here is what all of the gold and silver ever mined into existence looks like:

ALL THE GOLD IN THE WORLD
166,500 TONNES
DEMON OCRACY . INFO

ALL THE SILVER EVER MINED
1,411,475 TONNES
** IN EXISTENCE | LOST **

Now imagine that these amounts, divided into coins and bars

for use as money can buy all products and services that currently exist and that will EVER exist.

This is the root of the ever-increasing purchasing power of sound money!

Sure, miners will continue to mine gold and silver and add that to the money supply, but any marginal increase in these precious metals from year to year can in no way outstrip the ever-increasing productive abilities of hundreds of millions of people in a truly free division of labor economy!

Secret of Wealth #8: **Under a fiat money system, you and I are essentially slaves. While you and I can still get wealthy under today's fiat money system, the wealth you could enjoy in your life would have been, and would continue to be into the future, considerably greater under a sound money system. By design, through the insidious toll of planned inflation, your purchasing power erodes daily. Intentionally. It is taken from you no differently that if by a thief on the street with a gun.**

- What they count on is that you WILL keep producing;

- And since you will produce, there are things you can do until the system changes:

  - Produce 'ahead of the curve," ahead of

inflation. Become more productive than ever;

- Bank Cash and precious metals: Save more from the results of your productivity;

- Become financially independent of the banking system;

- Invest in something to counteract inflation; and

- Plan to not only weather the storm, but benefit from the inevitable mass wealth transfer that is coming.

- Now that you are aware, you cannot claim ignorance. You, as a man, have an obligation to fight this insanity at whatever level you choose, even if it is just protecting you and your family.

Moral of the Story

It is beyond your immediate control that you are a slave. You are now, however, an educated and hence dangerous slave. Work towards wealth, yes. You are a man and have no choice, but RAISE A VOICE at every opportunity to shut down the insanity.

Support those who fight for individual liberty!

Evil IS powerless if the good are unafraid.

Secret #9 — Savings Be Good

Savings and Capital Accumulation: Pay me now or pay me later.

"To the extent we consume today, we cannot become wealthy tomorrow. The less we in society save and forego consumption today—the more of our incomes we spend today — the exponentially less wealth we can possibly enjoy tomorrow."

"Those who are free save substantially for the future in the expectation there will BE a future worth saving for."

I do not intend to try to turn you into an economist.

For most of us that would be exceedingly boring.

What I DO want to do is introduce to you the necessity and power of savings and the creation of capital that results directly from savings.

If what drives our desire to produce is our unlimited imaginations, then what drives our actual physical ability to produce is capital in the form of money for investment into business enterprises, specifically as short term "expenses" such as for utilities and rent, and for long-term investment in capital goods (machinery and buildings) that are progressively more technologically advanced and which thus increase the productivity of labor.

Capital and capital goods derive from savings that are invested into productive business enterprise— Savings by businesses themselves out of profits that are ploughed back into the business to make it grow, and savings from wages by employees that are invested into businesses.

The more and the more technologically advanced capital goods that we produce permits us not only to produce more and higher quality consumers goods, but also progressively more technologically advanced capital goods for the ever expanding continuation of the production process.

Apple's ability to build the latest iPhone™ stems directly from the technological advances and capital goods that were available back when they built the original iPhone.

Apple's ability to produce the original iPhone stemmed directly from the technological advances and capital goods that were developed in earlier decades of computing.

If the technology that built the original iPhone had not been developed, Apple could not have progressed to the technology and manufacturing methods that built the latest iPhone. And the same is true whether one speaks of bridges, or microwaves, cars, wrist watches, or spaceships. But in order for earlier technology to even exist, and for that earlier technology to be used to spring-board to new productive technologies, there MUST be an ever expanding degree of savings by both individuals and businesses.

This stuff is really cool so stick with me here to get to my main point and why you should give a damn in the Moral of The Story below. By the way most of what I talk about here I learned from Dr. Reisman, who in his book Capitalism, a Treatise on Economics, provides an absolutely superb expanded explanation of all of this.

Again, none of this is new! It's been talked about by a wide variety of sane economists for at least 200 years; prior to now it's been a secret to you only because no one ever told you.

First, let's cover some basic definitions here:

- Capital is savings that is devoted to investment in business enterprises for the production of a product or service. Capital may consist of short term investment funds for use in the purchase of rapidly consumed business expenses such as wages, utilities, insurances, maintenance and the like, and long-term investment funds typically called capital expenditures which are used to purchase things like plant improvements, new machinery, etc....things that are more durable and which are consumed over longer periods than daily business expenses.

- Capital Goods are the machines and tools and other material objects used in the physical production of a product or service. It's the power plants, railroads, factory buildings and equipment of an industrial enterprise. It's also the pickup truck, lawn mowers, rakes, hoes, and leaf blowers of your local gardener.

- Savings is the accumulation of money over one's expenses for the purpose of investing for the future. Savings by wage-earners, businesses and investors is what permits the production and accumulation of progressively more advanced capital goods as the precondition to the production of ever more technologically advanced and higher quality consumer's goods in ever greater quantities.

- Capital Accumulation is the building up of capital funds and capital goods for use in production in individual businesses, specific industries, and in the economy as a whole. The more capital and capital goods that are accumulated, the greater the variety of productive technologies that can be developed and the greater is the productivity of labor overall.

- Time preference is the simple truism that if we desire something, we generally desire to have it in our possession sooner than later.

Savings and Time Preference

According to the principle of time preference, a person values goods and services available to him in the present more highly than goods or services in the future, and goods in the nearer future more highly than goods in the more remote future. You generally prefer a house or car now more highly than one year from now, etc.

From Reisman:

> *Time preference is implied in the very nature of valuation, and, indeed, of human life itself. All other things being equal, to want something is to want it sooner rather than later. ...The nature of human life implies time preference, because life cannot be interrupted. To be alive two years from now, one must be alive today. Whatever value of importance one attaches to being alive in the future, one must attach to being alive in the present, because being alive in the present is the indispensable precondition to being alive in the future. The value of life in the present thus carries with it whatever value one attaches to being alive in the future, of which it is the precondition, plus whatever value one attaches to life in the present for its own sake.*

> *Time preference manifests itself in the extent to which individuals make provision for the future relative to their current consumption. An individual with an extremely high time preference will have no savings. He will consume his entire income and not use any of it to provide for his future consumption. By the same token, an individual with a very*

low time preference will seek to accumulate savings to a substantial multiple of his current income and consumption.

The continued development of capital goods that are progressively more technologically advanced depends upon a large degree of saving and capital accumulation, which in turn depends upon a low so-called "time preference" which in turn depends upon how rational we are about our future.

What do I mean by this?

...Time preference is the lower the more rational and the freer a society is. The more rational people are, the more they are aware of the future: the more they can mentally project it and the greater is the reality for them of such projections; in addition, the more are they aware of themselves as self-responsible causal agents, capable of affecting the course of future events to their own advantage by means of saving. Similarly, to the degree that people are free and enjoy the security of property, they know that they can benefit from whatever provision for the future they decide to make in the present. Thus, to the degree that a society is dominated by the values of reason and freedom, the more conducive it is psychologically and politically to saving and providing for the future, which is only another way of saying that it is more conducive to a low time preference and to all that that implies about capital accumulation and economic progress.

But as it turns out, even if we behave more rationally and

provide for the future far more than we behave irrationally and provide for the range-of-the-moment satisfaction of our desires in the present, our preference for better stuff in the future has its limits and actually governs the accumulation of capital and thereby contributes the scarcity of savings and capital, or more fundamentally to the scarcity of labor that we have already learned about in Secret of Wealth #3.

What must be stressed here is that time preference prevents the existence of profit and interest from always resulting in saving and the accumulation of additional capital. For example, if the rate of profit and interest is 5 percent, the implication is that by saving and investing $100 this year, one can have and consume $105 worth of goods next year. The reason that people do not all rush to save as much as possible, despite the fact that doing so would enable them to consume more in the future, is that they have time preference. Time preference results in people preferring and additional $100 of consumption today to $105...of consumption a year from now. It thus acts to limit the extent of saving and capital accumulation and to contribute to the scarcity of capital.

Such capital accumulation comes to an end because of time preference. Once people [wage earners or business people] succeed in accumulating a certain amount of capital relative to their incomes, they feel that they have done their duty by the future and can now turn more heavily toward enjoying life in the present. Thus, they stop accumulating capital relative to their incomes, even though the accumulation of still more capital relative to their incomes would provide them with still higher incomes in the future.

So, always it comes back to this: what limits our ability to produce is our limited ability and willingness to work—to the literal scarcity of labor and the implied ability of additional labor to result in the possibility of greater savings, savings for use as capital in capital accumulation for technological progress, increased production, and a progressively higher standard of living.

Like labor, there is always a shortage of capital in the progress of human welfare. Each of us is only willing to work so much, and out of our incomes we are only willing to save so much before we think we have 'done our duty by the future' and decide to play more in the present.

Of course, as we have learned in Secret of Wealth #2, there is STILL no limit to what we what we need and desire. **But the key here is that even though our nature automatically limits how far we will go to provide for a better future, we will faster create the wealth to satisfy this need and desire to the extent we behave rationally, value freedom and self-responsibility, and thus hold a shorter time preference.**

If the majority of people in a society hold values that are anathema to rationality then time preference increases, less provision is made for our individual and business futures, more consumption takes place in the present, and less and less saving and capital accumulation takes place, resulting in progressively deteriorating standard of living as even the capital required to merely maintain our existing productive ability (things wear out and have to be replaced) becomes harder and harder to come by.

This has been the case in our country for the past several decades: what matters is not "equity" created in stock, bond, and housing bubbles, but investment in new capital goods. Government anti-free market policies and those of the central bankers necessarily cause the de-cumulation of capital and the resulting decline in the average man's standard of living!

Savings and the Division of Labor

You don't need to memorize this but you DO need to understand it because of its link to the division of labor, and thus directly to your personal welfare.

Knowing the importance of a fully-functioning division of labor economy (Secret of Wealth #5) in the creation of an progressively elevated standard of living, it is now important that you understand that the very existence and functioning of that division of labor economy cannot occur without savings and capital accumulation, and thus a low time preference in the vast majority of us.

Saving and capital accumulation lays the groundwork for the

division of labor in four ways:

1. They make possible the production of goods other than the food required for the next meal. They are necessary to release people's labor from the immediate production of food, so that they can produce other things, including tools for the better production of food. In the absence of saving and capital, everyone's labor would be devoted almost exclusively to securing his next meal;

2. They raise the productivity of labor in food production so that progressively more people can devote time and energy to the production of products and services that satisfy higher-level needs, which makes possible the further increases in the productivity of labor even for food production. Saving and capital accumulation are the source of demand for ever more advanced factors of production which increase the productivity of our labor...not just in food production, but in all fields of production other than food, initially enabled themselves by savings and capital;

3. They make possible for early and reliable payments for labor so that the time which elapses between the performance of labor and the receipt of payment by the producers is relatively short, no matter how long is the time which must elapse between the performance

of labor and payment by the ultimate final consumers. Basically, without saving and the accumulation of capital funds by the business owner out of profits from previous sales, the wage earner (and intermediate level producers) wouldn't get paid for his part in making widgets or cars until the final consumer buys the widget or car whereupon his wages would be taken from the sales revenue. Recall our refutation of Marx's Exploitation Theory in Secret of Wealth #7? Savings and capital accumulation from profits is where wages come from; they enable producers to be paid (and subsequently wage earners) within a reasonable period of time after the completion of their work. In the absence of savings and capital in terms of money, any significant division of labor would be impossible, because it would then be necessary for many producers (and their employees) to wait years, decades, or generations before being paid; and

4. They provide the foundation for larger-scale production and thus the basis for carrying the division of labor further at any given stage of production.

Secret of Wealth #9: Saving and capital accumulation by individuals and business enterprises in the form of money and capital goods are necessary to even HAVE a division of labor economy within which you and I can prosper. And saving and capital accumulation occur only to the degree

that we act rationally and promote and defend individual freedom in our society.

- The continued development of capital goods that are progressively more technologically advanced depends upon a large degree of saving and capital accumulation, which in turn depends upon a low time preference, which in turn depends upon how rational we are about our future.

- Although a short time preference causes savings and capital accumulation, it also operates to maintain a scarcity of savings and capital and therefore of labor. This emphasizes the need for more labor, and thus an ever increasing productivity of what labor we have available and choose to expend.

The Moral of the Story

So what? What good does all this high-falutin' talk about savings and capital accumulation have to do with me in my quest for a better life in wealth?

Well, it is this: If you want a better life for yourself and your kids, and their kids (better, longer, more enjoyable) then you want an enlarged fully-functioning DOL, which depends upon savings and capital accumulation by all of us (individuals and businesses), which depends upon a pervasive low time preference in society, which occurs when we behave more rationally in terms of being self-responsible causal agents.

These fundamentals of time preference and saving are what underlie the ideas expounded in the popular book Rich Dad Poor Dad by Robert Kyosaki. If you want to get wealthy you must not only save but invest your savings in assets and productive enterprise...either yours or someone else's...and expressly` NOT in current consumption of the latest cars, gizmos, vacations, etc.

As Rick Rule said, if you want to be wealthy you must save absolutely ruthlessly.

Of course we are to a large degree prevented from acting on a low time preference even if we are rational by the sheer theft of our ability to save caused by the fiat funny-money perpetual-inflation machine that we live at the mercy of.

All of this ties in with other things you have learned thus far about our unlimited need and desire for wealth, our nature to be productive, the ineradicable shortage of labor, the necessity to increase our productivity, the necessity and source of profits, and sound money.

We are limited in our ability to be productive out of the starting gate! So why compound this 'economic problem' as Reisman puts it by abandoning reason and sound economic science for the sake of huge government (deficit spending on wars and unambiguously failed social programs), and living range-of-the-moment by consuming everything we produce?

All of it comes down to this: if you want a better future you want wage earners and business people to act more rationally, to have a generally lower time preference—by being made responsible and accountable for their own futures as "self-responsible causal agents"—and thus cause all of us to save more so that capital accumulation can occur, and so that products and services of ever increasing quantity and quality can be produced, with the resulting progressive enrichment of everyone.

And to do this we (you and me) ought to be out there advocating for reason and individual freedom and the institutions of capitalism, and the dramatic roll-back in the size and scope of government and the replacement of the funny-money system with sound money.

Rationality in our economic affairs, what is most important to our very survival and thriving, has to replace the "lying, stealing, and cheating" mentality that Yaron Brook talked about. To the extent lying, stealing and cheating takes place in business today, it is as a result of government policies that permit it to happen, and even promote it. Lying, stealing, and cheating are an aberration in a free society and is normally dealt with swiftly and effectively by free markets.

You want a better life? Save and invest and encourage your

family and neighbors to be rational enough to do the same, and in the same effort work to destroy and replace this current abomination we call government that hamstrings the good working man at every turn.

If you understand what I have been telling you, then you must realize that <u>there is no other way.</u>

Secret #10 — The Other Elephant in the Room

Resources Aplenty, Technological Progress, Human Adaptability, and Sustainability Nonsense

As an alternate means of pushing the environmentalist agenda as a tool of controlling human beings acting in raw freedom the enviro-nutjobs are today hanging their hat on the concept of "sustainability."

According to Wikipedia this means "the practice of maintaining processes of productivity indefinitely—natural or human made—by replacing resources used with resources of equal or greater value without degrading or endangering natural biotic systems."

The United Nations in its drive for Agenda 21 coined the term "sustainable development" to mean "development that meets the needs of the present without compromising the ability of future generations to meet their own needs." As used by the United Nations the term incorporates both issues associated with land development and broader issues of human development such as education, public health, and standard of living.

This would appear on the surface to be entirely rational,

right?

Who wouldn't want to "maintain" productivity indefinitely and "replace resources" without "endangering natural biotic systems?" Do you not want to meet the needs of the present without compromising the ability of future generations to meet theirs?

I for one do not.

Let me explain what they are getting at here, and it's NOT to your benefit.

This entire jingoistic concept of 'sustainability' implies the same severe limitation on individual self-interested human behavior that we have already talked about.

It's just the latest ruse used to sell it.

Google Agenda 21 and read both sides of the issue. Glenn Beck does an excellent job of exposing this on-going disaster so Google Agenda 21, Glenn Beck as well. Or read Rosa Koire's Behind the Green Mask, U.N. Agenda 21 at Amazon.

Read and learn.

The concept implies that our world of resources is limited. That we are running out of "resources" from which to make things. It implies we are on the verge of destroying the planet because of our rampant exploitation of "resources." You have heard it: peak oil. Peak fish in the ocean. Peak this, and peak that. Pending water wars from peak fresh water. And on and on and on.

And of course this fits in well with the global man-made climate change bugaboo. Not only are we using up precious resources but in the process we are again, destroying the planet.

How convenient.

If you understand what I have been saying about an ever expanding division of labor driven by ever increasing technological progress, then that coupled with the fact that the planet is nothing but a big ball of resources, you should conclude on your own that, IF WE ARE LEFT FREE, we will ALWAYS find a way to create products and services that use nature-given factors of production—minerals, and water, and trees, and the ocean, and the air— in the most efficient manner possible because it is in our individual interests to do so!

It is the most profitable way to do so.

If we run short of mineral X, we either find a replacement/ alternate mineral or minerals, devise an alternate production process, and/or develop technology that incorporates both to work past the relative shortage.

I won't recount the uncountable instances of this occurrence over just the past century. They should be obvious to anyone who is aware.

My point is that we, if left free, will ALWAYS find ways to produce with what we have and we will ALWAYS find ways to get at what we do not have in way of nature given resources.

Read the book Abundance as a recent prognostication of what technological progress will do for us in solving worldwide basic human problems and elevating the great masses throughout the world from lives of poverty, sickness, and starvation to lives where their life expectancy will double or triple.

Secret of Wealth #10: **"Sustainability" in the sense used by enviro-nutjobs is as bogus an idea as global man-made climate change. The world is nothing but a huge ball of nature-given resources and man, if left free, will continue to increase his standard of living forever through technological progress (and of course everything that this implies).**

- Enviro-nutjobs, the willful handmaidens of TTK and elitist bureaucrats, use the sustainability argument to control and limit "development" out there in the material world by free individuals acting in their own self-interest to mutual benefit.

- Man can, and if left free absolutely will, eventually

remake the entire surface of the planet into one huge modern version of the Garden of Eden. And then, just as he does today in redevelopment of inner-city slums, he will remake it again, only better.

- ALL of this making and remaking of the world into an ever more blissful place will be done by free individuals acting in their own interests. And it is precisely this that TTK do not want.

The Moral of the Story

If you want to remain free, fight this 'sustainability' insanity along with all of the other scare tactics of climate change, terrorism, etc., and rest assured that if this latest buzz word doesn't gain traction, TTK will devise another one.

Secret #11 — Capitalism: The Only Solution

The World Has Not Yet Seen Capitalism

"…economics is the science that studies the production of wealth under a system of division of labor and capitalism is the essential requirement for the successful functioning of a division-of-labor society, indeed, ultimately for its very existence. It is implicit in these propositions that the ultimate source of the importance of the division of labor and capitalism, and of the science of economics, is wealth. This is because, in the last analysis, the division of labor, capitalism, and the science of economics are all merely means to the production of wealth."

What we have for a social system is not Capitalism.

The world has not yet seen Capitalism!

What the world needs in order to vastly alleviate human suffering and to tremendously increase the degree of psychological and material welfare, and thus to a very large degree happiness throughout the world, is Laissez-faire Capitalism (Wikipedia).

Webster's dictionary defines Laissez-Faire Capitalism as: 1) a doctrine opposing governmental interference in economic affairs beyond the minimum necessary for the maintenance of peace and property rights; and 2) a philosophy or practice characterized by a usually deliberate abstention from direction or interference especially with individual freedom of choice and action.

In economic terms, essentially what it means is "government, leave us the hell alone!" and has often been described as a general expression of a stringent "separation of economy and state."

Philosophically speaking, Laissez-Faire Capitalism is the only moral society IF we choose to exist in peace and harmony with one another, trading with each other to mutual benefit.

From Ayn Rand:

A social system is a set of moral, political and economic principles embodied in a society's laws and institutions and government which determine the relationships, the terms of association among the men living in a given geographical area.

There are only two fundamental questions or different sides of the same question that determine the nature of a social system: Does a social system recognize individual rights and does a social system ban the use of physical force from human relationships...

Is man a sovereign individual who owns his person, his mind, his life, his work and his product, or is he the property of the tribe, the state, the society, the collective that may dispose of him in any way it pleases, that may dictate his convictions, prescribe the course of his life, control his work and expropriate his product. Does man have the right to exist for his own sake, or is he born in bondage as an indentured servant who must keep buying his life by serving the tribe but can never acquire it free and clear; this is the first question to answer; the rest is consequences and practical implementation; the basic issue is only: Is man free; In mankind's history capitalism is the only system that answers 'yes."

Capitalism is a social system based on the recognition of individual rights, including property rights, in which all property is privately owned, the recognition of individual rights entails the banishment of force from human relationships.

As I have said, Capitalism is the social system that best supports and promotes a fully-functioning Division of Labor economy. Remember that the DOL is the means of maximizing the productivity of labor, and thus of producing the greatest amount of wealth per capita, and thus the greatest material welfare of each individual, for the greatest degree of maintenance, extension, and enjoyment of each individual's life.

Laissez-Faire Capitalism implies all of the institutions and characteristics of Capitalism, and the core values that underlie these.

The Fully-Functioning Division of Labor IS Capitalism

Human life and well-being depend upon the production of wealth. The production of wealth depends upon the productivity of labor (POL) which vitally depends upon the division of labor (DOL).

In turn, the DOL depends upon the institutions and characteristics of Capitalism. Thus, a fully-functioning DOL society is in its very essence a Capitalist society.

If one cares to reason from first principles, which is what you are here to do, then the moral justification for Capitalism runs something like this:

- The world exists and man is part of it. The universe, the physical world, exists independent of whether you and I are around or not, but while you and I are here, we are a natural part of the universe. And in this universe, things are what they are and they act the way they are supposed to act. Things will do what they are meant to do. That's called the Law of Identity. An apple is an apple. An apple is not an orange. A human being is a human being. A human being is not a slave. The distinguishing trait of we humans is that we possess the ability to reason; our means of survival is not automatic like it is for a coyote, an amoeba, or a coconut tree; we have choose to act out there in the world using reason to survive and thrive, or we die.

- We possesses a specific nature in that we can use our brains to understand our world. The world is knowable to us: things are what they are and nature operates in accordance with the Law of Cause and Effect, including how to best for a man to survive and prosper and how best to live with other men in a society. All we have to do, we the ones with the brains, is observe what we see and reason from there.

- In his nature, a man is an end in himself, and while on this rock his life MUST be his standard of value, and he is morally right in taking actions necessary to maintain, extend, and enjoy his life. Man as an individual being, in his very nature, is the supreme value on this rock; each man takes his life as his supreme value, and whatever may exist or not exist as an afterlife, life in this world is worthy of full enjoyment as an end-value in itself.

- Since the world is a physical world and man must live in it, man's nature dictates that he alter his material surroundings to maintain, extend, and enjoy his life. Not only is it right to produce and prosper, it is absolutely necessary for man's fulfillment as a rational being. He is designed to be productive in order to

thrive. Parasitism and dependency by choice is
sickness and abnormal;

- The naturalness, the necessity, the rightness of being
concerned with material self-improvement is of
necessity a leading force in an individual's life.
Individuals identify themselves as self-responsible
causal agents with the power to improve one's life.
Individuals give a sense of present reality to life when
envisioning the decades to come. Individuals adopt
the outlook that hard work pays and responsibility for
one's own future is met by saving some of what one
produces.

- The rightness of being productive implies the Right to
Life: the right to take all the actions required by the
nature of a rational being for the support, and
furtherance, the fulfillment and the enjoyment of
one's life.

- Because all men seek to maintain, extend and enjoy
their lives, each man must live with other men in a
manner that is not only non-conflicting, but mutually
beneficial;

- We do the DOL, as a consequence of living in freedom,
as the only way for rational men to beneficially coexist;
the DOL is the natural effect of free and independent

men living with one another in society, where each man contributes what he can out of the pure self-interested motive and actions of pursuing his own life.

- By definition, the institutions and characteristics of a fully-functioning DOL are those of Capitalism.

- Capitalism IS a fully-functioning Division of Labor society.

Because Capitalism is a society that not only welcomes but encourages all to be productive to the best of their ability, it is the solution to worldwide unemployment and poverty, and an antidote to worldwide uncertainty, fear, despair, and suffering!

Do you want the maximum possible elevated physical and psychological welfare for everyone the world over?

Then what you want is more and bigger and better capitalists and not the fascists, crony capitalists, moochers, and other con-men on the take that skulk around in our current deplorable scheme seeking personal benefit, the rest of humanity be damned.

Again, from George Reisman:

Economic activity and the development of economic laws and institutions do not take place in a vacuum; they are profoundly influenced by the fundamental philosophical convictions people hold. In order for people to adopt laws and institutions that facilitate economic well-being, it is critical that they understand the basic principles that govern the development, and functioning of the division of labor, AND accept a this-worldly, pro-reason philosophy that underlies a man's right to life, and all the corollary rights that this most fundamental right entails. If they do not, it is a matter of time before more and more destructive laws and institutions are adopted, stopping economic progress, causing economic decline, and ever-progressing human misery.

A widespread knowledge of, a cultural establishment of, pro-capitalist laws and institutions is important to businessmen and capitalists because it assures the continued existence of the very activities of businessmen and investment, the activities prohibited under socialism. Business activities can endure and flourish only in a society in which the average citizen at least intuitively understands the role of wealth, the operation of the division of labor, appreciates their value, and thus the value of businessmen and capitalists. The value of pro-capitalist economics to businessmen is not to teach you how to make money, but of getting you to thoroughly understand that it is to the self-interest of everyone why businessmen and capitalists should be free to make money.

Government intervention and socialism merely create anti-freedom impediments or outright destruction of the division of labor and of capitalism, through creation of the symptomatic problems of inflation, shortages, recessions and depressions, and mass unemployment, and declining

*capital   accumulation   (decumulation)   and   falling
productivity of labor.*

So what are the institutions and characteristics of Capitalism...
of a free fully-functioning DOL society?

Institutions of Capitalism

- Private Property and Private Ownership of Means of Production
- Financial Self Interest and Profit Motive
- (Freedom of) Economic Inequality
- Freedom of Competition
- Saving and Capital Accumulation
- Exchange and Money
- Price System
- Rule of Objective Law
- Limited Government

Characteristics of Capitalism

- Harmony of Rational Self-Interests of All Men
- Integration and Harmony Of Material Interests Of All Who Participate
- Mutually Beneficial Voluntary Trade
- Ubiquitous Respect for Individual Rights
- Personal Self-Esteem and Sense of Self-Responsibility
- Ever Increasing Scientific and Technological

Knowledge
- Technological Advancement and Economic Progress
- Full Employment and Pervasive Individual Motivation to Contribute
- Ever Increasing Purchasing Power of Money
- Peace and Tranquility as the Natural State – Absence of War, Racism, Poverty, Altruism
- Continuously Rising Standard of Living for Everyone

Secret of Wealth #11: The fully-functioning DOL society is a Capitalist society. Due to the enormous benefits provided to anyone who participates in the DOL to the best of his ability, the DOL, Capitalism, is the solution to worldwide suffering and strife, and the sole means of elevating the personal mental and physical welfare of the great majority of human beings now living or that ever will live.

- When people like you and I throughout the world behave in accordance with our nature out of pure self-interest, we engage in productive effort that makes us happy, engage the help of others because we can't do it alone, and trade with others to mutual benefit for the vast majority of the things we need and desire;

- When we are so engaged, we have no time or patience for racism, the tribal mentality of group-against-group, my gang against your gang, or wars.

- In the process of being so engaged, we in the same stroke eliminate unemployment and poverty throughout the entire world.

The Moral of the Story

It is the institutions and characteristics of capitalism (IOC) that promote the DOL, increase the POL and lead to a continuously higher standard of living (SOL) and ever higher quality of life (QOL) for everyone who participates in this system of individual freedom:

$$IOC \Rightarrow DOL \Rightarrow POL \Rightarrow SOL/QOL$$

Capitalism is THIS unleashed.

Capitalism is the way.
What we have is NOT Capitalism.
The World Has Not Yet Seen Capitalism.

As I said before, regarding the ideas at stake, there's nothing new under the sun. What I am teaching here regarding Capitalism has been around for over a century. But it may be totally new for YOU. For additional information, read Ludwig von Mises, George Reisman, or any number of other Austrian

School, pro-capitalist advocates.

Secret #12 — All That a Man Needs

Be a Simple Kind of Man.

Not ignorant, just simple.

Because of the in-depth look at some philosophical topics in this section, I strongly recommend that you start this Secret of Wealth with a completely fresh and alert mind. Don't delve into this right after the other Secrets. Take a break and come back when you are fully rested.

....

All that a man needs to become successful at anything are freedom (rights), a dream, and conviction that your dream will be realized.

More specifically what you must have are freedom from coercion by others, a dream and vision of what you want your life to become, and rational, grounded-in-reality beliefs and the conviction of those beliefs.

Everything else that I have been talking about, or will talk about through the end of this book are fundamentals that underlie these three.

I have put this 'Secret of Wealth' last on my list of twelve because of the special focus I want to devote to the concept of rights and their place as the foundation of any ability to actually act on your convictions and beliefs.

In essence, if your rights are not protected, if you are not free from coercion, you cannot act. To the degree that you are not free from coercion by others you are incapable of acting for your own benefit, regardless of what you believe regarding your aptitude and abilities.

As implied in Secret of Wealth #11 regarding Capitalism and the division of labor, both Capitalism and a fully-functioning division of labor are dependent upon freedom. In turn, **freedom for you and me in society depends upon the identification of, the full awareness of, and the protection of valid rights.**

There is one main reason that I have included this material on individual rights in my book and that is the toxicity of the weak-minded simps of the environmental movement, of course the rampant anti-man values of the statists, and the total perversions of rationality that they all spew (you may safely surmise that I despise rabid environmentalists and dead-ender statists).

Among the final reasons that I decided to include this lengthy expose' on rights is my reading of the recently published and highly acclaimed book Abundance by Peter Diamandis and

Steven Kotler.

The book is terrific in opening the reader's mind to the wonderful possibilities opening up via new technologies that are in the works this very day. The book talks about achieving all this new technology but does not identify by whom all of this technology will be created.

The book implies that governments will create it—that through all the inefficiencies, lack of accountability, capricious bureaucratic controls, ridiculous capital misallocations, and cronyism inherent in statism will somehow manifest all of these magical wonders into existence.

Of course I see that the technological wonders described in the book cannot come to pass without their creation by individuals taking individual actions that lead to a sum, which for me implies an expansion of Freedom in a developing world, NOT the expansion of government controls and infringement of freedom that necessarily comes with each new "program."

As wonderful and as breathtaking and as vision-inspiring the scope of the book, the authors give short shrift to the absolute necessity of individual freedom that will be required to make all of this happen, and of course the required commensurate respect for and protection of individual rights. It seems to me that they almost ignore the very root cause of any of it, or otherwise attribute all future success to the actions of government.

It is an unstated background theme of the book that it is they, the authors and other brainchilds of the technology, that as part of a TTK sub culture will alone have the wisdom and foresight to envision the possibilities and petition the government for the special dispensations that will be required to create and run the official Czar-doms that are going to be necessary to manage government-provided deficit- and stolen-via-taxes funding. There's not much talk in the book about the profitable (i.e. economic) implementation of any of these ideas, which in and of itself implies feel-good endless funding without concern for risk-reward or cost-benefit analysis. After all, these budding TTK are doing it for the poor and especially the poor children.

Never mind that the average Joe or Jane like you and me will get shafted again as we have with the stupendously successful multi-decade War on Poverty that still rages.

Their book is just a typical modern indication of the general state of awareness that people have regarding their rights and what freedom of the individual implies with respect to their own personal welfare.

So let's spend some time on rights.

Freedom and Rights

There are lots of talking heads out there yammering about all kinds of rights: individual rights, group rights, tribal rights, animal rights, gay rights, women's rights, environmental rights—without a strong personal constitution it is literally enough to drive you to drink.

If you believe that frogs and amoebas and stink bugs have rights, then you might as well chuck this book in the garbage because by that belief you negate virtually everything we have covered to this point.

I harp on rights extensively here because understanding what a right is and what your fundamental rights are is absolutely crucial to your personal welfare and happiness, AND to the welfare and happiness of every human being on the planet that lives now or ever will live. Certainly if more people had a sounder understanding of what truly constitutes a right and why, we would not be in the predicament of world-wide violence of man against man that we are in today and have been for the last 100 years.

Although rights come from our understanding of human nature, which is a very philosophical endeavor, my intent is not to turn you into a philosopher. Just as my intent is not to turn you into an economist.

However, as I stated at the outset of this book, I will not

speak down to you or dumb down what I have to say; it is your responsibility as an entity capable of self-respect to seek growth—to raise your own bar of understanding and challenge yourself to expand your mind.

So here goes....

Let's begin with a quote from Ayn Rand:

If one wishes to advocate a free society — that is, capitalism — one must realize that its indispensable foundation is the principle of individual rights. If one wishes to uphold individual rights, one must realize that capitalism is the only system that can uphold and protect them. And if one wishes to gauge the relationship of freedom to the goals of today's intellectuals, one may gauge it by the fact that the concept of individual rights is evaded, distorted, perverted and seldom discussed, most conspicuously seldom by the so-called "conservatives."

Every political system is based on some code of ethics. The dominant ethics of mankind's history were variants of the altruist-collectivist doctrine which subordinated the individual to some higher authority, either mystical or social. Consequently, most political systems were variants of the same statist tyranny, differing only in degree, not in basic principle, limited only by the accidents of tradition, of chaos, of bloody strife and periodic collapse. Under all such systems, morality was a code applicable to the individual, but not to society. Society was placed outside the moral law, as its embodiment or source or exclusive interpreter — and the inculcation of self-

sacrificial devotion to social duty was regarded as the main purpose of ethics in man's earthly existence.

Since there is no such entity as "society," since society is only a number of individual men, this meant, in practice, that the rulers of society were exempt from moral law; subject only to traditional rituals, they held total power and exacted blind obedience — on the implicit principle of: "The good is that which is good for society (or for the tribe, the race, the nation), and the ruler's edicts are its voice on earth."

The most profoundly revolutionary achievement of the United States of America was the subordination of society to moral law.

The principle of man's individual rights represented the extension of morality into the social system — as a limitation on the power of the state, as man's protection against the brute force of the collective, as the subordination of might to right. The United States was the first moral society in history.

All previous systems had regarded man as a sacrificial means to the ends of others, and society as an end in itself. The United States regarded man as an end in himself, and society as a means to the peaceful, orderly, voluntary coexistence of individuals. All previous systems had held that man's life belongs to society, that society can dispose of him in any way it pleases, and that any freedom he enjoys is his only by favor, by the permission of society, which may be revoked at any time. The United States held that man's life is his by right (which means: by moral principle and by his nature), that a right is the property of an individual, that society as such has no rights, and that the only moral purpose of a government is the protection of individual rights.

Definition of Rights

Exactly what IS a right?

Here are predominant definitions for the noun "right":

- Merriam-Webster's Dictionary: "behavior that is morally good or correct; something that a person is or should be morally or legally allowed to have, get, or do"; something to which one has a just claim; the power or privilege to which one is justly entitled;"

- Cambridge Dictionary: "your opportunity to act and to be treated in particular ways that the law promises to protect for the benefit of society;"

- Oxford Dictionary: A moral or legal entitlement to have or obtain something or to act in a certain way;

- Google Dictionary: "That which is morally correct, just, or honorable; a moral or legal entitlement to have or obtain something or to act in a certain way."

- Wikipedia: "Rights are legal, social, or ethical principles of freedom or entitlement; that is, rights are the fundamental normative rules about what is allowed of people or owed to people, according to some legal system, social convention, or ethical theory."

I have been all over this territory over the years and have not yet found a better definition of what a right is than that provided by Ayn Rand herself:

"A right is moral principle defining and sanctioning a man's freedom of action in a social context. It means freedom from physical compulsion, coercion or interference by other men. Thus, for every individual, a right is the moral sanction of a positive — of his freedom to act on his own judgment, for his own goals, by his own voluntary, uncoerced choice. As to his neighbors, his rights impose no obligations on them except of a negative kind: to abstain from violating his rights."

"Rights are a moral concept—the concept that provides a logical transition from the principles guiding an individual's actions (ethics) to the principles guiding his relationship with others (politics)—the principle that preserves and protects individual morality in a social context—the link between the moral code of a man and the legal code of a society, between ethics and politics. Individual rights are the means of subordinating society to moral law."

"By its nature, the concept of a 'right' pertains only to action—specifically freedom of action."

So what does this mean in plain language? It means that a

right is a sanction to independent action by individual man. It means that by your very nature you are entitled to take certain actions.

The opposite of acting by right is acting by permission.

So what actions? Specifically what actions are you, as a human being, entitled to take?

The Only Valid Rights

You have ONE fundamental right from which all others are derived and upon which all others depend: You have the right to your very life.

You are entitled to your life. You have the title to your very life if you will.

The Right to Life means that you are by your very nature entitled to sustain, protect, extend, and enjoy your life. It means that in your natural state of being, of being free, you are entitled, you enjoy the unhindered freedom, to "take all actions required by the nature of a rational being to the preservation of your life."

As a derivative from the right to your life you have the Right to Liberty. To maintain, extend and enjoy your life, by your very nature you must be free to gain knowledge, choose values, and then act in accordance with your own judgment in pursuing those values. The right to liberty is the right to think, choose, and act on your judgment.

Also derivative from the right to your life, you possess the Right to Property. In order to maintain, extend, and enjoy your life in the physical world, you require and thus are entitled to the material means to accomplish these. You are entitled to gain, to keep, and to dispose of material values. Says Ayn Rand:

> *"Without property rights no other rights are possible. Since man has to sustain his life by his own effort, the man who has no right to the product of his effort has no means to sustain his life. The man who produces while others dispose of his product, is a slave. Bear in mind that the right to property is a right to action, like all the others: it is not the right to an object, but to the action and the consequences of producing or earning that object. It is not a guarantee that a man will earn any property, but only a guarantee that he will own it if he earns it. It is the right to gain, to keep, to use and to dispose of material values."*

Also derivative from the right to your life is that you are entitled to pursue your happiness. Your nature requires that you act to maintain, extend, and enjoy your life—to pursue your personal welfare as your central purpose in living. The Right to the Pursuit of Happiness is the entitlement to live for your own sake and fulfillment.

Interdependence of Rights.

As Peikoff states:

Since man is an integrated being of mind and body, every right entails every other: none is definable or possible apart from the rest. There can be no right to think apart from the right to act: thinking (for a rational man) is a guide to action; the process consists of setting the ends and means of one's action through the identification of facts and of values. Similarly, there can be no right to act apart from the right to own: action requires the use of material objects (even the act of speaking requires a patch of ground on which to stand). Freedom—like man—is indivisible."

"Rights form a logical unity. ...It would be a crude contradiction to tell a man: you have a right to life, but you need the permission of others to think or act. Or: you have the right to life, but you need the permission of others to produce or consume. Or: you have the right to life, but don't dare pursue any personal motive without the approval of the government."

"Man is a certain kind of living organism—which leads to his need of morality and to man's life being the moral standard—which leads to the right to act by the guidance of this standard, i.e., the right to life. Reason is man's basic means of survival—which leads to rationality being the primary virtue—which leads to the right to act according to one's judgment, i.e., the right to liberty. Unlike animals, man does not survive by adjusting to the

given—which leads to productiveness being a cardinal virtue—which leads to the right to keep, use, and dispose of the things one has produced, i.e., the right to property. Reason is an attribute of the individual, one that demands, as a condition of its function, unbreached allegiance to reality—which leads to the ethics of egoism—which leads to the right to the pursuit of happiness."

Rights Have Meaning Only in a Social Context

Rights have no meaning or use outside of men living with one another in a society. Rights only have meaning or applicability when one man interacts or has the potential to interact with others.

Peikoff:

"If a man lived on a desert island, there would be no question of defining his proper relationship to others. Even if men interacted on some island but did so at random, without establishing a social system, the issue of rights would be premature. There would not yet be any context for the concept or, therefore, any means of implementing it; there would be no agency to interpret, apply, or enforce it. When men do decide to form (or reform) an organized society, however, when they decide to pursue systematically the advantages of living together, then they need the guidance of principle. That is the context in which the principle of rights arises. If your society is to be moral (and therefore practical), it declares

you must begin by recognizing the moral requirements of man in a social context; i.e., you must define the sphere of sovereignty mandated for every individual by the laws of morality. Within this sphere, the individual acts without needing any agreement or approval from others, nor may any others interfere."

Finally, Ayn Rand's definition of right above uses the word "sanction" which by definition means one is "officially allowed or granted effective or authoritative approval or consent to take specific actions."

Note that this only applies to a man living in society with others. In a capitalist society, government of the people by the people and for the people, as the protector of individual rights, is the entity that sanctions freedom of action in society for the individual by way of objective law that upholds the moral code required by individual man. More on the role of a proper government below...

The Source of Rights—Roots in Philosophy: Ethics v. Politics

The source of man's rights is not a supreme deity or the edicts of a legislature, but from nature. Again, whatever the source of your creation, you possess a specific discoverable nature. The source of rights is human nature as discovered via the field of philosophy called metaphysics—the academics word for the study of what is real, of what exists. More specifically, the Law of Identity which states that A is A. A thing is what it is and not something else at the same time. A man is a man, a turnip is a turnip, and no amount of word-smithing or parsing can change that.

Rights do not come from the State or the group. Rather, their requirement is inherent in human nature. As Ayn Rand states:

The concept of individual rights is so new in human history that most men have not grasped it fully to this day. In accordance with the two theories of ethics, the mystical or the social, some men assert that rights are a gift of God — others, that rights are a gift of society. But, in fact, the source of rights is man's nature.

The Declaration of Independence stated that men "are endowed by their Creator with certain unalienable rights." Whether one believes that man is the product of a Creator or of nature, the issue of man's origin does not alter the fact that he is an entity of a specific kind — a rational being — that he cannot function successfully under coercion, and that rights are a necessary condition of his particular mode of survival.

The source of man's rights is not divine law or congressional law, but the law of identity. A is A — and Man is Man. Rights are conditions of existence required by man's nature for his proper survival. If man is to live on earth, it is right for him to use his mind, it is right to act on his own free judgment, it is right to work for his values and to keep the product of his work. If life on earth is his purpose, he has a right to live as a rational being: nature forbids the irrational.

It cannot be otherwise!

If man is to live on this planet as the rational being that he is, then he is entitled to the actions described above.

Period.

Now, what's all this talk about morality? That is an awfully stern, restrictive, and emotionally charged word, right? And its most often associated with religious fervor. What the hell is morality? Are you getting all religious and stuff on me here, Joseph?

Morality is nothing more than ethics, the branch of philosophy that studies how a man should live, how he should act. And a moral a code of values is a set of core values that a man lives by. A man can possess a lousy set of values and his moral compass is commensurately off-kilter, or a code of values that is proper to his life and which properly guides his life as a rational being.

In essence, morality teaches us that a man should act in a way that promotes life and not in a way that destroys life. Obviously the moral code of a murderer is not the equivalent of the moral code of a rational business man. Note that morality applies to your life regardless if you interact with others or not. A moral code guides your life even if you live on a desert island.

Politics, as a branch of ethics that studies how men should live with one another in society, is what mandates that rights to be required as a matter of law—embodied in a written moral code that men should live by when amongst each other in a society. It is only the existence of society that gives rise to politics and rights. Recall Ayn Rand's definition of a right:

> "A right is moral principle defining and sanctioning a man's freedom of action in a social context."

> "Rights are a moral concept—the concept that provides a logical transition from the principles guiding an individual's actions (ethics) to the principles guiding his relationship with others (politics)—the principle that preserves and protects individual morality in a social context—the link between the moral code of a man and the legal code of a society, between ethics and politics. Individual rights are the means of subordinating society to moral law."

This being understood, Peikoff formulates corollaries to the source of rights (emphasis is mine):

- All rights rest on the fact that man's life is the moral standard. Rights are rights to the kinds of actions necessary for the preservation of human life. Just as it is only the concept of life that makes the concept of 'value' possible, so it is only the requirement of man's life that make morality, and thus the concept of 'rights' possible.

- **All rights rest on the fact that man is a productive being.** Rights presume that men can live together without anyone's sacrifice. If man merely consumed objects provided in a static quantity by nature, every man would be a potential threat to every other. In such a case the rule of life would have to be that which governs the lower species: seize what you can before others get it, eat or be eaten, kill or be killed.

- All rights rest on the ethics of egoism (it is right and proper to live for one's own sake and to reap the rewards of one's independent judgment and actions). Rights are an individual's selfish possessions—his title to his life, his liberty, his property, the pursuit of his own happiness. Only a being who is an end in himself can claim a moral sanction to independent action. If man existed to serve an entity beyond himself, whether God or society, then he would not have rights, but only the duties of a servant."

Bastardized Rights. Invalid Rights. Non-Rights.

Rights pertain ONLY to individual humans as rational, volitional beings and NOT trees, tribes, unions, races, sexes, dogs, society or governing bodies!

Regarding conflict of rights among men (Peikoff):

> *If rights are defined in rational terms, no conflict is possible between the rights of one individual and those of another. Every man is sovereign. He is absolutely free within the sphere of his own rights, and every man has the same rights.*

> *This doesn't mean that individuals will not disagree and possibly require compromise to mutual benefit...perhaps even to the point of pursuing the intervention of the courts to resolve a dispute. What it does mean is that there is no ethical conflict between individuals who possess the same rational rights.*

> *If one detaches the concept of "rights' from reason and reality, however, then nothing but conflict is possible, and the theory of "rights" self-destructs. Just as bad principles drive out good, so false rights, reflecting bad principles, drive out proper rights—a process that is running wild today in the proliferation of such self-contradictory verbiage as "economic rights," "collective rights,"... and "animal rights."*

> *"Economic rights" in this context means a man's right,*

simply by virtue of existing, to man-made goods and services, such as food, clothing, a home, a job, education, day care, medical care, a pension. All such claims involve a contradiction: if my right to life entails a right to your labor or its product, you cannot have a right to liberty or property.

"Collective rights" means rights belonging to a group qua group, rights allegedly independent of those possessed by the individual. Thus we hear of the special rights of businessmen, workers, farmers, consumers, the young, the old, the students, the females, the race, the class, the nation, the public. ...All such collectivist variants reflect the ethics of self-sacrifice; all the variants divide men into beneficiaries and servants, masters and slaves, and thus negate the concept of "rights." Substituting for it the principle of mob rule.

"Animal rights" are an absolute abomination. Words mean things. A man is a man; an animal is an animal. Rights are a moral concept, and moral concepts pertain to beings with conceptual minds complete with the power of reason and volition—the power of evaluating and choosing a course of action. This is precisely what animals do not possess. Animals act range-of-the-moment and automatically—the ONLY way their perceptual level of consciousness allows them to.

They cannot choose their course of as we humans do.

Animals may bond with us, we may develop such close associations to them as pets that some of us cannot live without them. We may grieve for them when they die. We may rationally value them as better than certain humans. As rational animal we certainly don't wish them unnecessary harm and in fact we are quite adept at animal husbandry, but an animal simply is not the equivalent of a human being.

Animals possess NO rights. If you wish to delve more into the reasons that animals do not have rights, Google "Objectivism and animal rights" and read. There is an entire field of philosophy, Epistemology, that deals with how we know what we know...the arguments and refutations are all out there to research if you care to.

I warn those of you who subscribe to animal rights: those who have convinced you of this idea have placed you as the moral equivalent of a human-killing virus or any random bacterium. If the idea ever gains widespread fanatical fervor, then virtually ANYTHING you now own or do that can possibly harm the minutest of organisms will wind you up on death row.

There are nut jobs out there today who advocate wiping out the human race for this very reason. (In my opinion, enviro-nutjobs are the worst kind of hypocrites in voluntarily remaining alive one more instant while they have bugs splattered all over the windshields of their favorite speed-machines, while they saunter up to Napa in the finest leather apparel to ogle the vineyards and enjoy the wines where other insect and rodent species have met their horrible deaths at the hands of the vintners. My god, who speaks for these innocent intrinsically-valuable creatures?! The horror. These two-faced hypocrites should grow a pair and in being consistent with their blathering, just end their existence. As Forrest Gump would say, that is all I have to say about that.)

Now, understanding that rights pertain only to human beings, Ayn Rand clarifies what a right is NOT in this context:

If some men are entitled by right to the products of the work of others, it means that those others are deprived of rights and condemned to slave labor. Any alleged "right" of one man, which necessitates the violation of the rights of another, is not and cannot be a right. No man can have a right to impose an unchosen obligation, an unrewarded duty or an involuntary servitude on another man. There can be no such thing as "the right to enslave." A right does not include the material implementation of that right by other men; it includes only the freedom to earn that implementation by one's own effort.

Observe, in this context, the intellectual precision of the Founding Fathers: they spoke of the right to the pursuit of happiness — not of the right to happiness. It means that a man has the right to take the actions he deems necessary to achieve his happiness; it does not mean that others must make him happy.

The right to life means that a man has the right to support his life by his own work (on any economic level, as high as his ability will carry him); it does not mean that others must provide him with the necessities of life.

The right to property means that a man has the right to take the economic actions necessary to earn property, to use it and to dispose of it; it does not mean that others must provide him with property.

The right of free speech means that a man has the right to express his ideas without danger of suppression, interference or punitive action by the government. It does not mean that others must provide him with a lecture hall, a radio station or a printing press through which to express his ideas.

Any undertaking that involves more than one man, requires the voluntary consent of every participant. Every one of them has the right to make his own decision, but none has the right to force his decision on the others.

There is no such thing as "a right to a job" — there is only the right of free trade, that is: a man's right to take a job if another man chooses to hire him. There is no "right to a home," only the right of free trade: the right to build a home or to buy it. There are no "rights to a 'fair' wage or a 'fair' price" if no one chooses to pay it, to hire a man or to buy his product. There are no "rights of consumers" to milk, shoes, movies or champagne if no producers choose to manufacture such items (there is only the right to manufacture them oneself). There are no "rights" of special groups, there are no "rights of farmers, of workers, of businessmen, of employees, of employers, of the old, of the young, of the unborn." There are only the Rights of

Man — rights possessed by every individual man and by all men as individuals.

Property rights and the right of free trade are man's only "economic rights" (they are, in fact, political rights) — and there can be no such thing as "an economic bill of rights." But observe that the advocates of the latter have all but destroyed the former.

Remember that rights are moral principles which define and protect a man's freedom of action, but impose no obligations on other men.

Inalienability of Rights

A right is a prerogative that cannot be morally infringed or alienated. This is what we mean when we say rights are inalienable.

Evil exists and men can be robbed or enslaved. But the victim's rights are still inalienable: the right remains on the side of the victim; the criminal is wrong.

A man's rights cannot be taken from him morally, as a matter of acting properly towards other men.

While a man can be deprived of his ability to act to maintain, extend and enjoy his life, the rightfulness of him having the freedom to act does not go away, and the correction of violations of his rights is the basis for justice in accordance with a codified objective Rule of Law that is designed to protect those rights.

Rights and Force. The Violation of Rights.

Ayn Rand:

To violate man's rights means to compel him to act against his own judgment, or to expropriate his values. Basically, there is only one way to do it: by the use of physical force. There are two potential violators of man's rights: the criminals and the government. The great achievement of the United States was to draw a distinction between these two — by forbidding to the second the legalized version of the activities of the first.

The Declaration of Independence laid down the principle that "to secure these rights, governments are instituted among men." This provided the only valid justification of a government and defined its only proper purpose: to protect man's rights by protecting him from physical violence.

Thus the government's function was changed from the role of ruler to the role of servant. The government was set to protect man from criminals — and the Constitution was written to protect man from the government. The Bill of Rights was not directed against private citizens, but against the government — as an explicit declaration that individual rights supersede any public or social power.

The result was the pattern of a civilized society which — for the brief span of some hundred and fifty years — America came close to achieving. A civilized society is one in which physical force is banned from human relationships — in which the government, acting as a policeman, may use force only in retaliation and only against those who initiate its use.

This was the essential meaning and intent of America's political philosophy, implicit in the principle of individual rights.

I like what Leonard Peikoff says regarding violation of rights versus the everyday tragedies that may befall us in our interactions with others:

"An individual can be hurt in countless ways by other men's irrationality, dishonesty, injustice. Above all he can be disappointed, perhaps grievously, by the vices of a person he once trusted or loved. But as long as his property is not expropriated and he remains unmolested physically, the damage he sustains is essentially spiritual, not physical; in such a case, the victim alone has the power and the responsibility of healing his wounds. He remains free: free to think, to learn from his experiences, to look elsewhere for human relationships; he remains free to start afresh and to pursue his happiness. Only the crime of force is able to render its victim helpless. The moral responsibility of organized society, therefore, lies in a single obligation: to banish this crime, i.e., to protect individual rights."

And the banishing of this crime is the subject of the next section....the only legitimate role of government.

Government Role Regarding Rights

I realize you may think that I quote excessively, but on the criticality of understanding what rights are and how your very welfare depends upon them, AND on the role that our government should be taking in regard to our rights, I cannot apologize.

The excerpt from Ayn Rand below is enormous. It is the best explanation of the role of government that I have found, and because my intent with this book is to provide you with an integrated, philosophically-sound and practical, actionable approach to life, I must include it here in its entirety. I have no desire to reinvent the wheel and rehash all of her ideas into my words as it would be a complete waste of time. If you think you "get it" regarding the concept of rights, do yourself a favor and make it complete by absorbing this last quote of the section.

Just buckle down, FOCUS, and read it and understand it. If you ever in the future need to fall back on the foundations and purpose of rights, you will know where to go.

Also, you may be under the influence that anarchy or "competing governments" is the way to go as so many Libertarians believe these days. If so, this passage will cause you to question that belief. Unless you and I can revive in others a proper understanding and respect for rights, and hold our government accountable, we are, as they say, "toast".

I pray we are not too late.

Now, Miss Rand in all her wisdom and eloquence:

A government is an institution that holds the exclusive power to enforce certain rules of social conduct in a given geographical area.

Do men need such an institution—and why?

Since man's mind is his basic tool of survival, his means of gaining knowledge to guide his actions—the basic condition he requires is the freedom to think and to act according to his rational judgment. This does not mean that a man must live alone and that a desert island is the environment best suited to his needs. Men can derive enormous benefits from dealing with one another. A social environment is most conducive to their successful survival —but only on certain conditions."

"The two great values to be gained from social existence are: knowledge and trade. Man is the only species that can transmit and expand his store of knowledge from generation to generation; the knowledge potentially available to man is greater than any one man could begin to acquire in his own lifespan; every man gains an incalculable benefit from the knowledge discovered by others. The second great benefit is the division of labor: it enables a man to devote his effort to a particular field of

work and to trade with others who specialize in other fields. This form of cooperation allows all men who take part in it to achieve a greater knowledge, skill and productive return on their effort than they could achieve if each had to produce everything he needs, on a desert island or on a self-sustaining farm.

"But these very benefits indicate, delimit and define what kind of men can be of value to one another and in what kind of society: only rational, productive, independent men in a rational, productive, free society."

A society that robs an individual of the product of his effort, or enslaves him, or attempts to limit the freedom of his mind, or compels him to act against his own rational judgment—a society that sets up a conflict between its edicts and the requirements of man's nature—is not, strictly speaking, a society, but a mob held together by institutionalized gang-rule. Such a society destroys all the values of human coexistence, has no possible justification and represents, not a source of benefits, but the deadliest threat to man's survival. Life on a desert island is safer than and incomparably preferable to existence in Soviet Russia or Nazi Germany.

If men are to live together in a peaceful, productive, rational society and deal with one another to mutual benefit, they must accept the basic social principle without which no moral or civilized society is possible: the principle of individual rights.

To recognize individual rights means to recognize and accept the conditions required by man's nature for his *proper survival.*

Man's rights can be violated only by the use of physical force. It is only by means of physical force that one man can deprive another of his life, or enslave him, or rob him, or prevent him from pursuing his own goals, or compel him to act against his own rational judgment.

The precondition of a civilized society is the barring of physical force from social relationships—thus establishing the principle that if men wish to deal with one another, they may do so only by means of reason: by discussion, persuasion and voluntary, uncoerced agreement.

The necessary consequence of man's right to life is his right to self-defense. In a civilized society, force may be used only in retaliation and only against those who initiate its use. All the reasons which make the initiation of physical force an evil, make the retaliatory use of physical force a moral imperative.

If some "pacifist" society renounced the retaliatory use of force, it would be left helplessly at the mercy of the first thug who decided to be immoral. Such a society would achieve the opposite of its intention: instead of abolishing evil, it would encourage and reward it.

If a society provided no organized protection against force, it would compel every citizen to go about armed, to turn his home into a fortress, to shoot any strangers approaching his door—or to join a protective gang of citizens who would fight other gangs, formed for the same purpose, and thus bring about the degeneration of that society into the chaos of gang-rule, i.e., rule by brute force, into perpetual tribal warfare of prehistoric savages.

The use of physical force—even its retaliatory use—cannot be left at the discretion of individual citizens. Peaceful coexistence is impossible if a man has to live under the constant threat of force to be unleashed against him by any of his neighbors at any moment. Whether his neighbors' intentions are good or bad, whether their judgment is rational or irrational, whether they are motivated by a sense of justice or by ignorance or by prejudice or by malice-the use of force against one man cannot be left to the arbitrary decision of another.

Visualize, for example, what would happen if a man missed his wallet, concluded that he had been robbed, broke into every house in the neighborhood to search it, and shot the first man who gave him a dirty look, taking the look to be a proof of guilt.

The retaliatory use of force requires objective rules of evidence to establish that a crime has been committed and to prove who committed it, as well as objective rules to define punishments and enforcement procedures. Men who attempt to prosecute crimes, without such rules, are a lynch mob. If a society left the retaliatory use of force in the hands of individual citizens, it would degenerate into mob rule, lynch law and an endless series of bloody private feuds or vendettas. [Hatfields and McCoys come to mind]

If physical force is to be barred from social relationships, men need an institution charged with the task of protecting their rights under an objective code of rules.

This is the task of a government—of a proper government —its basic task, its only moral justification and the reason why men do need a government.

A government is the means of placing the retaliatory use of physical force under objective control—i.e., under objectively defined laws.

The fundamental difference between private action and governmental action—a difference thoroughly ignored and evaded today—lies in the fact that a government holds a monopoly on the legal use of physical force. It has to hold such a monopoly, since it is the agent of restraining and combating the use of force; and for that very same reason, its actions have to be rigidly defined, delimited and circumscribed; no touch of whim or caprice should be permitted in its performance; it should be an impersonal robot, with the laws as its only motive power. If a society is to be free, its government has to be controlled.

Under a proper social system, a private individual is legally free to take any action he pleases (so long as he does not violate the rights of others), while a government official is bound by law in his every official act. A private individual may do anything except that which is legally forbidden; a government official may do nothing except that which is legally permitted.

This is the means of subordinating "might" to "right." This is the American concept of "a government of laws and not of men."

The nature of the laws proper to a free society and the source of its government's authority are both to be derived from the nature and purpose of a proper government. The basic principle of both is indicated in the Declaration of Independence: "to secure these [individual] rights, governments are instituted among men, deriving their just powers from the consent of the governed . . ."

Since the protection of individual rights is the only proper purpose of a government, it is the only proper subject of legislation: all laws must be based on individual rights and aimed at their protection. All laws must be objective (and objectively justifiable): men must know clearly, and in advance of taking an action, what the law forbids them to do (and why), what constitutes a crime and what penalty they will incur if they commit it.

The source of the government's authority is "the consent of the governed." This means that the government is not the ruler, but the servant or agent of the citizens; it means that the government as such has no rights except the rights delegated to it by the citizens for a specific purpose.

There is only one basic principle to which an individual must consent if he wishes to live in a free, civilized society: the principle of renouncing the use of physical force and delegating to the government his right of physical self-defense, for the purpose of an orderly, objective, legally defined enforcement. Or, to put it another way, he must accept the separation of force and whim (any whim, including his own).

Now what happens in case of a disagreement between two men about an undertaking in which both are involved?

In a free society, men are not forced to deal with one another. They do so only by voluntary agreement and, when a time element is involved, by contract. If a contract is broken by the arbitrary decision of one man, it may cause a disastrous financial injury to the other—and the victim would have no recourse except to seize the offender's property as compensation. But here again, the use of force cannot be left to the decision of private individuals. And this leads to one of the most important and most complex functions of the government: to the function of an arbiter who settles disputes among men according to objective laws.

Criminals are a small minority in any semi-civilized society. But the protection and enforcement of contracts through courts of civil law is the most crucial need of a peaceful society; without such protection, no civilization could be developed or maintained.

Man cannot survive, as animals do, by acting on the range of the immediate moment. Man has to project his goals and achieve them across a span of time; he has to calculate his actions and plan his life long-range. The better a man's mind and the greater his knowledge, the longer the range of his planning. The higher or more complex a civilization, the longer the range of activity it requires—and, therefore, the longer the range of contractual agreements among men, and the more urgent their need of protection for the security of such agreements.

Even a primitive barter society could not function if a man agreed to trade a bushel of potatoes for a basket of eggs and, having received the eggs, refused to deliver the potatoes. Visualize what this sort of whim-directed action would mean in an industrial society where men deliver a billion dollars' worth of goods on credit, or contract to build multimillion-dollar structures, or sign ninety-nine-year leases.

A unilateral breach of contract involves an indirect use of physical force: it consists, in essence, of one man receiving the material values, goods or services of another, then refusing to pay for them and thus keeping them by force (by mere physical possession), not by right—i.e., keeping them without the consent of their owner. Fraud involves a similarly indirect use of force: it consists of obtaining material values without their owner's consent, under false pretenses or false promises. Extortion is another variant of an indirect use of force: it consists of obtaining material values, not in exchange for values, but by the threat of force, violence or injury.

Some of these actions are obviously criminal. Others, such as a unilateral breach of contract, may not be criminally motivated, but may be caused by irresponsibility and irrationality. Still others may be complex issues with some claim to justice on both sides. But whatever the case may be, all such issues have to be made subject to objectively defined laws and have to be resolved by an impartial arbiter, administering the laws, i.e., by a judge (and a jury, when appropriate).

Observe the basic principle governing justice in all these cases: it is the principle that no man may obtain any values from others without the owners' consent—and, as a corollary, that a man's rights may not be left at the mercy of the unilateral decision, the arbitrary choice, the irrationality, the whim of another man.

Such, in essence, is the proper purpose of a government: to make social existence possible to men, by protecting the benefits and combating the evils which men can cause to one another.

The proper functions of a government fall into three broad categories, all of them involving the issues of physical force and the protection of men's rights: the police, to protect men from criminals—the armed services, to protect men from foreign invaders—the law courts, to settle disputes among men according to objective laws.

These three categories involve many corollary and derivative issues—and their implementation in practice, in the form of specific legislation, is enormously complex. It belongs to the field of a special science: the philosophy of law. Many errors and many disagreements are possible in the field of implementation, but what is essential here is the principle to be implemented: the principle that the purpose of law and of government is the protection of individual rights.

Today, this principle is forgotten, ignored and evaded. The result is the present state of the world, with mankind's retrogression to the lawlessness of absolutist tyranny, to the primitive savagery of rule by brute force.

In unthinking protest against this trend, some people are raising the question of whether government as such is evil by nature and whether anarchy is the ideal social system. Anarchy, as a political concept, is a naive floating abstraction: for all the reasons discussed above, a society without an organized government would be at the mercy of the first criminal who came along and who would precipitate it into the chaos of gang warfare. But the possibility of human immorality is not the only objection to anarchy: even a society whose every member were fully rational and faultlessly moral, could not function in a state of anarchy: it is the need of objective laws and of an arbiter for honest disagreements among men that necessitates the establishment of a government.

A recent variant of anarchistic theory, which is befuddling some of the younger advocates of freedom, is a weird absurdity called "competing governments." Accepting the basic premise of the modern statists—who see no difference between the functions of government and the functions of industry, between force and production, and who advocate government ownership of business—the proponents of "competing governments" take the other side of the same coin and declare that since competition is so beneficial to business, it should also be applied to government. Instead of a single, monopolistic government, they declare, there should be a number of different governments in the same geographical area, competing for the allegiance of individual citizens, with every citizen free to "shop" and to patronize whatever government he chooses.

Remember that forcible restraint of men is the only service a government has to offer. Ask yourself what a competition in forcible restraint would have to mean.

One cannot call this theory a contradiction in terms, since it is obviously devoid of any understanding of the terms "competition" and "government." Nor can one call it a floating abstraction, since it is devoid of any contact with or reference to reality and cannot be concretized at all, not even roughly or approximately. One illustration will be sufficient: suppose Mr. Smith, a customer of Government A, suspects that his next-door neighbor, Mr. Jones, a customer of Government B, has robbed him; a squad of Police A proceeds to Mr. Jones' house and is met at the door by a squad of Police B, who declare that they do not accept the validity of Mr. Smith's complaint and do not recognize the authority of Government A. What happens then? You take it from there.

The evolution of the concept of "government" has had a long, tortuous history. Some glimmer of the government's proper function seems to have existed in every organized society, manifesting itself in such phenomena as the recognition of some implicit (if often nonexistent) difference between a government and a robber gang—the aura of respect and of moral authority granted to the government as the guardian of "law and order" —the fact that even the most evil types of government found it necessary to maintain some semblance of order and some pretense at justice, if only by routine and tradition, and to claim some sort of moral justification for their power, of a mystical or social nature. Just as the absolute monarchs of France had to invoke "The Divine Right of Kings," so the modern dictators of Soviet Russia have to spend fortunes on propaganda to justify their rule in the eyes of their enslaved subjects.

In mankind's history, the understanding of the government's proper function is a very recent achievement: it is only two hundred years old and it dates from the Founding Fathers of the American Revolution. Not only did they identify the nature and the needs of a free society, but they devised the means to translate it into practice. A free society—like any other human product— cannot be achieved by random means, by mere wishing or by the leaders' "good intentions." A complex legal system, based on objectively valid principles, is required to make a society free and to keep it free-a system that does not depend on the motives, the moral character or the intentions of any given official, a system that leaves no opportunity, no legal loophole for the development of tyranny.

The American system of checks and balances was just such an achievement. And although certain contradictions in the Constitution did leave a loophole for the growth of statism, the incomparable achievement was the concept of a constitution as a means of limiting and restricting the power of the government.

Today, when a concerted effort is made to obliterate this

point, it cannot be repeated too often that the Constitution is a limitation on the government, not on private individuals—that it does not prescribe the conduct of private individuals, only the conduct of the government— that it is not a charter for government power, but a charter of the citizens' protection against the government.

Now consider the extent of the moral and political inversion in today's prevalent view of government. Instead of being a protector of man's rights, the government is becoming their most dangerous violator; instead of guarding freedom, the government is establishing slavery; instead of protecting men from the initiators of physical force, the government is initiating physical force and coercion in any manner and issue it pleases; instead of serving as the instrument of objectivity in human relationships, the government is creating a deadly, subterranean reign of uncertainty and fear, by means of nonobjective laws whose interpretation is left to the arbitrary decisions of random bureaucrats; instead of protecting men from injury by whim, the government is arrogating to itself the power of unlimited whim—so that we are fast approaching the stage of the ultimate inversion: the stage where the government is free to do anything it pleases, while the citizens may act only by permission; which is the stage of the darkest periods of human history, the stage of rule by brute force.

It has often been remarked that in spite of its material progress, mankind has not achieved any comparable degree of moral progress. That remark is usually followed by some pessimistic conclusion about human nature. It is true that the moral state of mankind is disgracefully low. But if one considers the monstrous moral inversions of the governments (made possible by the altruist-collectivist morality) under which mankind has had to live through most of its history, one begins to wonder how men have managed to preserve even a semblance of civilization, and what indestructible vestige of self-esteem has kept them walking upright on two feet.

One also begins to see more clearly the nature of the political principles that have to be accepted and advocated, as part of the battle for man's intellectual Renaissance.

Belief

Ok, you have now officially been bludgeoned to death on rights and the proper role of government.

Let's shift to Belief.

Beliefs are nothing more than a feeling of certainty about something.

Thus, there are rational beliefs and irrational beliefs out there because you can be right and you can be wrong about the foundation of your beliefs. If you believe the witchdoctor can heal you by blowing peyote smoke in your face, I'd say you possess a decidedly irrational belief. If you believe you can heal your body by clinically proven homeopathic or modern medicine then you have a more valid belief.

What amazes me is that while most people can clearly distinguish between these two examples, they have a tremendous degree of difficulty in distinguishing between valid and faulty beliefs when it comes to figuring out the best way to live and prosper in a society. Huge numbers of people literally believe in their souls that it is vitally important that what has been earned by others should be taken and redistributed to them.

And of course, we know that powerful beliefs can change the world, for good or for bad depending upon the belief. One cannot rationally argue that murderous beliefs of Adolf Hitler were more beneficial to man on this planet than the certainty of success of a Henry Ford or Andrew Carnegie.

The main point that I want to drive home is that the beliefs required for prospering must be founded on reality, and that the only beliefs that will aid you in succeeding are empowering beliefs that derive from your acceptance of the nature of man in a benevolent universe.

And by empowering beliefs I mean those that compel you to take action. Beliefs that drive you to jump out of bed in the morning anxious to take on the challenges of the day.

You've hear the admonition that you should act on the conviction of your beliefs. Well, if you possess tremendous conviction in your beliefs I tell you that you cannot help but act on them! "Believing in yourself" is not something that has to be fought for if you have convictions and are totally committed.

THAT is the second step.

The very FIRST step is your world view and outlook.

To be successful at anything one must come from a place of certainty and courage and not fear and doubt. And to come from a place of courage and certainty, your foundational ideas that cause your courage and certainty must be grounded in what's real...on the benevolent universe world view and in proper core values.

Take either away and you can do nothing.

Permit and promote both and the results are the western world and the inevitable transformation of the world into a Shining City on a Hill.

There is NO LIMIT to what individual man can create if he rationally believes in his productive genius and others believe as he does.

Secret of Wealth #12: The two things that a man needs to be successful in prosperity in the acquisition of wealth are the respect for his individual rights by others, and an

empowering, compelling belief in himself that he can achieve his values and dreams.

- Everything else discussed in this book is foundational to these two.

The Moral of the Story

If you want to be successful, stand up for your rights and those of your fellow man, develop empowering beliefs based in reality, act on the conviction of your beliefs, and find others who believe as you do to assist you in the creation of the vision for your life.

Now, speaking of visions....

CHAPTER FOUR

Visions of that Shining City on a Hill

Adopt a Personal Vision of an Incredibly Bright Future

"The sun never shone on a cause of greater worth. 'Tis not the affair of a city, a county, a province, or a kingdom; but of a continent-of at least one eighth part of the habitable globe. 'Tis not the concern of a day, a year, or an age; posterity are virtually involved in the contest, and will be more or less affected even to the end of time, by the proceedings now. Now is the seed-time of continental union, faith and honor. The least fracture now will be like a name engraved with the point of a pin on the tender rind of a young oak; the wound would enlarge with the tree, and posterity read it in full grown letters."

—Thomas Paine, 1776

The United States of America has been described as the Last Great Bastion of Freedom and the Last Great Hope for Mankind.

And I believe that it is.

It still is even though we have gone so far down a path of

degradation as to make the country unrecognizable from even the relative freedom of just 10 years ago.

American Exceptionalism

The United States in its founding principles is unique in history.

The United States as founded is exceptional.

https://youtu.be/s4F2kphfqmg

And I use the word exceptional expressly because it is a word that evokes such an emotional response in its detractors.

No other country in the history of the world was founded on freedom and individual liberty as the bedrock principles of its existence. No other country was founded not only on individual rights and the primacy of the individual, but that such rights are innate to human nature and not given to a man by any government; a man's right to his very life and ALL that this implies is naturally his from birth.

In accordance with its fundamental principles of individual rights and supremacy of the individual a valid government is necessarily at the consent of the governed for the express purpose of securing individual rights.

We have an incredibly unique tradition. When you go back and research the history of those early times from the 1600s to the late 1700s, one cannot help but be amazed at what led up to the founding of this country.

Life was not perfect back then, no more than it is today, and no more than it will be 100 years from now. Things were a mess. There were terrible, seemingly intractable problems to deal with in that time, not the least of which was a relatively short life expectancy exacerbated by conflict stemming from competing imperialistic world views (England, France, and Spain all wanted their piece of North America).

At the time of revolution, there was probably more uncertainty, fear, and anxiety over the future as in any time in our history, perhaps even including the Civil War.

That's what makes the story even more amazing...is that with all of the trials and tribulations, and differing opinions and philosophies, and opposing factions, and all the failings of human beings, a group of men called the founding fathers cobbled together enough of a consensus on the very nature of what man is—of what it means to be men—to actually codify the requirements of our nature into the very founding principles of a new country: that each man was entitled by the fact of his every existence to the pursuit of his life, his liberty, and his own happiness. A man by right fact of his very being alive is entitled to act out of self-interest and in that very process of acting for self-preservation, creating a harmony of interests among all free men who chose to live in society with other free men.

Understand that this concept is profoundly unique in the annals of history!

It is powerful and it still motivates today those of us who can still see—who still have a sense of life, a yearning for freedom.

If you are a student of history, you must come to the conclusion that their accomplishment was simply stupendous. And it was seen that way at the time as well! They knew what they were doing; they understood the magnitude of what it was they were attempting to create. But even though the odds were stacked well against them, they did it anyway.

Think about it. The horrible institution of slavery was still an intractable problem when the Bill of Rights was adopted. Many of the men involved in the founding were slave owners! There was an intense debate about the abolition of slavery in the original constitution because it was so ingrained an economic aspect of the southern colonies. Few Americans realize that Thomas Jefferson's first draft of the Declaration of Independence called for the abolition of slavery, even though he still owned slaves!

But even though slavery was not resolved at the founding of our nation, these men still had the courage, fortitude and foresight to proceed with the establishment of a nation founded on individual freedom. Because of the challenging issues of the day, it was a grueling, messy, contentious process.

But they did it anyway, and they did it knowing that such major issues such as slavery would have to be addressed as the nation grew, IF it grew, IF it survived even the first few years.

And what motivated them, what drove them, was a **vision of what the world could be like** if the citizens of this new country would only choose, continuously choose, to adhere to the founding principles of the country as the guiding principles of their own lives over the decades and centuries of this new and unique nation's existence.

That is why I briefly delved into American Exceptionalism. Grab hold of your birthright and begin to imagine what your life can be. Show respect for your heritage by showing you are worthy of it by dreaming again, and then making your dream, whatever it is for you, a reality.

Life is Naught... Without a Vision

I am supremely optimistic about our country and the world, but it has occurred to me that the time that I felt the most positive about where our country was headed was when Ronald Reagan was president. The reason? Reagan was an optimist whose optimism was based on his convictions regarding the power of the individual. He had a vision of what the world, certainly the country, could be, if men would only be left free.

He believed in his soul of the inviolate rights of man and in individual liberty.

I realize that many of you younger than about 45 probably cannot identify with an "old guy" like Reagan. It's just like I have a hard time identifying with a guy like Dwight D. Eisenhower. But we all have our influences in our life and this is my tribute to Reagan. Hopefully you can similarly identify with someone in your own generation...

Ronald Reagan is the only leader/politician of my entire 40 some adult years that I thought of as a true leader because he spoke often and passionately of individual liberty. Although I could not agree with him philosophically on many issues and policies, and although he was only partially successful in office, I respected him tremendously because of his heartfelt clarity on the need for individuals to be free.

You could tell it burned in the man's soul.

It wasn't a bye-line, a bromide, a salesman's pitch, a means to get elected; it was part of his core being. And I strongly identify with that. As imperfect and as misguided at times as I think he was, and as mixed-results his efforts were, he was nevertheless a man who championed that all men should be free because it is man's nature to be free.

He knew the power in the productivity of a free people and what they could create if men were left free and not inhibited by the shackles of an excessive government. A favorite quote of his from his Farewell Speech, January 1989 reads:

I hope we once again have reminded people that man is not free unless government is limited. There's a clear cause and effect here that is as neat and predictable as a law of physics: As government expands, liberty contracts.

Reagan internalized the concept of the 'Shining City upon a Hill'; he had to of necessity because of his convictions about individual liberty, because of his convictions for a limited government and what was possible with a free people.

That was the 80s.

I remember the 80s. It was a time when the majority of American's felt optimistic. I felt optimistic. I felt that there was nothing I could not accomplish. And I felt this way not because of how I was raised.

I felt this way because I had a visceral response to a leader who spoke directly to my innate need and desire...my yearning to be free.

There is a reason he won the Presidency twice in landslide victories...he was a vocal leader who championed the individual.

It was a time, when, even with a large government presence in our lives, we still busted our asses and produced greater than ever before because we had a leader who actually openly spoke out for unfettered individual liberty via limited government, and the inevitability of prosperity for all.

Unfortunately, the majority of us have forgotten that dream. A large percentage of us have literally passed away and several new generations have grown up without such a leader.

Generations who have been the victim of a statist mentality, who have known nothing else, and who to a large degree are responsible for the insanity in government control and social chaos that reigns today.

We have taken serious steps backwards since Reagan left office. Of course things were not perfect back then; even

Reagan's administration succumbed to financial mistakes that have contributed to the disaster of today's world financial woes (David Stockman does an excellent job of detailing this in his book The Great Deformation).

But we have nevertheless digressed from an elevated place.

We are certainly less free than we were back then.

We are less optimistic.

We, you and I as men who desire to live like men, must revive that vision of The Shining City.

Not only must we revive it as a vision for the country as a whole—for what the country can represent to all of us and to the world as he states in his speech, but first and foremost we have to create it for ourselves, for our own lives, and in that very process create it for the world.

We have to create a Grand Vision for ourselves as to what we want our lives to look like five, ten, thirty years into the future....in consonance with that grand vision of the country.

In fact, it is the individual Grand Visions that we create for ourselves and our families that will ultimately, in aggregate, manifest themselves in that Shining City.

And because truly no man is an island, a crucial part of the Grand Vision that we create for ourselves must be our personal vision of how we all live with each other in society.

Do we choose to live in a society where we are freer or where we are less free than we are today?

Do we choose to live in a society where we are perpetually at each other's throats, or where we see our fellow man as equals and as benefactors in our mutual desire to work and be happy?

After what I have shown you, it should not be difficult for you to realize that as individual liberty erodes, so does the opportunity for wealth erode, and thus the likelihood that you or I will become wealthy or maintain our wealth once we have acquired it.

As parasitism grows, not only will there be there fewer and fewer producers, but as the gulf between the haves and have-nots widens, the remaining producers will be vilified even more than they are today. The fewer and more vilified the producers in society, the less wealth that is available to everyone, and the lower the standard of living and quality of life of everyone.

Look And You Shall See!

I want you now to work with me to envision a United States in which each of us is truly free.

To borrow from John Lenin, it isn't difficult if you try.

We are often urged to 'become a child again' when it comes to creating our goals, dreams, and aspirations without pre-conceived limitations acquired from a life of experiences in the 'real world.'

In a similar sense, open your mind here and become not a child with no experience, but a rational self-serving child-like adult who, in the context of all you have experienced in your past life, is coming to understand for the first time the magnitude of what is at stake if we do not first value freedom and act to be free, and who also sees in child-like wonderment the future as full of possibilities with no limitations.

Let us envision a world where each of us is a free, independent and sovereign individual and where we are, as a fundamental guiding principle, respected, honored, highly valued and championed as such by all other free, independent, and sovereign individuals.

In such a vision, ultimately what one is truly free of, or from, in society is the initiation of the use of force.

Let us envision a society where each individual is left alone to be free and independent, to deal with one another on a mutually-beneficial basis out of self-interest in the pursuit of one's own life as his primary purpose.

Where each of us, in all of our glorious inequalities in talent and ability, contributes what we can from our own hand to a market that is as unhampered by government interference as it is from common criminals, where each of us freely trades with other men for the values that they create that we want.

A society where no one is made to give up the product of his mind to those who have not earned it...neither out of compulsion (e.g. taxes) or out of any asinine altruistic obligation or sense of guilt for what we are or have (the goal of the egalitarians and collectivists).

A society where NO ONE receives the unearned or undeserved.

Rather, a society where each of us, out of pursuing values in self-interest—out of seeking value for value for personal gain, trades with other men to mutual benefit, to the extent of our own contribution.

In such a country, no rational man, no good and decent man initiates the use of force against another nor seeks the aid of government to do his dirty work.

In such a country, there is perpetual peace.

In such a country peace and harmony is the norm.

War, class warfare, and domestic strife are aberrations. Crime, especially violent crime, is an ever diminishing abnormal condition among men.

It is a country where no straight-thinking man is interested in violence against another because one would in his soul understand that to do so it would be extremely harmful to oneself personally. In a word, it would be abhorrently irrational.

Initiating an act of violence, such as through theft, fraud, or acting viciously out in envy, etc., would be to injure oneself by violating a fundamental core principle, a social contract, often embodied in a rational interpretation of the words "do unto others as you would have others do unto you."

Violence caused by the initiation of force of one man or group of men against others destroys the productive capacities of the victims of force, and thus their ability to produce wealth and contribute, and thus their prospects for physical and psychological welfare, of the ability to maintain, extend, enhance, fulfill and enjoy their lives.

More powerful words from Reisman:

The capitalist society we want to achieve is a society in which individual rights are consistently and scrupulously respected—in which, as Ayn Rand put it, the initiation of physical force is barred from human relationships. We want a society in which the role of government is limited to the protection of individual rights, and in which, therefore, the government uses force only in defense and retaliation against the initiation of force. We want a society in which property rights are recognized as among the foremost human rights—a society in which no one is made to suffer for his success by being sacrificed to the envy of others, a society in which all land, natural resources, and other means of production are privately owned. In such a society, the size of government would be less than a tenth of what it now is in terms of government spending [written in late 1990s, so more like 1% now]. Most of the government as it now exists would be swept away: virtually all of the alphabet agencies and all of the cabinet departments with the exception of defense, state, justice, and treasury. All that would remain is a radically reduced executive branch, and legislative and judicial branches with radically reduced powers. To the law-abiding citizen of such a society, the government would appear essentially as a "night watchman," dutifully and quietly going about its appointed rounds so that the citizenry could rest secure in the knowledge that their persons and property were free from aggression. Only in the lives of common criminals and foreign aggressor states would the presence of the government bulk large.

Can you imagine such a world?

I can imagine it. I can see it. I get excited at the prospect.

For all of us I eagerly want it to happen.

I can imagine a country where that great sense of optimism prevails, where the vast majority of citizens have internalized the value of freedom and aggressively defend and protect individual rights as the sole means of attaining whatever unique degree of happiness and fulfillment that each desires.

Where we as individuals embrace and jealously value our inequalities and differences as nature-given opportunities to define a central purpose for our lives. Where we then aggressively pursue this purpose with a vehicle of productive activity that is chosen by us as uniquely suitable to us as to no other being on the planet, whether its motherhood, basket weaving, or rocket science.

Focus here and envision with me more of what that Shining City will look like in practice....

Radically Changed Personal Outlook. First and most fundamentally, the average Joe and Jane out there would relish in his or her selfishness. It would be OK to be selfish. It would not only be OK, but it would be cool to recognize selfishness as one of your personal character traits. It would be an accolade to be recognized as selfish, rationally selfish, by others. I mean here selfishness in the truest, rational sense of the word, and not in any sense synonymous with, and in fact the exact opposite of, non-compassionate, uncaring, or unemotional detached coldness.

Selfishness is in fact profoundly compassionate and universally beneficial to all in its consequence. When you and I act out of rational self-interest, meaning in a manner that furthers our own life and happiness, we necessarily need and actively seek the help of others in the quest of our personal Grand Vision, and we highly value men of similar stripe.

Rational men have a powerful genuine, heart-felt, well-wishing affection for like-minded men.

Antithetically speaking, those who act out of irrational self-interest act in a way that damages and destroys life and happiness. It is these parasites who seek personal gain not by contribution but by theft, by taking without producing. It is these people who actually despise and hate those of us who see the light.

Fortunately, in our vision of a heroic new world, such men are an irrelevant minority....

Think about it. For each and every one of us, everything we do now we do for purely selfish emotional reasons (re-read Secret of Wealth #7).

You love and adore your children and work hard to see that they are healthy and happy. NOT because you are "selfless," but ultimately because you value how it makes you feel to see them healthy and happy. You value their very lives because of what their lives mean to YOU. Why do you not value the lives of other's children as intensely as you do yours? They are all children, yes? It's because of what your kids mean to YOU. It is because of the value that YOU place on their health and happiness.

Mother Theresa was purely selfish. She did what she did for people because doing so was important to her—of value to her—for whatever her reasons and emotional needs, whether you agree with them or not. Mother Teresa didn't value being materially poor. She simply valued helping others more than being materially rich. She lived an ascetic lifestyle because she valued the daily helping of others in pain more than she valued stuff for increasing her personal comfort. All the talk of her being so-called "selfless" is incorrect.

I challenge you on this. I stipulate that you do everything you do for purely selfish emotional reasons. EVERYTHING. I challenge you to identify anything you do as a purely 'selfless' act...where you obtain nothing in return for your actions. This does not mean that you will always do things for rational motives—we are human and make mistakes—but it does mean you do everything you do ultimately to satisfy an emotional need.

Acting out of selfishness IS our nature: It cannot be otherwise. It's just that nobody has ever pointed this out to us, and those who have an interest in keeping people feeling guilty about their talents or possessions have been trying to teach us what they call selflessness—altruism...which is nothing more than a bastardized, convoluted distortion of the meaning of true selfishness.

In the old society, before our Shining City was created, TTK and their hordes of minions had taught altruistic self-sacrifice by teaching you to give up what's important to you for what is not important to you and trying to get you to do it out of guilt by appealing to your innate human attribute of selfishness.

You should sacrifice out of supposed personal interest they would say. It is good, they would say, for you to give up what you value and to give it to someone who has not earned it and who does not deserve it, and to do so out of selflessness, out of loving others more than yourself because THIS is the true meaning of a moral life. 'Selflessness' of course being their code word for the naturally selfish act of avoiding a pain...only it was the pain of a false and vicious guilt instilled by them. A guilt for your natural desires and abilities planted in you by them, where in a normal healthy person there would be no guilt.

In the heroic new world, we would all value, relish, and celebrate selfishness as a cardinal virtue. It is ONLY in being purely selfish that one is able to contribute the most that he is able.

And because of this, we would all pursue self-interested productiveness with an intense, almost maniacal vigor, with the accompanying commensurate boom in the plenty of wealth and the standard and quality of living for virtually everyone on the planet.

We would be universally encouraged to pursue our goals, dream, and aspirations out of pure self-interest.

We would be a far, far happier people....setting an example for people the world over on the benevolent nature of a man living for himself with his life as his supreme value and productively fulfilling his life as his primary guiding code of action.

Governance and Law: Our governments, primarily local in extent, would be small and unobtrusive in our lives. They would function primarily in the form of courts, local police, and the defense of the nation.

All branches of government would be severely limited in their powers as was intentionally designed, however flaw-fully into the Constitution.

In our Shining City, politicians would routinely speak passionately of protecting individual liberty because for perhaps the first time since the American Revolution, it would, like Reagan, burn in their souls, be an inseparable part of their character, and the driving force of their actions.

Politicians would be LEADERS who would actively champion the businessman, the capitalist, the productive; they would justly castigate the lazy, the parasitical, and the undeserving, and yet be hugely compassionate and outspoken for the truly unable and helpless among us.

Politicians would be part-time servants who would voluntarily serve short terms while pursuing their normal lives.

The age of career politicians would be over.

The age of becoming rich as a career politician through legalized graft, favoritism, and placement above the law created for the rest of us could never happen again.

The age of the citizen statesman would be revived. Men and women would be asked to serve by their neighbors, not based on what interest groups can gain from them or from any personal lust for power, but on their standing in their communities where they are respected by people just like you and me as honest, hard-working, productive, liberty-loving, life-values oriented, and thus as honorable people— deserving of honor—deserving of the honorable position as a publicly recognized guardian of liberty through temporary government service.

Good men and women would accept an appointment to serve as any humble person accepts any accolade, as a temporary personal honor in recognition of the good that they represent.

Such citizen-politicians would be motivated to serve from the honor granted them, but they would be equally anxious to return to their productive private lives; they would view serving in government and government actions and expenditures almost as necessary evils, to be tolerated only to the extent they are absolutely required.

Out of motivation to jealously protect our liberties from ever being infringed on as they had in the past, we individually would assume more responsibility to remain aware and active in local, state, and federal issues. But because government would be severely limited in size and scope, and because the majority of men would have ingrained in their characters the indelible traits of sovereignty, independence, and desire for liberty, the amount of time that being active in political goings-on would be inconsequential to the rest of our lives.

Police would be empowered to aggressively pursue criminals

while scrupulously upholding individual rights. They would not be the militarized thugs that tend to populate the police departments today, but your neighbors...people just like you who actually value the Bill of Rights as highly as you do, and who endeavor to succeed in their own businesses someday.

Justice would return to the very simple principle of 'you will be treated the way you deserve to be treated while living in a society of free men.' To wit: If you do not intentionally injure others and you work to better your own life to the best of your ability, you are just. You are good. You are free to live and enjoy your life unfettered by anyone in government, to the extent that your own abilities can carry you.

However, if you intentionally injure others, you will provided an opportunity to correct yourself through civil due process. Should you continue to injure others, you be removed from society and placed in a severely minimalist existence jail or prison until you can demonstrate that you can return to society and live like any respectable man should live in freedom with other men.

But in such a society, the percentage of the population incarcerated would be exceedingly small compared to the overcrowding of a permanent population that is now exhibited in our prisons.

Literally everything besides the police, courts, executive and legislative branches at the local level, and the additional state, military, and treasury at the federal level would be privatized and deregulated.

The nation would return to live under a true Rule of Law, objective law (as opposed to arbitrary and capricious) where any man can easily on his own find, read, understand, and rely upon a simple code for what he cannot do in society, such restrictions being limited solely by the principle of the non-initiation of physical force against another.

And it is this specifically, the Rule of Law, which would define our legal/state system as a Constitutional Republic and emphatically NOT a democracy. The vast majority of us would consciously recognize that democracy without a sound moral code embodied in objective laws is nothing more than gang rule.

We would once again become a nation of well-defined, concrete, limited-in-scope, objectively-worded laws where each of us is equal under the law with no exceptions for politicians, politician's cronies, the wealthy, or the influential.

This would be a country where there would be no doubt in any responsible thinking person that 360 million votes to silence your voice would mean nothing. It would mean that the vast majority of citizens understand what "inalienable rights" means.

The lobbying and pressure groups that work to infringe on freedoms could not exist because the limits upon what a government can do would prohibit such influence; those parasites who attempt to game the system to curry favor from government officials would be shamed and castigated so mercilessly by their peers and the public that they would lose any economic status they had theretofore achieved, and remain an outcast until they could once again demonstrate their value.

Of course, individuals, through group representation, could still petition their representatives for change, but the content and tone of proposed changes would be cast in terms of how best to protect freedoms, NOT on how best to impinge on others freedoms to the advancement of the personal gain of the members of one's group.

We as a people would adhere to the credo: if you cannot achieve it out in the free market, you cannot achieve it— especially including the sale of ideas.

Each of us would feel secure in our property and know that we would not have to fear arbitrary and capricious behavior of rudderless government officials.

Citizens would not fear their government.

Government servants would fear the wrath and justice of the

citizenry.

As it should be.

Respect for Property Rights: The people in our state and local governments would have complete respect for private property and of course all of the rights that depend upon this. This would be so because enough of us would hold property rights to be of such vital importance to our personal welfare and happiness that we simply would not tolerate politicians who would attempt to usurp power and color outside the lines.

Confidence from knowing that our fellow man honors our own personal sovereignty and hence our property would create and foster an ever-growing goodwill among all of us, and our civility would be the beacon of hope for the good people of other countries who yearn to be free.

Citizens would not fear confiscation or control of their property by their government.

Taxes: In our heroic new society, there would be no mandatory state or federal personal or corporate income tax, capital gains tax, inheritance tax or any other form of taxation of productive capacity such as mandatory workman's compensation insurance.

No longer would capitalists and businessmen have to deal

with the enormous cost of preparing quarterly tax statements.

Businessmen would cease becoming tax-collectors for the government.

Because the welfare state would disappear, businesspeople would no longer pay the enormous sums of money required to keep track of social security, Medicare, Obamaramacare or any other of the current myriad of taxes and other forced benefit deductions.

No longer would you and I as workers have our money removed forcibly taken from our paychecks or ever again have to prepare and file tax returns.

While there may very well be some type of formal system in place for the funding of limited legitimate government functions, such a system would be voluntary, for limited objectives, and stringently controlled by a politically active, voting, local public. And whatever voluntary tax system was emplaced, citizens would physically write a check for those taxes so that they feel the pain and enormity of what a tax is and so recall this pain anytime they are tempted to appeal to their government to raise taxes.

But aside from this minimal requirement to fund a severely limited government, each of us could save the vast majority of our incomes if we so chose; the capital accumulation that would occur by businesses would cause a tremendous increase in the technological progress and productivity of labor in virtually every industry.

It would be extremely hard to ever again enact any kind of forcible tax system on a society where men truly understand and value their freedom.

Mandatory taxes would be seen for what they are: an outright theft of the produce of your mind.

Freedom of Production and Trade: We would not be inhibited in any way by government interference except as a consequence, via the police and courts, to the extent that we as citizens initiate the use of force against other citizens.

There would be no government licensing requirements for any industry; any such certifications or licensing would be voluntary and only be offered by private trade associations or industry advocate groups as a means of maintaining voluntary professional standards. It would be the consumer who would determine the value of such certifications, not the government—something that in the age of information would be relatively easy to research, discern, and make informed individual judgments about which to rely on and support.

People would understand that today's labor unions artificially raise wages, dramatically decrease productivity, and contribute heavily to unemployment—all the while making union bosses ridiculously rich for what they 'contribute': the loss of wealth to the rest of us that would otherwise be produced by free men in a free Capitalist society.

Labor unions, while completely legal, would naturally become useless rather quickly and eventually disappear; men of independence and self-respect would deem it in their interest to find their own value to other men on their own terms via mutually-beneficial trade. It would become absolutely abhorrent to any independent productive person to turn over his independence and freedom to such parasitic pressure groups in a society that champions and rewards individual initiative and productiveness.

Pro labor union legislation would be repealed and labor unions could only operate on a purely voluntary basis. They would have to compete in the free-market arena of ideas like any other political movement, without the use of force embodied in such legislation, to include forced membership or dues.

Freedom of Inequality and Competition: We would recognize and celebrate the completely natural inequality in abilities among us as part of the foundation of a fully-functioning division of labor.

Each of us would be proud of what we could contribute, and recognize that we are each free to rise above the challenges we face in life to achieve what we are each, individually, capable of achieving, whether on our own or through the help of others.

Each of us would champion and cheer on both the more capable and the less capable among us in the recognition that we ALL benefit immeasurably in freedom under the division of labor. We would champion each other because we would, as a reflection of ourselves, highly value the productive man, no matter his background, current station in life, or level of ability.

We would be immensely grateful for each other, not as sources of what can be taken, but as sources of what can be contributed in the process of each of us maintaining, extending and enjoying our lives.

The zero-sum mentality would not be tolerated, and parasitism would once again return to its status of evil and be severely chastised as a poor choice in a society where so much opportunity abounds and there is such a tremendous need for human labor.

Envy, among the most destructive of human emotions, would be an aberration, quickly identified and called out by the good among us and corrected as a poor choice—as aberrant behavior originating in faulty parasitic, anti-life values.

Those who in accordance with their lesser abilities contribute a little would be rewarded little, but would be nevertheless rewarded. Think about it: those who contribute a little in the fully functioning division of labor benefit significantly more for what they contribute and risk than does the billionaire for what he contributes and risks.

Those who contribute greatly will reap great rewards, with all of us in recognition that such rewards were justly earned, are profoundly honorable, and are to be applauded.

Savings and Capital Accumulation: Capitalists and consumers would save more of what they earn. Why? Because we would be a little less loony and plan better the future as self-responsible causal agents. Go back and review what you learned.

Technological Progress: Because of tremendously increased savings and capital accumulation by capitalists, there would be the wherewithal to fund an explosion of discoveries, inventions, and technological progress beyond anything currently imaginable.

It is technological progress that vastly increases our productivity and ultimately results in a vastly higher SOL and QOL, including a much longer average life expectancy due to inevitable advances in medicine and healthcare.

Money: Today's fiat-money fractional reserve currency system manufactured by a central bank would be a thing of the past.

That system would be so thoroughly discredited as a fraud, and people would be so ingrained with the knowledge of what it had done to their lives, of the literal loss and pain it had caused them, that any talk of the reestablishment of a central bank, with its necessary policy of inflation and wealth destruction, would simply not be tolerated and only identified as a seriously bad joke.

Public reaction to any serious attempt by politicians to create a new central bank would be immediate and visceral on a massive scale with the intensity and seriousness of Andrew Jackson.

(Start at minute 2:34 in following video)

https://youtu.be/_Jm42AS9tko

Amazing story eh?

Our money would consist of gold and silver.

Only gold and silver.

Period.

The bits of green paper we all carry around would be a mere convenience; they would be 100% backed by gold and silver. Each of us could go to any bank and exchange our green dollar bills for gold and silver anytime anywhere because the banks would be prohibited from loaning out the money that you deposited with them to multiples of other people as is done today under the fractional reserve system.

Public scrutiny of banks would be merciless; fraudulent bankers would be aggressively prosecuted and go to jail for conducting business the way that they do today.

Never again would your purchasing power be diminished month after month, but rather, it would literally <u>increase</u> month to month, year after year, decade after decade, as our aggregate productivity soars through the roof and the progressively increasing quantity and quality of wealth that is available for us to purchase explodes.

Finally, because inflation causes the economic booms and busts in an economy, recessions would no longer occur. Production would occur on a continuous ever-expanding scale. Isolated industries could and would experience booms and busts as a natural part of a free market, but economy-wide and world-wide recessions and depressions that we now experience on a regular basis would no longer happen.

Wages and Income: Wages, like the prices of anything else, would be completely determined by price discovery function of the free-market.

Those who choose to be employees would be paid what they are worth in the free market. They would be paid a wage that is truly commensurate with their productive contribution as determined by those who require their services.

People would be free to bid wages up or down depending upon the value assigned to their personal productive contributions via the dictates of the free market in labor.

There would no minimum wage.

This does NOT mean that workers would be forced to accept 'subsistence' wages...wages so low that one could barely survive.

No!

In Capitalism, wages can fall only so far because capitalists must compete for competent reliable workers in an open market, and it behooves a capitalist to pay more than the next closest bidder if he wants to obtain the quality of labor he wants in the quantities that he wants.

Thus, all workers would feel secure in that they could always not only obtain employment because of the perpetual scarcity of labor, but that they would be paid a wage that is just with respect to their abilities.

And even if worker's wages should fall as dictated by a free market in labor, the real wages that they represent would be continuously increasing due to the ever-increasing technological progress and resulting higher productivity of labor.

No one could permanently lose real wages/purchasing power in the completely free market of our Shining City.

Unemployment and Poverty: Unemployment would disappear.

Would that not be awesome?

The insanity represented by the 20%+ unemployment rate of today simply could not exist. The virtual unlimited need for labor in a fully-functioning DOL would ensure that anyone who wanted to work would be able to find employment at a commensurate wage.

Again, justly so, those that contribute little would earn little compared to those who contribute more.

The war on poverty would end because it would no longer be necessary. The trillions previously spent in the war on poverty would instead be invested by private enterprise. The resulting perpetual boom in production would demand all the labor it could acquire.

The inner cities would eventually be redeveloped and flourish simply because of the valuable real estate and the sheer availability of labor there.

Death of Welfare and the Blossoming of Charity: Government expenditures for welfare programs would cease and government-provided welfare would vanish.

The immense increases in productivity and wealth, and the new mentality of abundance and giving that foster them would ensure that the number of private charities and donations to these charities would blossom.

The seeming permanent fixture of the homeless in our inner cities, and the panhandlers at intersections these days would be a thing of the past.

ANYONE who truly needed a helping hand would easily obtain it until they could get on their feet again. For those truly indigent, infirm, and aged, charity could be provided for life.

There would be more than enough! Out of sheer gratitude for the abundance that we would experience, not to mention the cessation of taxes, each of us would be more and more inclined to give to the charities of our choice.

Again, in the age where information is at our fingertips, as individuals we could easily discern what charities are respectable, and which are fraudulent, abusive, or have excessively high expenses compared to what actually goes to the needy. As in competition for anything else, those charities that cannot compete on a cost-effective basis for our dollars simply fall by the wayside and quickly become irrelevant or go out of business.

Racism: Because of the social contract of and between free men, there is little racism, or any other -ism. And because we are not perfect, what -ism persists in the minds of the unintelligent and ignorant would be rendered completely irrelevant. Violence against others based on race, religion, sex, etc., would be dealt with like any other crime—in the courts based on objectively defined laws.

Productive people simply have no patience for such things; free men in pursuit of wealth and happiness need the help of others; they are interested in obtaining the best value from other men regardless of their skin color, sexual preferences, etc. Those who provide value in their work efforts are rewarded with positions remunerated based on the free market for labor.

Everywhere there would be tremendous demand for all honest labor.

All else is irrelevant to the equation. Race, religion, sex, or any other −ismness would simply become irrelevant. The only thing that would matter in the world of productive trade is as Martin Luther King put it—the content of one's character, as evidenced by the rationality of one's work ethic.

Workers who choose to provide no value or are destructive of the social contract out of −isms are simply ignored as irrelevant, and at the extreme, spend time in jail for instigating violence, not because of their race, but because they choose not to be productive—to contribute, having chosen instead not to live in peace with other free men.

Capitalists and businesspeople that offensively discriminate based on any human attribute would be dealt with harshly and justly through loss of business and profits by the boycott of rational consumers once their practices were made known.

War and Peace: Envision a United States where we are fighting no wars, and such wars as are necessary to fight are only in response to direct physical aggression by foreign governments.

Where none of our brightest, youngest minds are being uselessly wasted on some foreign battlefield. There would be no more of young men losing their lives for unjust causes; no more tragedies of lives destroyed in their primes, or young soldiers returning home maimed, disfigured or mentally damaged for life.

I am speaking of a society where the government-military-industrial complex is so tamed and controlled, that modern imperialistic tendencies to go to war by faulty-valued politicians are cut off at the root before they can even see the light of day, and in the modern-day equivalent, are tarred and feathered and run out of town on a rail.

National Interests would be rationally, narrowly, and specifically defined to principally mean the protection of the lives and property of U.S. citizens. This would certainly not entail forcing other nations to sell us their natural resources. If we cannot freely trade value for value with other free nations in the acquisition of the natural resources we require, then our nation simply does without until we develop our own or until such free trade can be established.

There would be NO wars over the control of resource-rich territories.

A truly free society is characterized by peace and harmony at home and internationally, unless, as is the case in relations among individual men, force is initiated against us by foreign governments, or other foreign entities such as is currently presented by the militant Islamic state and terrorist groups.

With respect to defending our nation, liberty oriented politicians would openly and loudly advocate a policy of staying home, speaking softly in setting an example for the world, but carrying a damned big stick.

Here, the big stick is a continuously updated modern military machine that is fully capable of overwhelming and annihilating any potential enemy, and several enemies simultaneously, without the use of nuclear weapons, though nuclear weapons would certainly remain part of a free country's arsenal.

We would adopt a just foreign relations policy where free men are left alone to be treated by other free men in the world as they should be with honor and accolades and riches, while thugs are treated as they should be with the fist. We would operate on the premise that the only thing a thug understands is a bloody nose from an overwhelmingly powerful punch from an angered innocent victim.

We would close our military bases overseas as soon as possible except perhaps for the territories that United States citizens spilled their blood for in the defense of liberty, as long as the contractual terms with host countries remain in effect.

Commensurate with setting an example for the world, while we vigorously and diligently strive to uphold our principles of individual liberty at home, our statesmen would actively criticize and campaign to end, without violence, dictatorial regimes throughout the world. Our statesmen would speak often and loudly of individual freedom and publicly chastise so-called 'world leaders' who operate oppressive governments such as Kim Jung Un, Castro, and Maduro, and speak directly to their people about fighting for the benevolent wonders of freedom and the supremacy of the individual.

<u>Domestic Police and Prisons</u>: Our local police departments would be demilitarized.

The military might that is constantly exhibited against the average citizen today is insane.

The threat posed to the average citizen today by the local police department is much greater than that from local street gangs.

The police would be reduced to the proper role of "night watchmen" as Reisman puts it that is little noticed and has little impact on the lives of good citizens.

While the reality of that Shining City is possible, no rational person is a Pollyanna. Individuals remain free to harm others, and it is the role of the police and courts to catch criminals and prosecute crimes, and if need be, remove offenders from society until they can reform.

As with foreign policy, the only thing a thug understands is a bloody nose. Jails and prisons, while remaining humane in basic human care, would become a loathsome place to spend time. Certainly for the worst hardened criminals, they would be converted from the relatively posh lifestyle establishments that we have today to cold, hard, unhappy places where days are spent in tedium, devoid of digital entertainment and frolic, and in misery from the constant reminder of the self-caused privation of freedom.

Prison would be a place where perhaps the only entertainment is books consisting of the classics of history, literature, economics, the physical sciences, music, and art, and physical exercise, and manual labor. Educational programs could be provided by charity but consist only of these core classic topics.

Gangs would be completely and utterly destroyed and prevented from festering in the big house, even if that means the physical isolation of individuals for the entire duration of their imprisonment.

As a result, prison sentences would become shorter as the harsh, mentally painful, but humane prison living conditions would serve to seriously motivate those with any remaining spark of humanity to change their lives in short order and work hard to rejoin the civilized world.

Those criminals who cannot or will not reform will simply fade away and die in prison as completely irrelevant to the rest of us on the outside.

Drugs: There would ultimately be absolutely no government prohibition on what an individual can put in their body, since this would be a clear initiation of force by the government against individuals.

Each of us would acknowledge as proper that neither the government nor any majority of voters owns anyone's physical body; that we each own our bodies and what we do with it is our business—unless we, as workers, initiate the use of force against an employer by showing up to work in a doped-up daze and unable to perform our function to the level for which he is employing us.

The Drug War would cease at the same time laws are enacted both to free an individual to do what he wants with his body in private, AND commensurately, to advocate that businesspeople are encouraged to discriminate against those who cannot fully function because of their self-induced stupors.

Each of us would come to recognize that drug use is not life-promoting and is in fact actually life-destroying, and no one would be forced to associate with or be penalized for discriminating against mind-altering drug use, especially including businessmen and capitalists.

Absolutely no charity or aid would be provided to those who are intent on destroying their lives through habitual drug use, other than entry into and completion of charitable rehab programs.

Similarly with racism, sexism, etc., companies that excessively harass employees regarding drug testing, etc., would suffer from public condemnation and the resultant loss of profits, and courts would remain in full effect for the adjudication of civil lawsuits and even class-action lawsuits.

Essentially, free men of the Shining City would abhor drug use as a crutch of weak minds attempting to evade reality...of short-circuiting the necessity of producing as the means to fulfillment...especially in an age of incredible abundance. Because drug use and living in a drug-induced stupor is so antithetical to a free, independent man of self-esteem, such a stigma would become so attached to drug use as to render the problem inconsequential in comparison to what it is today.

Courts and Tort: The courts would be limited in their power to the letter of the law and have no authority to "legislate from the bench" in interpreting laws as a judge sees fit even to the point of making new law in their adjudications.

The only change to tort law, other than ensuring the law is objective, like any other law, might be to severely penalize plaintiffs who bring proven unjust and frivolous lawsuits.

Otherwise, if a judge can be found to hear the case, anyone can sue anyone for any reason at any time with no limitations other than this threat of severe penalty (fine and jail time) for fraud.

In our Shining City, we would all be cognizant of the true purpose of the courts...to settle civil disputes among honorable men (for disagreements will always exist among volitional beings), and to remove criminals.

In our new society, the number of cases brought would drastically decrease as more and more people appreciated each other as productive citizens doing their best to make their way in the world, instead of looking at each other as threats to their own livelihood.

The backlog in the courts would diminish and then cease as fewer and fewer lawsuits would be brought as men learned to solve their differences peacefully outside of the court system, until and unless there was no other option. As anyone knows who has been involved in a lawsuit, to get the courts involved without first working hard to settle disputes amicably detracts from productive enterprise, and thus destroys the very quality of life of everyone involved.

Mediation outside of the court system would play a larger role in a freer, more just society.

Immigration: In the heroic new world, the borders would be open to free immigration as long as the welfare state is dismantled prior to establishing such an open border policy.

With the presence and persistence of an ineradicable scarcity of labor, capitalists and entrepreneurs would seek good workers no matter where on the planet they hail from. In fact, in a fully free market, the clamor for new labor would be so enormous that not only would full employment of US citizens ensue, but the need for new labor, especially for entry-level work, could only be obtained by fresh immigration.

However, immigrants in our Shining City would have to support themselves by the sweat of their brow and could not rely on welfare programs, because the programs would long since have been dismantled.

And, as a corollary, as freedom spreads throughout the world, the demands for labor in one's own country would rise dramatically and the very need and desire to come to the United States to live life well would diminish commensurately. It is entirely conceivable that Americans would migrate to other countries for the same reasons that foreigners immigrate here now....a better quality of life by means of productive work of choice that is better available elsewhere.

Medicine and Health Care: As with any other area of needless government interference, the health industry would be completely privatized and deregulated and government health agencies to include the DHS, FDA, VA, and on and on, would all be dismantled.

The result would be a radical positive change in medical care as it all becomes profit driven. No different than any other industry, those medical practices and hospitals that served the consumer best would make the most money. Those that earned a poor reputation would fall by the wayside no different than any gas station that goes out of business because of its inability to compete in satisfying consumers.

The technological advancements in medicine would expand exponentially with the result that disease, including cancer, would be radically reduced or eliminated within our lifetimes, and our average life expectancy would easily be in the 100s within a few decades.

Deregulation would allow, among many other benefits, the competition of insurance products across state lines, something that is so obvious a fix to current high health care prices as only to be prohibited by state and federal government agencies in their quest to protect their turf and propagate themselves—the consumer be damned.

As with insurance, or contractor licensing, or any other form of certification, private groups and associations would provide oversight function for consumers. Again, especially in this day of immediate access to mass information, you and I would easily find, rate, and pay private medical review and evaluation services in our search for the best medical care.

Those who cannot compete in trusted quality services simply lose and fade into irrelevance, or cease to exist.

Those who compete and contribute, win.

Education: Public education at all levels would no longer exist….from pre-school on up to government-provided funding or scholarships at universities.

Education would become entirely privatized with intense competition taking place in attempts to win the consumer's dollar.

In a society where vastly more people are grounded in the life-promoting values of reason, purpose and self-esteem, most educational institutions in competing for profits would return to focusing on providing more of a classical education that celebrates Western thought and progress.

Western culture would become valued far more highly than

any other because it is based on individual liberty. Multiculturalism, the practice of valuing all cultures equally, would fade from the scene as free individuals simply could not equate the way of life and the values of cannibals, knife-wielding, stone-throwing religious sects, or dictators, with those of a capitalist.

Online education would explode...the massive growth of which today is only prevented by the lobbyists of large public educational institutions and entrenched bureaucrats in academia.

Because of its importance to everyday life, philosophy would be taught as part of a well-rounded education. This would include of course ethics (the branch of philosophy that addresses what principles men should use to guide their actions), which includes the sub-fields of politics (how men should live with each other in a society), and economics (the science of production in a division of labor society).

Energy: The energy industry would be completely privatized and deregulated.

Capitalists would be set free to pursue energy production as never before.

Our statesmen would expound policies that would promote energy-independence, free trade, and technological progress.

Subsidies and favoritism legislation that support one energy industry over another would be repealed; consumers would vote for the most cost-effective producers of energy in the same manner they do for the cars they buy.

Foreign Policy: We would maintain close friendships with other capitalist or near-capitalist countries.

There would be absolutely no government-provided aid to any foreign entity.

We would recognize that the best thing we can do for the rest of the world is produce, seek other freedom-loving peoples to promote free trade, and set an example as described above.

Environment: Environmentalism as we know it today would be dead. Its proponents long since disgraced and embarrassed—their theories long since debunked and thrown onto the ash heap of the Great Con.

In our Shining City, we would recognize the old environmental movement for what it really was...a man-hating movement to curtain human action, severely restrict human productive activity, and as a necessary consequence, return our society to the age of feudalism characterized by mass loss of human life, poverty, misery, and shorter life spans for those who manage to survive (See Chapter 2 if you have forgotten what a wonderful benefactors the socialist environmentalists are).

To a productive rational people, the earth is just a big ball of natural resources, and we as individuals in taking action to promote our lives, could and probably eventually will use and reuse this great ball of resources to remake the face of the earth a thousand times over, turning it into more of a garden each and every time.

Much of the world is already a literal garden. And because it's natural beauty is pleasing to human beings, its natural beauty would continue to be valued...and improved countless times. Places previously beautifully developed by man would be redeveloped and made more beautiful than before because we value creativity and the reshaping our world to foster our well-being and happiness.

Even so, no rational person intentionally or excessively pollutes the physical world in which he must live!

It is precisely because we would value our created environments that we as individuals would become even more vigilant in protecting our physical surroundings from unnecessary damage from toxins and pollution than ever before, not out of hyped up fear of manufactured threats as is currently pushed by today's environuts, but out of personal self-interest in maintaining, extending, and enjoying our lives to the maximum extent possible.

Overall SOL-QOL: In that Shining City upon a Hill, we would all enjoy an absolutely stupendous increase in physical wealth, and thus in our individual standard of living and quality of life.

Just as the average 'middle-class' person of today lives with a standard of living higher than kings of the 1700s or 1800s, so would the 'new' poor would live lives comparable to the millionaires of today.

There is literally nothing but time and the continuous march of freedom, technological progress and the productivity of labor that will allow relatively poor individuals of perhaps the last half of the 21st century to live in a luxurious garden environment comparable to that of Versailles, replete with the modern amenities of the home of a present-day billionaire.

Stop for a minute and consider one main attribute of our Shining City—longer average life expectancy into the 100s. Those of you in your 50s and older can especially relate to this. Whereas now you become more cognizant of your mortality the older you get, we tend not to start thinking seriously about growing old and death until our late 50s or so, especially as we begin to see friends of ours pass away at what seems to be young age in their 50s and early 60s. Think now how it would change your life if you didn't seriously contemplate death until your 80s because you knew that on average you stood a really good chance of living healthfully to

120!

Given the restrictions to our freedom to produce since the early 1900s, I postulate that we would already be there or beyond had our predecessors been left truly free.

So not only would our Shining City be characterized by wealth in an abundance that would be considered absolutely unimaginable today, we would also be around a hell of a lot longer to enjoy it, and into old age in much better health and thus much more able to enjoy it.

Capitalism Unleashed is what will create that Shining City on a Hill.

And for Capitalism to Be Unleashed, Each of Our Minds Must be Unleashed

From Our Own Self-Imposed Prison of a Diseased World View—Of a Faulty Mental Outlook

Towards That Shining City...

From where we are now, transforming the United States into a completely capitalist society could be achieved by a few simple steps.

Simple but not easy.

I do not want to focus on these in this book except to provide them as a realistic roadmap to a free country to get you to understand that the transformation IS possible; I will expound on these in subsequent programs, videos, and other venues.

Granted, we are a long, long, long way from making the Unites States resemble what I paint for you below, but I DO believe it can happen.

Certainly not in my lifetime, but possibly in yours.

The simple steps for transforming the nation we have into a Capitalist utopia are the following (courtesy of and roughly following Reisman):

- Restoration of Respect for Individual Rights, principally the right to Property, that right upon which all others depend;

- Full Privatization of Property;

- Restoring Full Freedom of Production and Trade;

- Abolishing the Welfare State;

  - Elimination of Social Security, Medicare, Medicaid, Obamacare

  - Elimination of Public Welfare

  - Elimination of Public Hospitals including the VA

  - Firing Government Employees and Ending Subsidies to Business

  - Elimination of Price Controls (Rents, Energy...)

- Abolition of Income, Capital Gains, and Inheritance Taxes;

- Establishment of Gold and Silver as Money;

- Procapitalist Foreign Policy;

  - Freedom of Immigration

  - Friendly Relations with Other Capitalist or near-Capitalist Countries

  - Elimination of Foreign Aid

  - Removal of Military Installations Abroad

- ○ Set an Example for the World: Speak Softly and Carry a Big Stick.

- Separation of State from Education, Science, and Religion;

  - ○ Abolition of Public Education-Promotion of Rational Private Education Based on an Objective View of Human Nature

  - ○ Separation of Government and Science

  - ○ Separation of State and Church

Two Visions of a World in Need. The Choice is Very Clear...

Capitalism...the unfettered Division of Labor...represented

by the beauty of a modern-day Seattle:

- Unrestricted individual liberty characterized by individual sovereignty, and inviolate and universally respected individual rights;
- Virtually NO taxes. Any taxes are local and voluntary;
- Complete privatization of all property;
- Ever increasing savings, capital accumulation, technological advancement, and productivity of labor;
- Continuously elevated demand for labor, virtually NO unemployment;
- Ever increasing quantity and quality of wealth;
- Ever increasing purchasing power of a sound money;
- Ever increasing standard of living and quality of life.

Or, Socialism...the Prevention, Hindrance, and Destruction of a Fully-functioning Division of Labor...Like the Dinginess of a Modern-day Havana, Cuba, or Caracas, Venezuela, or even a Detroit, Michigan:

- ○ Severely restricted individual liberty;
- ○ Progressively onerous state theft from individuals via taxation and regulation;
- ○ Ubiquitous violation of individual rights;
- ○ Control and nationalization of private property;
- ○ Ever increasing consumption of savings, decreasing capital accumulation, technological stagnation, and continuously lower productivity of labor;
- ○ Perpetually high unemployment of 30%+;

- ○ **Ever decreasing quantity and quality of wealth, degradation of existing wealth as stuff wears out without being replaced by new and better;**
- ○ **Shortages of common household wares and food in response to price controls and frequent economic crises**
- ○ **Ever decreasing purchasing power of a fiat money;**
- ○ **Progressively higher percentage of income that must be spent on life's necessities;**
- ○ **Ever decreasing standard of living, and quality of life...**

History is replete with examples of failed socialism-statism, the most obvious of course is the failed Soviet Union. If you never read the book The Russians, by Hedrick Smith, it would open your eyes as to what life is like in a totalitarian society.

All one has to do is look at the world and see.

But of course, the abject failure of socialism-communism-statism does not necessarily ensure the embrace of its opposite.

As a famous philosophy professor states: "The collapse of a negative, however, is not a positive. The atrophy of a vicious version of unreason is not the adoption of reason. If men fail to discover living ideas, they will keep moving by the guidance of dead ones; they will keep following, by inertia, the principles they have already institutionalized."

Knowing what you now know from your discovery of living ideas I have tried to impart to you, since you have a choice of the kind of society you want to build for yourself and leave for your heirs, you have but one rational choice to make...

Work to Build the Shining City

By Making Your Personal Grand Vision a Reality...

...By Being Productive

CHAPTER FIVE

Want to Be Wealthy? Change Your Mind.

The Critical Choice That You Make Consciously or Subconsciously

Want to get wealthy? Want to be happy? Get right with the universe.

You know, it is easy to get discouraged with all that we can find wrong with the world.

The easiest thing in the world is to give in to the crap in life, the negative influences, the bad stuff, and let it affect how we feel and how we look at the world, and thus everything we do and everyone we love.

Regardless of whatever negative aspects of reality are at work around you, you CAN be happy in your life, and not only happy but absolutely joyful as an on-going, frequent, even continuous state of mind.

And most of being happy, as I have endeavored to show, is your attitude, your outlook on life, your worldview...or as Ayn

Rand would call it, your "sense of life."

Most of being happy is also therefore what you subsequently do with your life in the pursuit of your purpose.

You literally have a choice here: You can go through your days with a lousy attitude, as a "miserable deadbeat full of excuses" as a hero of mine used to say—because you choose to focus on all of the negatives out there and allow all the crap in life to bring you down to the point of discouragement, disillusion, ambivalence and apathy, and even depression, hatred, and abject fear.

Or, you can simply choose to accept the given current state of affairs out there as reality, but a reality that you choose not to affect your outlook and attitude.

Rather, a reality which you actively work to change as a consequence of—and in the process of—pursuing your own life, by fighting for your own happiness in your own little corner of the universe.

There will ALWAYS be negative stuff that you can choose to focus on.

Always.

The world is a dangerous place, people are not perfect, and bad stuff happens to good people. That's just the way it is.

The social issues may change from time to time, but there will always be negative stuff out there.

EVERYONE has problems. And it's easy for any of us to fall back into negativity if we have not learned yet to condition ourselves to catch ourselves sliding down that slope.

Of course, the really good news is that there is always so much more good in your life that you can choose to focus on than there is bad. And focusing on the good, the life-promoting, is what leads to happiness.

One of my favorite contemporary quotes is from Tony Robbins. He said "Your life is what you feel."

At first take, if you're not used to thinking this way, this might seem kind of fufu and fruity to you.

But it is a very powerful statement once you grasp its meaning.

His statement is so ridiculously true because everything we do, we do for emotional reasons. We do the things we do because somewhere along the way we came to associate the actions we take with obtaining the emotional states of either avoiding pain or gaining pleasure.

This is all very well known. There is nothing new in this.

The gist of all this is that **the quality of your life is the type**

and intensity of the emotions that you allow yourself to experience on an on-going basis.

If you allow yourself to be sucked in by the negative influences in your life, and subsequently act in ways contrary to your own health and happiness, then the emotions you experience on a continual basis are not going to be very uplifting emotions and you're going to be miserable.

But if you can manage to remain positive in the context of a proper world view and attitude towards life and living, if you can manage to continuously choose to focus on the good, your life will be far more likely to be wonderful and filled with happiness and all of the good things that we humans normally wish for one another in good will.

And the real mind-job comes when it finally hits you that it's as easy to pursue one path as it is the other!

Look, I am not a Pollyanna. We all have to deal with stuff in life that isn't pleasant. We all have bad days. Sometimes dealing with the stuff is more difficult than at other times. But we always manage to get through it, right?

We always come out the other side relatively unhurt, and once we do, we often realize that our imagination as to how bad or tough something was going to be was way off the mark. Have you ever noticed that 99% of the stuff you worry about never even happens! And if it does, it's never as "bad" as we thought it was going to be.

The trick is to realize this beforehand and go into the inevitable stuff that's going to come up with an empowering attitude and mindset.

It's all a matter of choice and conditioning...

The Operable Words Are "Choose" And "Focus."

Your ability to focus and what you focus on—what you think about—depend entirely on what you choose as your core values. And your core values are determined by how you choose to view your own nature, the nature of the world, and your place in it.

The kicker here, the very crux of being happy, is your ability to 1) continuously focus, and 2) to continually focus on the good (the good being that which maintains, extends, and fulfills your life and the lives of those you love).

The great news is that you can take actions to condition yourself to do this just as easily as you have taken actions in the past that conditioned you to wallow in a negative state.

And the way to condition yourself to be happy, in fact to do anything is perhaps, in my mind, the greatest contribution that personal development guru Tony Robbins has made to mankind.

To see what Tony teaches, check out his Personal Power® and other products. I will not spend too much time on what he teaches except to the extent needed to get across to you that you CAN change your life by changing your attitude by changing your core values, mental outlook and world view.

And incidentally, I have no association with Tony Robbins and make nothing from the sale of his products. I borrow from what he teaches to get my point across, but if you want to shake yourself up, see his material for the nuts and bolts of conditioning yourself for permanent change.

If you have some of Tony's stuff, I suggest you go back through it again.

Conditioning Yourself to Think

One of Tony's main principles is that of self-conditioning.

When you are in a strong negative emotional state, anything you do, including thinking, while you are in that state tends to be linked up with the state, such that down the road when you find yourself doing what you were doing then, that emotional state will tend to return and cause the same negative, destructive behavior.

Similarly, when you are in a strong and powerful positive emotional state, anything you do consistently while you are in that powerful state tends to be linked up with that state as well, such that down the road when you find yourself doing what you were doing then, that positive emotional state will tend to return and again manifest itself in your behavior, but this time in a much more empowering life-generating behavior.

So the key of course is how to stop yourself from experiencing negative emotional states, replace the negative emotional states with positive emotional states, and then do something concrete while you are in that new positive state that your brain links up with the replacement emotion.

For example, someone one used a rubber band around his wrist as a tool to condition himself to break bad habits or poor states of mind. When he found himself falling into a poor state of mind or revisiting bad habits he would painfully sting his own wrist by snapping the rubber band against it.

This action interrupted the mental process that he was stuck in (it hurt) and woke him up, whereupon he regrouped his mental powers and refocused his mind on empowering thoughts, positive habits and desired emotions in order to keep himself on track with what he had to accomplish to achieve his goals.

I think he has since outgrown this tool because in using it over time he has conditioned himself to react automatically to destroy bad habits or negative states without the aid of the rubber band.

Another example is my own.

I have learned over the years through a lot of hard knocks in life that I intensely dislike wasting my life on negative emotions and upset, or even wasteful sloth and laziness. I hate it. It makes me angry if I catch myself slipping up and indulging in emotions that do not serve me. I hate the very thought that I might waste what precious life I have totally out of control and awash in negativity...whether the emotions are anger, fear, disappointment, guilt...whatever. I have linked up in my mind that my life is too valuable to spend wallowing.

And you can learn like I did that it's not what happens…it's what you do.

We ALL feel negative emotions, and they do serve a purpose. They can serve to make us stronger as the saying goes. Negative emotions are part of being human. But the key is what you do with them—what you do when you experience them—if and how you re-channel that energy.

After exposing myself to Tony's program countless times over the years, I have literally conditioned myself to almost instantly snap out of negative emotions before they even have a chance to take hold. I still sometimes use a physical movement to snap myself out of it, but my response has now become 90% automatic and the physical motion is now part of an automatic response. I say 90% and not 100% because I am by no means perfect. I am not a machine and I fall down just like the next person. But I will gladly take the 90%!

The automated response that I have conditioned myself with is to say to myself in one form or another (sometimes out loud when in private): "NO! I do not want to feel this way! I will NOT feel this way! Feeling this way does not help me. This does NOT serve me. This hurts me, it is a waste of my life, and I absolutely REFUSE. I want to feel happy and positive and in control! I FEEL happy and positive and in control! And I FEEL happy and positive and in control because I have the power to feel this way and I deserve it! I am worthy of these positive empowering emotions. I am worthy of a happy life!"

Sometimes just saying "No!" to myself is all it takes now. It happened this morning just as I was getting ready to sit down and write these very sentences. What set me off is not important. What is important is that I controlled how I feel. I did it. And I did it consciously in control.

It feels great to have that kind of power!

Sometimes the replacement of my negative state with the emotions that I want to feel is seared into my brain by subtly clenching my fist in a certain way in a self-directed show of power. And any time I clench my fists like that I instantly put myself back into those powerful states.

I literally KILL negative emotions of doubt, fear, anger, whatever, as soon as they pop up. In my mind I usually see myself flinging them off and away from me.

Sounds silly maybe.

BUT IT WORKS.

If you can learn this one skill of controlling your emotional state, you will have taken a MAJOR step towards getting what you want in life. And you don't even have to be that good at it!

What is required is that you condition yourself to change your own emotional state and behaviors at will, anytime that you want to.

Folks, everyone who succeeds goes through their own self-conditioning process! Even multi-gazillionaires. **If you are feeling frustration about your life, you should feel AWESOME that you are at that point where you are wrestling with this! Embrace it. Be excited about you being here, at this point of frustration! The really good news is that eventually you will change how your head works and it will become more automatic and easier.**

By the way, I have been mildly chastised for stating a negative in my rant...that "I DON'T want to feel this way." But for me it works...I think it works because for me stating the negative reinforces the powerful human need to run away from pain. I follow it up with the positive thing that I want to run towards.

And listen, don't be naïve about this. Sometimes negative emotions can be so wrapped up with something in your life that it is extremely difficult to control these emotions while that something, that stimulus, still affects you.

Most of the time this has to do with other people in your life.

Well, part of winning is being tough. And sometimes you just have to cut people loose from your life and stop associating with them. Sometimes, as long as the stimulus remains, you will continue to experience the same negative emotional response. Sometimes that response is too difficult to overcome, usually because that stimulus (person) is opposed to your core values, and usually because it is justified and rational.

Sometimes you brain is telling you to get out.

Sometimes you just have to remove the stimulus from your life.

Figure out what works for you and if you need help call Tony.

Conditioning Yourself to Focus

But, as awesome as what Tony teaches is, and it is truly revolutionary, there is something that he doesn't thoroughly address: And that is HOW do you actually continuously get yourself to focus on conditioning yourself like this? <u>How</u> does one actually make oneself aware on a continuous basis of the need to change to begin with, and then <u>stay</u> focused so you can actually consciously think about what's important and what to do next?

How do you develop the ability and willingness, even eagerness, to focus your brain so that you can think about what you're supposed to think about?

"If I could just <u>focus</u>, If I could just keep this stuff top of mind, I could do this….I know I could!" I hear you say.

HOW do I begin to focus?

HOW do I maintain my focus?

What is the secret key to being able to continuously focus on what I need to do?

What powerful force allows a person to even THINK about snapping themselves out of a stupid mental state at will?

What is the key to being able to focus to the extent necessary to mentally consolidate all of my daily actions into a single integrated planned purpose that will compel me to achieve my goals, my dreams, and my visions?

I am going to provide the answer. Read on.

See, when we first start out in earnestly, massively changing our lives, we all tend to feel this way. Initially we get all hyped up and excited, and many of us stay excited for a long, long time. But most of us let the feeling wane because we don't know how to hang on to it through all of life's daily goings-on.

We seem to be able to stay motivated for certain periods of time, but end up losing the drive because "life gets in the way."

The following is from a very astute student of Mike Dillard and Robert Hirsch at their Elevation Group on one of the conference calls that I participated in last year (we'll call him Bernie):

"This is definitely one of the most comprehensive information products I've ever come across about business building – thumbs up for your great work... The importance of the correct mindset is so totally clear to me, and yet I find it hard to fully assume it – I think the "how" part is the missing link in all the "self-help" issues of changing mindsets and making real, lasting change. Could you please share your best practices about assuming the

right mindset and elaborate on HOW you actually make things shift in the thought patterns? How you begin to live the thoughts the truthfulness of which you totally realize at a surface level. Thanks!" - Bernie

Robert's live response to him involved belief, as in believing in yourself. As Robert couched it: "Seeing to believe v. believing to see" and "what you think becomes what you say becomes what the universe manifests for you: Thought equals word equals manifestation."

In essence, Robert directed him to control his thoughts and the rest will follow...all of which I agree with. But he did not go far enough in his answer.

The key is what I have been telling you all along.

The key is your values, and more fundamentally, your outlook on the world and living.

What matters here are your operable day-to-day values and goals that guide your daily actions, but most importantly your core values from which all other day-to-day values and goals are derived, and even more fundamentally, the foundation and origination of your core values.

Ultimately, what you discover, and learn, and adopt as your mental outlook and your worldview are what matter.

And you discover these once you finally go through an

objective earth-shaking, root-cause extrospection process of seeing what the universe and your very nature IS, and a similar process of objective introspection of deciding what it is you should DO.

Let me explain what I mean graphically using what is commonly called Cognitive Behavior Therapy (CBT).

I debated about use a graphic for this, but oftentimes a picture is worth a thousand words. So please bear with me because it may help some of you who may be struggling with all of this.

CBT is what many of the mindset gurus out there teach as to how the change conditioning process works. CBT is a type of psychotherapeutic treatment that helps patients understand the thoughts and feelings that influence behaviors. The underlying concept behind CBT is that our thoughts and feelings and even physiology play a fundamental role in our behavior. The theory states that once faulty thinking, lousy emotions, and poor physiology lead to poor behavior, all of these factors can be reinforcing in a vicious down-spiraling self-feeding loop.

For example, let's say that someone gradually becomes conditioned to be a no-account slouch because of adopting a cavalier attitude towards taking care of themselves, and being lazy and non-productive, and time is spent just carelessly plopping themselves on the sofa in front of the boob tube.

Well, repeatedly plopping onto the couch in front of the tube can instantly reinforce the poor thought patterns and negative emotions that turned them into a slouch to begin with.

This is because that person is linking the powerful force of physiology with a lousy state of mind.

So when challenging external events happen to this person, and they plop themselves down on the sofa to think about what to do or get away from the events, that simple physiological action will likely reinforce their no-account slouch mentality.

Such a person could very well wind up adopting the mental outlook and worldview, at least subconsciously, that he world is brutal, people take advantage of you, that making changes in their life is too hard and that it's better to just lay low, not stick their neck out and take risks, work as little as possible while mooching as much as possible, and drink beer for a living.

Let's then say that they hear news that someone is making a ton of money in their business and are living a life of happiness and fulfillment, their response may be to despise them, attribute their gains and happiness as pure luck and even unjust, and they may likely retreat into their slouch mentality as a safe-haven, secure in their perception that it's best not to risk anything because it's all either just blind luck or a game rigged against them, neither of which they stand much of a chance against—it's easier and safer to do their minimum wage job and watch TV and be a no-account slouch than to risk failure.

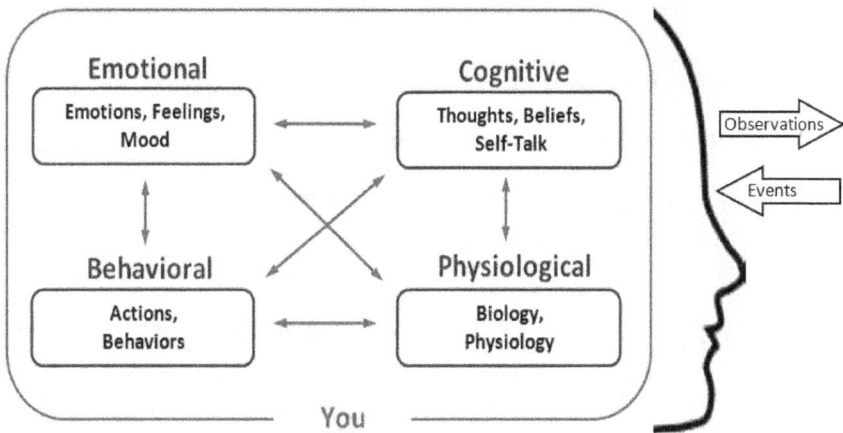

The gist of the beneficial therapy part is that if you can control what you think, you can control your emotions, your physiology and thus your behavior.

If you think in a positive manner the entire loop becomes self-enhancing and positively reinforcing instead of self-defeating and negatively reinforcing. One online source stated that "The goal is to alter cognitive processes (how and what you think) by increasing self-awareness, better self-understanding and improving self-control by developing more appropriate cognitive and behavioral skills."

Sounds simple. Sounds reasonable, right?

It almost sounds easy.

But there is something crucial missing that to me stands out like a sore thumb.

Can you see it?

Increasing self-awareness, better self-understanding and improving self-control based on what? What standard is someone supposed to use to know if one is on the right track?

Is the increased awareness, self-understanding, and self-control of a slouch's slouchiness as valid as the same process in an aspiring entrepreneur or committed mother?

Clearly not.

One is decidedly anti-life and one is pro-life in the most naked and fundamental sense of the terms.

Again, the key is your values!

The criticality of values is so obvious to me that there seems to be an intentional evasion in most of these types of "therapies" in not addressing the issue of values being the source of behavior, and exactly what are correct values that underlie successful therapy.

What I mean is that the CBT process implies that there is such a thing as proper human behaviors, and that there are proper values that drive those behaviors, but this fundamental piece of the puzzle is totally neglected.

What does one change their thinking to? What IS proper behavior and why?

Can one use one's emotions as a guide for behavior? ...People feel strong emotions all the time and in fact use them as a guide for their behavior, often destructive behavior...But why?

How does one know the therapy is successful?

What is the standard for proper thinking and behavior?

What are we comparing to?

And who decides?

Why do the proponents of CBT not come right out and just state what the proper values are?

I will tell you why: Because of the pervasive attitude in this progressive era that values are relative. My values may not be your values, but mine are just as valid as yours.... THAT mentality.

Listen to me here: Our values, whether we are aware of them consciously or not, underlie everything you and I do.

What matters are the core values that we choose for our life.

...The core values that you and I <u>choose</u>.

...The <u>core</u> values that you and I choose.

Let me formulate this:

1. **What you and I choose to do** (our behavior, our outward actions) **depends upon how and what we think.**

2. **How and what you and I think about** (including derivative values goals and actions) **depends upon our ability to focus.**

3. **Both our ability to focus AND what we think about depends entirely on what we choose as our core values.**

4. **And our core values are determined by how you and I choose to view our own nature, the nature of the world, and our place in it** (what I call worldview and mental outlook).

We'll talk about core values in a minute...

So with this in mind, here is my picture version of what I think CBT should be. Granted it probably won't pass muster with professional shrinks, but I think it is useful. Maybe I should call this Josephied cognitive behavioral therapy or JCBT. Or simply values-based-behavioral-therapy (VBT).

Hah! This'll turn the shrinks out there purple!

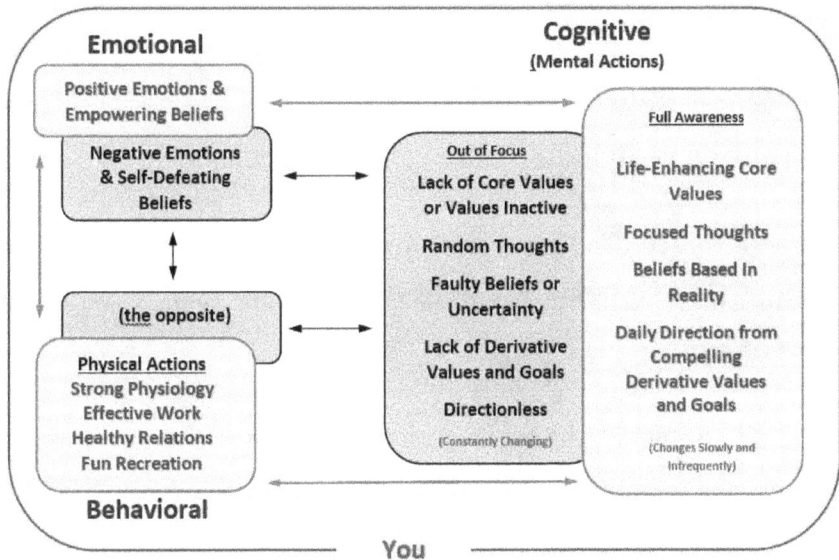

Emotional

Positive Emotions & Empowering Beliefs

Negative Emotions & Self-Defeating Beliefs

(the opposite)

Physical Actions
Strong Physiology
Effective Work
Healthy Relations
Fun Recreation

Behavioral

Cognitive
(Mental Actions)

Full Awareness

Out of Focus
Lack of Core Values or Values Inactive

Random Thoughts

Faulty Beliefs or Uncertainty

Lack of Derivative Values and Goals

Directionless

(Constantly Changing)

Life-Enhancing Core Values

Focused Thoughts

Beliefs Based In Reality

Daily Direction from Compelling Derivative Values and Goals

(Changes Slowly and Infrequently)

You

If we are reasonably healthy, early on in life we formulate some version of a mental outlook, a view of ourselves, a view of the world and our place in it. In effect, this allows us to answer the questions we all have to answer continuously throughout our day: "What does this mean?" and "What should I do?"

At some point, we develop some manner of core values... what's really important to us, at first usually subconsciously-held values about our life and health and other people, but later hopefully, we consciously choose core values that define who we are and what we need to maintain, extend and enjoy our lives. What we need to be happy.

We create beliefs, feelings of certainty, based on these core values, and go on to create derivative values and goals that are subordinate to our core values. These derivative values and goals are what we can use a guides for our daily actions; they cannot help but guide us because they are derived from our conviction about our core values and beliefs.

We experience emotions and physiological states that form a constantly reinforcing feedback loop to our values, whether good or bad.

If we are healthy and aware we proceed in the green loop in my VBT diagram and we experience a relatively happy life.

Again, this is if we are healthy and have proper raising and good role models, etc.

If we are not healthy and unfocused, we experience the grey loop to some degree.

For most of us, this is not a conscious, deliberate process. For most of us this process is totally subconscious, haphazard, and disjointed and results in a terribly toxic mush of conflicting values and beliefs and poor behavior and performance in life.

We get stuck in the grey loop, which, hopefully, because it is purely by chance, does not become too negative, anti-life, and happiness-defeating.

Without rational pro-life guidance, living in the grey loop we just kind of pick up stuff as we go through life and well, that's just who we end up being. Not our fault, right?

Living in the grey loop often results in what I call a "culturally relative mentality": "I am who I am. What makes me who I am is what it is. Live with it. My values are just as good as yours because you are no different than me in your random collection of core values and beliefs. Who are you to say what's right for me?"

Such a random undirected process can be terribly self-defeating and anti-life.

However, with proper outlook, a developed ability to focus and think, and a set of life-promoting beliefs, values and goals to guide us, we will likely experience very positive, empowering emotions as the manifestation of our life in the green loop.

We act in a manner that is proper for a rational person. We maintain our bodies and practice sound physiology (e.g. we stay fit, eat well, and don't ingest health destroying substances), we are productive in our work, we have healthy relationships, and recreate in a healthy life-restoring manner (e.g. a sunny day at the beach instead of spending the day at a bar getting into a drunken stupor).

And the more that we do all the things that are proper to a healthy human existence in the green loop—the more correct world view perspective, continuous focusing, thinking, believing, goal setting, feeling of positive emotions, and proper behavior that we practice and immerse ourselves in, the better we get at it and the more conditioned we are, and the more automatic and effortless it becomes in an upward-spiraling conditioning process that drives us on to be better and better.

My point here is that ultimately it IS a matter of choice. It's a matter of choice from a very young age.

It's just that relatively few people have very good guidance when they are young!

As Leonard Peikoff says, we don't have to behave rationally. We can elect NOT to focus and choose to drift, in which case our reinforcing positive conditioning stops until we regain focus (we all have bad days where we fall off the horse), or worse, we elect to forego focusing, relinquish our life-enhancing world view and digress into a downward-spiraling negative reinforcement conditioning that may be difficult to recover from.

Look, my intent is not to turn you into some half-baked self-shrink here. I want you to understand the process that we go through. And that we go through it either subconsciously and unfocused, with likely terrible results because of the state of today's society, or we can choose to go through it consciously and focused and based in reality, with tremendously powerful and positive life-promoting results.

Once you make the decision to go green, the real kicker is that it takes as much energy and effort to run the positive cycle as it does the negative.

So why run the negative?

Focus, Thinking, and Choice.

Let's focus more on focus and its relation to values because it is critical to your ability to be productive and happy because it underlies and is the precursor to even entering the green loop.

From Peikoff (**bold** emphasis added):

> *"Focus" names a quality of **purposeful alertness** in a man's mental state. "Focus" is the state of a goal-directed mind committed to attaining full awareness of reality.*

> *"Full awareness" does not mean omniscience. It means the awareness attainable by a man who seeks to understand some object by using to the full the evidence, the past knowledge, and the cognitive skills available to him at the time.*

> *To "focus" one's mind means to raise one's degree of awareness. In essence, it consists of shaking off mental lethargy and deciding to use one's intelligence.*

> ***Focus is not the same as thinking**; it need not involve problem solving or the drawing of new conclusions. **Focus is the readiness to think and as such the precondition of thinking.***

The act of focusing consists of the basic mental effort required to reach and/or maintain full awareness:

> *The exertion of such effort…never becomes automatic. The*

choice involved must be made anew in every situation and in regard to every subject a person deals with. The decision to focus on one occasion does not determine other occasions; in the next moment or issue, one's mind has the capacity to go out of focus, to relax its concentration, drop purpose, and lapse into a state of blur and drift. It retains this capacity no matter how long a person has practiced the policy of seeking full awareness. Focus never turns into a mental "reflex"; it must be willed continuously. This is inherent in calling it a matter of choice. The essence of a volitional consciousness is the fact that its operation always demands the same fundamental effort of initiation and then of maintenance across time.

As long as a man is awake (and his brain intact), he is conscious of reality in the sensory-perceptual form; this much is given to him by nature. But consciousness in the form required by his survival is not given to man; it must be achieved by a process of choice. Man's power of volition is the power to seek such awareness of reality or to dispense with it. His choice is to be conscious (in the human sense) or not.

The choice to focus is man's primary choice. *Primary here means: presupposed by all other choices and itself irreducible. Until a man is in focus, his mental machinery is unable to function in the human sense—to think, judge, or evaluate. The choice to (focus) is thus the root choice, on which all other choices depend.*

Nor can a primary choice be explained by anything more fundamental. By its nature, it is a first cause...not an effect produced by antecedent factors. It is not a product of parents or teachers, anatomy or conditioning, hereditary or environment. Nor can one explain the choice to focus by reference to a person's own mental contents, such as ideas. ...In short, it is invalid to ask: why did a man choose to focus? There is no such "why." There is only the fact that a man chose the effort of consciousness, or he chose non-effort and unconsciousness. In this regard, every man at every waking moment is a prime mover.

This is not to deny that a person's ideas can have effects, positive or negative, on his mental state. **If an individual... chooses to be in focus, he will gradually gain knowledge, confidence, and a sense of intellectual control. This will make it easier for him to be in focus.** *After he practices the policy for a time, focusing will come to seem natural* [a manner of conditioning], *his thought processes will gain in speed and efficiency, he will enjoy using his mind, and he will experience little temptation to drop the mental reins. On the other hand, if he...remains out of focus, he will increasingly feel blind, uncertain, and anxious. This will make the choice to focus harder. After a while he will experience focus as an unnatural strain, his thought processes will become relatively tortured and unproductive, and he will be tempted more than ever to escape into a state of passive drift.*

Both of these patterns, however, are self-made. Human volition produced each condition, and the opposite choices remain possible. ...The most conscientious man, though he may have every inclination to use his mind, retains the power not to think further. The most anti-effort mentality, despite all his fears and disinclinations, retains the power to renounce drift in favor of purpose.

Once one is focused, once he is aware, one has to choose what to do with his awareness. Thinking consists of choosing what goal, intellectual or existential, to direct his mental and physical efforts to, and of choosing the means of attaining the goal.

Physical action "out there" in the material world is the result of mental action—of thinking, of the content of one's mind...of ideas, of concepts, of factual knowledge, and of beliefs. In other words, the immediate cause of a man's actions in the pursuit of his goals, are his thoughts. And man chooses his thoughts.

"Man chooses the causes that shape his actions!"

And what guides one's actions—what one chooses to do with his awareness—the causes that shape one's actions— whether one recognizes it consciously or not, are one's values.

Certainly one must first simply focus and become aware, but subsequent willed focusing leads to adopting a world view and values as one looks out on the world and wonders about one's place in it. Thereafter however, derivative values and goals and successive successful action results from previous choices of outlook and values.

Always, what you and I do in action, whether mental action or physical action, requires choice in regard to VALUES:

Man's actions do reflect the content of his mind, but they do not flow from specific content automatically or effortlessly. On the contrary, action involves continued choice, even after one has formed a full range of mental content, including a comprehensive set of value-judgments.

In regard to action, a man's choice—one he must make in every issue—is: <u>to act in accordance with one's values or not</u>. To act in accordance with one's values...requires that one know what one is doing and why. He has to assume the discipline of <u>purpose</u> and of a long-range course, selecting a goal and then pursuing it across time in the face of obstacles and/or distractions. It requires that one heed the hierarchy, the relative importance, of his values. This means: that he keeps in mind the fact that some of his values are primary or immediately urgent, while others are subordinate or less imperative-and he determines the time and effort to be spent on a given pursuit accordingly. Thus he integrates the activity of the moment into the full context of his other goals, weighing alternative courses and selecting appropriately. And it requires that one choose the means to his ends conscientiously... All this is involved in acting in accordance with one's values. Yet all this is precisely what is not automatic.

A man can accept a set of values, yet betray them in action. He can actively evade the steps their achievement would require, or he can simply default on the responsibility involved. He can choose to live and act out of focus, to drop the discipline of purpose, ignore hierarchy, brush aside knowledge and surrender to the spur-of-the-moment. This kind of man lets himself drift through the day or life pushed by random factors, such as sudden urges, unadmitted fears, or importunate social pressures."

Core Values

So, focus leads to world view and values, which guides our thoughts and physical actions...including the continued ability and willingness to remain in focus—to remain aware —so that successful action may continue.

True, you don't have to live in accordance with your values.

A man can accept a set of values, yet betray them in action.

But, for you to even stand a chance at making your life work, you must have proper values.

And although many contemporary philosophers will virulently object to this assertion, there is such a thing as the right set of core values that is required by our nature in order for us to succeed at being fulfilled and happy.

If your core values are an integrated composite that is congruent with your nature as a rational being that is fully capable of thriving, of being happy, of being fulfilled in a knowable benign universe, then your focus on what is important, being conditioned by your core values into your very being, can become virtually automatic, and your chances of actually being happy and successful with your chosen purpose are damned good.

If they are not, then it does not, and your chances of life-

long happiness and success are slim to none.

It is no more complicated than this.

So my response to student Bernie above would have been:

"How do you stay focused Bernie?"

"By defining your core values."

"If your core values, and by core values I mean burning-in-your-soul values, are those which are indeed supportive of the supreme value of your very life—the maintenance, extension, and enjoyment of your life—then you will constantly, naturally, consciously and subconsciously think about and take action to achieve these values through the pursuit of all subordinate, derivative values and goals that you create for yourself."

"You will automatically begin taking all the necessary steps, all of the actions that are unique to you in order for you to attain all of the subordinate goals that are the stepping stones to achieving these core values in you."

"You won't have to consciously concern yourself with HOW you "assume the right mindset and actually make things shift in the thought patterns."

"You won't be able to help it."

Focusing on the proper things will come naturally and it will be easier to condition yourself to keep the negatives out of your life and stay on track with your chosen purpose.

When you are at this place of solid, congruent, non-conflicting, empowering core values, you will know what to do with your life, you will know what goals to set, and you will relentlessly take action until you achieve your goals.

You will automatically discover your purpose, what you are to produce with your life and how you will contribute. You will literally be driven to do what you have to do to achieve your goals.

You won't be able to help it.

Once you are in this place you will actually be profoundly unhappy if you do <u>not</u> pursue your goals in the fulfillment of your purpose.

I can attest to this personally.

But as I have said, what you choose as your core values depends upon how you choose to view your own nature, the nature of the world, and your place in it.

Proper Core Values

I tell you that it is literal blasphemy to the progressives and multi-culturists and modern-day statists that I would dare postulate that there are certain core values that a man must possess in order for him to be happy and fulfilled as a free and independent individual human being.

My answer to them is tough cookies.

A man does have a unique specific nature that requires of him to hold certain core values in order to be happy and thrive.

So here we go....

I subscribe to the definition of values as "that which we act to gain or keep."

We shop for a cell phone because we act to gain or keep a cell phone. We eat nutritious food and exercise because we act to gain or keep our health. We buy books like this one because we act to gain or keep a life of abundance and happiness. (Of course ultimately, at root, we do all these things to gain or keep an emotion that we value, but you get the point).

Proper values are that which we act to gain or keep for rational (i.e. life-promoting) reasons. What I mean by this is that proper values are those which promote the maintenance, extension, and enjoyment of your life.

Period.

Values that do not foster the maintenance, extension, and enjoyment of your life are faulty values.

The physiological high that one receives from meth is not a proper value....it is a value that is totally opposed to the maintenance, extension, and enjoyment of one's life. As in Yaron Brook's speech, the values of a Bernie Madoff are not proper values—clearly they did not promote the maintenance, extension, and enjoyment of Bernie Madoff's life.

Virtues are the means to values—proper virtues are the rational actions, the rational actions, which we take to achieve proper values. Virtues are the gaining and keeping actions. Proper virtues are the rational actions that we take to "gain or keep" the things that maintain, extend, and fulfill our lives.

Spending one's last nickel to buy cocaine to get high is not a virtue that is proper to a human being—human being properly understood to mean rational animal—the animal that has the ability to choose to take actions necessary for the maintenance, extension, and enjoyment of his life.

Now get this....

Happiness is the state of consciousness, the emotion, resulting from the achievement of values—meaning, the achievement of rational values.

Happiness is achieved, is experienced, in the rational actions to gain or keep.

Does this make sense?

Do you see the link between focus, world view/mental outlook, values, mental and physical action, and happiness?

If you choose to see yourself and your fellow man as helpless beings in an unknowable malevolent universe that is unfair and out to get you, and that happiness for anyone is a total crap shoot—a completely random and causeless event, then the faulty core values that you will act to gain or keep, if you have any, are likely to be a disjointed disintegrated mishmash of smallish range-of-the-moment irrational wishes and whim-ridden desires, self-hatred, victimhood, and parasitism.

In this grey mode, your life is then essentially consumed with fear, anxiety, envy, with getting even with the universe for dealing you a bad hand, and taking what you can from your fellow man before he takes from you.

It's a dog-eat-dog world for you.

This is certainly not a happy life.

But, if you choose to see yourself and your fellow man as powerful causal agents that are fully capable of living an immensely happy and fulfilled life by your own hand in a knowable, benevolent universe in harmony with your fellow man, then the core values that you will act to gain or keep will necessarily be:

- **Rationality**: You will act to gain and keep reason as your only tool of surviving and thriving in a physical world, which although very beautiful is also very dangerous; you will live your life in adherence to reality by acknowledging and respecting the laws of existence: of causality (this causes that) and identity (a thing is what it is and nothing else); you refuse to evade or try to cheat what's real in human nature and you will treat others accordingly (honesty and justice); you will know how to gain and use the full power of your mind, how to choose your associates, how to organize and live with others in society. You will know how to safeguard your life and limb against every danger that can be foreseen;

- **Purpose:** You will act to find, keep and pursue your reason for being, your cause, your central purpose, as the guiding focus of your life's energies and productive efforts; and

- **Self-esteem:** You will act to gain and keep self-confidence in the convictions that your life is the good; that you have the right to be the beneficiary of your actions; that you are right and good and moral as your own highest value; and that you deserve the best, can achieve the best, and are able and worthy of a happy life; that you have the power to remain in focus to create the life that you want for yourself; you will live in accordance with your values (integrity).

Once identified consciously, these necessary core values become the foundation of all of your subsequent derivative values and goals, and a conscious/subconscious guide to all of your actions.

All other conscious values that we create for ourselves and possess are derived from, are subordinate to, and supportive of these core psychological-philosophical values. Your choice of goals for material wealth, finances, health, love, friendships, business relationships, etc., will all be directly determined by and colored by these core values.

You won't be able to help it.

- You won't lie, steal, or cheat, or tolerate anyone who does. You will pursue honesty in everything you do.

- You will objectively identify how to overcome obstacles and you will persevere until you succeed.

- You won't be without a moral compass or rudderless. You will not be able to NOT have a purpose that drives you to succeed at what is important to you.

- You won't associate with a man or woman, either as a partner or as a friend, who are morally-debased slouches, slackers, misfits, or parasites. You will seek out only those who are worthy of your own ethics. You will love and cherish those who hold the same core values be they lover, relative, friend, associate, or business partner.

I don't subscribe to the idea that people are basically good, or basically bad. You come into this world tabula rasa—a blank slate.

Good people are good or bad because of the core values they hold, that they choose. Or because of the lack of such core values or the holding of a collection of conflicting core values.

And it is because of the types of resultant subordinate, derivative values and goals that they create and seek in all aspects of their lives, that thus necessarily controls how they deal with other men in society.

Although most of us have some set of core values, if even

subconsciously acquired as a mishmash of ideas we have been exposed to during our lives, few of us ever consciously sit down, analyze, and choose proper values to guide us. However, once you have consciously gone through this process, it becomes so ingrained in your psyche that you won't need to go through the process except infrequently in the event that you fall off the wagon and lose your way (being good doesn't mean you're perfect and you don't have to live in accordance with your values).

Once these become ingrained and subconsciously, automatically operative in your psyche, the identification and pursuit of all subordinate derivative values and goals that you design for yourself follow automatically.

As an example, in the realm of business, Mike Dillard of The Elevation Group® put out a video describing 15 core values for entrepreneurs to adopt and adhere to in the conduct of their businesses. Just tremendously sound wisdom is embodied in the 15 values. But, the only reason Mike can even identify these is because he is a "good" man. Meaning, he somewhere in his life has adopted the core values necessary as a precondition to even consciously identifying the 15.

Do you think a parasitic welfare-bound couch potato could ever conceive of the 15?

Are the values of a no-account couch potato slouch equivalent to those of a Mike Dillard?

Do you understand there is such a thing as values proper to the life of a man and those that are not?

And that the value-relativity of the multiculturalists is a bunch of damned nonsense?

Can you ever subscribe to the idea that the values of a whim-ridden witch doctor, or the socialist radical mealy-mouth are as valid as yours as a liberty seeking, life-loving, self-responsible causal agent?

Journey v. Destination

But even possessing the right set of core values doesn't by any stretch mean that you are guaranteed to achieve your goals.

There are no guarantees in the real world.

What it means is that you will have meaningful, compelling subordinate goals in your life, and you will feel the most fulfilled and happiest in your pursuit of these subordinate goals, because their pursuit is the very means, the very process, of maintaining, extending, and enjoying your life.

You see, we humans as rational beings pursue values in order to live; we pursue our values, our goals, in order to be fulfilled and happy in the maintenance, extension and enjoyment of our lives.

This is crucial to understand.

We pursue values in order to Live.

We do not live in order to pursue values.

This is a fine distinction but it's an important one.

We don't mundanely maintain and extend our lives on a tread mill in drudgery so we can then go out and pursue stuff, and in acquiring stuff become happy. We do not exist so that we can go out and blindly, meaninglessly create and acquire stuff, desperately seeking to constantly get rich for the very sake of getting rich, which we think in turn will somehow, someday make us happy.

We are not wired this way.

Many disturbed souls try this path but it is certainly not a road to happiness by any means.

No, we pursue values, initially rudimentary physical values and only later more psychological values because of the emotional state of well-being such values create for us.

We pursue food and clothing, safety and security initially because we want to survive...we want to achieve the very fundamental state of being ALIVE, and once those basic living needs are satisfied, we move up ole' Maslow's hierarchy and purse love, purpose fulfillment and self-actualization so we can live even better and happier in quality, variety, and style.

It's the difference between saying "I am alive, therefore I must eat and find shelter so I can continue living" versus "I am alive, therefore I must eat and find shelter so I can live in ease and peace and health and happiness."

It's the difference between saying "I am alive, therefore I must do/get something to make me happy" versus "I am alive, therefore I choose to be happy in the pursuit of something I love."

We pursue values in order to LIVE.

We do not live in order to pursue values.

It's the journey and not the destination. We become happy in the pursuit of our happiness, in the pursuit of the purpose that we have rationally chosen for ourselves, as concretized in the goals we set.

It is in the process of pursuing our values, our most heart-felt yearned-for values, in the living of our daily lives, that we find happiness, that we can BE happy.

It's the journey, not the destination.

Robert Hersch, co-founder of The Elevation Group®, describes the conceptual process of "Be-Do-Have."

He speaks of being the mental state that you value first, as the primary, because it is the mental state, the emotions derived from such a state that we are after. And only then, driven by that mental state, go and Do your purpose, your reason for being, and then as a consequence, Have or obtain the material or other manifestations of your purpose, of your actions, of your pursuit.

The BE part are the world view and compelling values that you hold dear; it is the philosophical core values and all of your ostensible subordinate values that are the cause of your DO. The reason for your DO.

The DO part is all of the actions (virtues) that you take in pursuit of your subordinate values and goals.

It is the congruence and integration of these two, the BE and the DO that cause you to be fulfilled and happy in your pursuit, and, in the form of wealth, HAVE their material manifestation.

Their congruence and integration is the driving force for the purpose that you have created (fueled by your values).

It is the expending of your mental energy, and the taking of the actions that you have devised, to manifest that purpose 'out there' that makes you feel fulfilled and happy and wealthy.

While actually achieving the goal at the end of a pursuit does give us temporal momentary satisfaction and joy, it only has meaning to the extent that we earned it. That we created it. That we pursued it. That we journeyed to get it.

Do you see?

Does anyone doubt that earning something that you want through hard work makes it more valuable to you than if it is merely given to you without any effort? You will likely pursue a self-help program more vigorously if you make the monetary investment yourself than if a friend gives it to you off-hand and unrequested.

Achieving a goal only has meaning to the extent that we pursued it, that we made it happen through a process that we designed to make it happen, and that we worked that process. That we earnestly acted—labored—to gain or keep.

And that action, that laboring to gain or keep values and goals in all areas of our lives, is called.....drum roll please....

Being Productive.

You and I are meant to be productive!

Since we are imaginative intelligent beings, there will always be another goal to achieve, another destination for you and me to reach, and in the process of pursuit of the next goal, in our productivity, lies our continued happiness and fulfillment.

By the very nature of our being, if we are healthy, it indeed becomes a Relentless Pursuit.

Does this make sense to you?

THIS is why I focus on you being productive at something you love as being the source of your happiness!

Being productive, and all that this implies -- defining your world view and mental outlook, core values and beliefs; maintaining your focus, defining your central pupose, dreams, visions and aspirations, and goals; i.e. developing on empowering abundance mindset -- is what makes a person happy!

Let me add here some important additional perspective on the pursuit of happiness with respect to the trials and tribulations of life with another excerpt from philosophy professor, writer, and speaker Leonard Peikoff:

> *"The moral man's concept of the good...is his fundamental standard of practicality. Such a man experiences no conflict between what he thinks he ought to pursue (self-preservation) and what he wants to pursue. He defines all of his goals, fundamental and derivative alike, by reference to reality. As a result, he pursues only objectives that are attainable by man, consistent with one another, and possible to him; he uses his mind to discover the means necessary to reach these objectives; and he applies his knowledge in action, refusing to evade what he knows, to drift purposelessly, or to sacrifice his interests. To pursue rational goals by rational means is the only way there is to deal successfully with reality and attain one's goals.*
>
> *This does not mean that success is guaranteed to a conscientious (person). No philosophy can alter the metaphysically given fact that man is not omniscient or omnipotent. Regardless of a person's virtue, he may fail in an undertaking (or even die) through simple error.*

Besides error of knowledge, one must also reckon with the factor of other men. If one's goals in an undertaking involves the cooperation of others, his own virtue (or knowledge) cannot ensure success. The ideas, the motivation, the skills, the character traits that he needs in others depend on their choices, not his.

Then there is the factor of accident. It is possible, through no fault of anyone, for men to encounter illnesses, earthquakes, plane crashes, and the like, which can cut an individual down prematurely or cause him to fail in some endeavor. Proper human action can reduce the power of accident enormously. But this does not mean that accident can be eliminated.

There is no cosmic overseer, who takes note of virtue and crowns it with success. Nor is this an injustice on reality's part; it is an expression of causality and identity—of causality in that certain causes lead to certain effects, whether one desires them or not; of identity, in that man, like every other existent, is limited.

Virtue is not automatically rewarded but this does not change the fact that it is rewarded. Virtue minimizes the risks inherent in life and maximizes the chance of success. Morality teaches one how to gain and use the full power of one's mind, how to choose one's associates, how to organize society so that the best among men rise to the top. It teaches one how to safeguard life and limb in principle and therefore against every danger that can be foreseen. This does not give men omnipotence; what it gives them is the means of preventing, mitigating, or counteracting innumerable evils that would otherwise be intractable."

And regardless of the pitfalls in life, happiness is not only achievable by all of us; it is the expected natural state of a normal human life:

> *"Pleasure is moral. Happiness, therefore, is not only possible, but more: it is the normal condition of man. Ayn Rand calls this conclusion the "Benevolent Universe" premise. "Benevolence" in this context does not mean that the universe cares about man or wishes to help him. The universe has no desires; it simply is. Man must care about and adapt to it, not the other way around. If he does adapt to it, however, then the universe is "benevolent" in another sense: it is "auspicious to human life." If a man does recognize and adhere to reality, then he can achieve his values in reality; he can and, others things being equal, he will. For the moral man, failures, though possible, are the exception to the rule. The rule is success. The state of consciousness to be fought for and expected is happiness.*

> *...a man on the benevolent universe premise is well acquainted with pain. His insignia, however, is his refusal to take pain seriously, his refusal to give it metaphysical significance. To him pleasure is a revelation of reality—the reality where life is possible. But pain is merely a stimulus to corrective action, and to the question such action presupposes. The question is not "What's the use?" but "What can I do?"*

The rejection of this premise, its antithesis, is the "malevolent universe" premise:

"This premise states that man cannot achieve his values; that successes, though possible, are an exception; that the rule of human life is failure and misery."

And more from Peikoff regarding the underlying core values that must precede happiness:

"Even though rationality does not lead to success automatically, it is more than a necessary condition of happiness. It is also a sufficient condition. Virtue does ensure happiness in a certain sense... Consider a moral man who has not yet reached professional or romantic fulfillment...at the point where (perhaps) he is alone in the world, barred from his work, destitute. In existential terms, such a man has not "achieved his values"; he is beset by problems and difficulties. Nevertheless...he is confident, at peace with himself, serene; he is a happy person even when living through an unhappy period. He does experience deprivation, frustration, pain; but, in Ayn Rand's memorable phrase, it is pain that "goes only down to a certain point," beneath which are the crucial attributes such a man has built into his soul: reason, purpose, self-esteem.

A man of this kind has "achieved his values"—not his existential values, but the philosophical values that are their precondition. He has achieved not success, but the ability to succeed, the right relationship to reality. The emotional leitmotif of such a person is a unique and enduring form of pleasure: the pleasure that derives from the sheer fact of a man's being alive—if he is a man who feels able to live. We may describe this emotion as "metaphysical pleasure," in contrast to the more specific pleasures of work, friendship, and the rest. Metaphysical pleasure does not erase the pains incident to daily life, but, by providing a positively toned context for them, it does blunt them; in the same manner, it intensifies one's daily pleasures. The immoral man, by contrast, suffers metaphysical pain, i.e., the enduring anxiety, conflict, and self-doubt inherent in being an adversary of reality. This kind of pain intensifies the man's every daily defeat, while turning pleasure for him into a superficiality that "goes only down to a certain point".

Metaphysical pleasure depends only on one's own choices and actions. Virtue, therefore, does ensure happiness—not the full happiness of having achieved one's values in reality, but the premonitory radiance of knowing that such achievement is possible."

Philosophical values, core values, are the precondition to metaphysical pleasure, to premonitory radiance, to knowing that achievement is possible, and thus to being happy in the pursuit and achievement of derivative values and goals.

Are you getting this?

There are no guarantees.

None.

Zip. Zilch. Nada.

You can do all of the right things, live the most virtuous life and be the epitome of the good, and still not achieve your existential values—your material, financial, romantic goals, etc. In fact you can get hit by a truck just when you are on the very verge of success.

But you can still be happy because it's the journey, not the destination that matters.

Achieving goals has meaning to you, or brings you joy, only because of the trials and tribulations and effort and successes and even failures of the journey you took to get there.

It's how you make the journey, create the journey, and not the specific goals that you seek to achieve.

It's who you become in the making of the journey....

As I said at the start of this chapter...you want to be happy? Want to get wealthy?

Get right with the universe.

Happily contribute.

Happily produce.

Make it the journey and not the destination.

CHAPTER SIX

ACT! How to Change Your Life...

Accept responsibility for your plight and act to change it

Ok, it's been a wild ride of philosophy and psychology, ethics, politics, and economics up to this point.

And lots of hand-waving soap-box street wisdom....

But I offered you a step-by-step plan of action in the first part of this book, so step-by-step here is what you need to do from here.

WARNING!

Some of us are more analytical than others. And to the extent we are analytical, we are susceptible to paralysis of analysis. Meaning, we can get too bogged down in 'systems' and 'programs" and endless planning and thinking-about-it, and end up never actually doing anything. The early industrialists did NOT do this process that I am showing you below—at least not consciously. They lived in a different era when people were far more independent, emotionally rugged, and freedom-minded than today. Those that saw what they wanted just DID. They just acted. Today something like a plan is needed by many of us just to recondition us back from the ways of improper upbringing, and to get us on a solid path. Some of you reading my book could probably write this book and need little guidance. However, some of you are like babes in the woods and prior to reading my book pretty much ignorant of most of what I have talked about. Most others are somewhere in between. So take what you need from what I lay out below and chuck the rest. **Do not force yourself into anyone's canned process!** Including mine. This is a GUIDE. Adapt it to your personality. Take only what you think will work for you and run with it!

The key to making these steps below work for you is to just start. I never forgot the words of a former boss of mine when admonishing a passel of us young second lieutenants to do our best at a particularly challenging time for our unit that would result either in success or utter disaster. Colonel Steve Purdy said: "I want people who are not afraid to fail!"

That's it.

DO NOT be afraid of screwing up! There IS no screwing up if you are progressing and growing. And if you are taking steps to change your life to take you to a better place, you ARE progressing and growing.

That said, I have broken "how to change your life" into two pieces:

1. Mindset stuff: the tools you need to get and keep your head straight; and

2. Daily action stuff: the tools that allow you to act out there in the physical world on a daily basis using your newly acquired empowering mindset.

So, without further delay, with everything presented thus far as necessary background fundamentals and context, here is "what to do" to re-program yourself to be productive for wealth and for being happy in its pursuit:

Part 1: Life Altering Foundations: Headsetting 101

Adopt an Empowering Mindset. These first several steps are the "Be" in the "Be-Do-Have" context. They are more macro-level, internal, introspective, broad-view, all-encompassing philosophic principles behind a proper mindset. This is the 40,000-foot overview perspective on things that you need to have in your mental makeup. Without these steps as the foundation, your daily actions end up being unguided, random and without long-term purpose, and you won't make any significant progress.

A proper mindset is the precondition for YOU even being able to being happy and creating wealth, forget actually doing it.

I already have a proper mindset and I use it to create for myself.

I cannot create for you.

You have to create for yourself.

Therefore, YOU need to have a proper mindset.

Regarding all the steps below of creating and maintaining an empowering mindset: this is your referral checklist of sorts. You should refer back to it once or twice a week because you cannot keep it all front of mind and most likely little of it is already part of your mental makeup.

These steps are part of conditioning, and part of conditioning is practicing fundamentals, and a HUGE part of practicing mental fundamentals is making them top-of-mind by re-associating to them on a regular basis in order for them to become second-nature and part of your character and personality.

After this first set of 13 steps of macro-level head-setting, the micro-level nuts and bolts action stuff that I describe in the next sub-section Changing Your Daily Reality you should do daily.

This first set you do twice a week or whenever you feel the need to get back to basics, to fundamentals—because like any sport, what determines your success or failure is how well you have consistently practiced the fundamentals.

Here are the 13 steps what I see as critical components of an empowering mindset:

1. **Choose <u>Now</u> to Focus**. Focus your mind. BE aware. Do not drift. BE present. Get your head in the game. Get focused and make yourself re-focus as often as it takes to get what you want. **Everyone who has ever fought for and achieved anything worthwhile in life has had to fight to remain in focus!** As shown above, your primary choice in life is whether or not you focus your

mind—whether or not you choose purposeful awareness. So DO it. Do it continuously. While you are engaged with me in reading this text you are likely fully focused. Yet you will fall off the wagon and lose focus. You're human. And when you fall off the wagon, get back on the wagon and re-focus. Do it again. And again. And again, and again, and again, and again until you get good at and it becomes second nature and then you won't have to work at it as hard. If you want to live a good life in happiness and abundance, there is no other way. Go here to learn again about focus.

2. **Adopt a Benevolent Universe Premise as your World View.** Understand, accept, and internalize that you must change your world-view—your mental outlook— how you look at the world; you must be vigilant and fight to retain this world view. STOP seeing the world from the point of view of malevolency and scarcity and lack! See the world as an incredibly beautiful place of abundance and possibility! The universe is not out to get you. The universe doesn't care! A normal healthy man sees himself in harmony with what naturally exists out there and understands that evil is man-made and it is an aberration in the benevolent universe! Evil flat-ass does not belong here! It is the exception and is easily defeated and inconsequential in the great scheme of Life! A healthy rational man sees only possibility and abundance and beauty and health and

happiness as the natural order of things. Go here to learn again about the Benevolent Universe.

3. **Adopt the Rational Core Values of Reason, Purpose, and Self-esteem**. Understand, accept, and internalize that you <u>must</u> change your core values. And once you adopt the proper core values I laid out for you above, hang on to them for all you are worth. You must fully associate to these values in order to make them an integral part of your being and, along with your benevolent universe worldview, make them the guiding beacons of the thoughts and actions of your daily life. Go here.

You know, we generally do hold these as of some value to us just as the result of being raised in a generally liberty-oriented society...especially reason. We mostly intuitively hold the process or the faculty of reason as value and use it in our daily activities and in relatively mundane matters such as walking the dog or grocery shopping. It is reason and logic that tell us not to walk our dog out in front of a moving car and that tells us to look for a lower price rather than higher for two products of comparable quality.

But our failure rate is high when it comes to using reason in matters of more critical import, such as in how to treat people as they rationally deserve to be treated or in evaluating and voting for freedom-supporting public policy and laws. Generally, in this sense we have to learn how to reason from first sound principles such as the law of identity (A is A; a thing is what it is and not what it is not) or the law of causality (If I do X and Y, then Z is the result).

Even as adults we must continue to learn.

Living in reason requires vigilance.

And among the most important things we must learn are the importance of holding reason as your guiding light, your purpose in life as your compass, as your reason for being, and personal pride of living with integrity as your badge of truly being and feeling like a man.

4. **Commit to Being Productive.** Understand and internalize the vital role that productiveness plays in your happiness. Productiveness as a cardinal virtue. Being productive, and all that goes into 'being productive'—defining your world view, mental outlook, maintaining focus, core values, and beliefs; defining your central purpose, goals, dreams, visions and aspirations; i.e. developing an empowering MINDSET—is what makes a person happy! Relish in your uniqueness. Your uniqueness is a priceless gift. Your uniqueness is the wellspring of your happiness; it is a critical key to YOU being productive. You are

uniquely you. Produce in all areas of your life in a way that is uniquely you and apologize to no one for it! It's the journey not the destination. It's YOUR journey.

Read Secret of Wealth #1.

5.   **Be Pro-Capitalist.** A critical part of mindset is highly valuing and pursuing the type of society that promotes your ability to become, remain, and grow in wealth and abundance. Understand and internalize that capitalism—the fully functioning DOL in individual freedom—is the society that best increases yours and everyone's chances of becoming wealthy, and that promoting the institutions of capitalism is the only way to ensure a life of abundance for you and your progeny. It is not necessary that you make yourself an economist....what IS necessary is that you understand 1) a few basic concepts as the foundation of the common sense and the intuition about things that you may already naturally have, and 2) that what we have is NOT Capitalism. Let the economists worry about the rest. Read Secrets of Wealth #11 and #12.

Now if you have the time and inclination to delve deeper into economic theory and its philosophical roots, I recommend that you read the following sources:

	Pro-Life, Pro-Capitalist (The good guys)	Anti-Life, Socialist-Statist (The bad guys)
Philosophy:	Ayn Rand, Leonard Peikoff	Immanuel Kant, Bertrand Russel
Political Economy:	Ludwig von Mises, George Reisman	John Maynard Keynes, Paul Krugman

"The value of pro-capitalist economics to businessmen is not to teach you how to make money, but of getting you to thoroughly understand that it is to the self-interest of everyone why businessmen and capitalists should be free to make money."

Look, Capitalism IS freedom—IS individual liberty in action. Either you are for individual rights or you are not; there is no middle ground for real men. A little bit of socialism is NOT ok. A little bit of socialism is a cop-out. It's an excuse and a crutch for the weak of mind and spirit. It's a crutch for those who don't know how to deal with reality.

Don't be a gutless pansy! Choose freedom and individual liberty or choose servitude.

And on the subject of the dismal subject of economics... Do you think that economics is only for university professors and useless credit-hour fodder for getting a college degree? Not so. EVERYTHING you do is based on "economic" calculation...from what you choose to spend your money on to how much sleep you get every night, and even the partner you date.

Virtually everything you do involves economic calculation in the sense of win-loss, cost-benefit, or good-bad analysis.

There is probably no more science so critical to your personal welfare than sound economics.

6.   **Adopt an Abundance Mentality.** Alas, repetition is the mother of skill: We have an unlimited need and desire for wealth. The earth is a humongous ball of resources. There are innumerable people and vast sums of money ready to help you. There is no limit to what we can create! So why on earth live in a scarcity mindset!? Go ye forth and produce and prosper and enjoy the abundance of what has been created and will be created in the future by all of us. In a free world the pie keeps growing! Remind yourself of what the Chinese entrepreneur and billionaire Wang Jing said with respect to his participation in the Nicaragua Canal Project: "If you can deliver, you will find all the world's money at your disposal."

7.   **Be Grateful.** Be grateful for all the Good that exists in your life in the present, be it in form of relationships, wealth, health, or whatever good that you enjoy. What presupposes the ability to experience gratefulness?

Humility before the universe (God if you like). Remember the rational man's take on pain? My word, be grateful for what you have now, in this very moment in time. Right now. This is NOT humility in the sense of subjugation to, or weakness or powerlessness before some higher authority 'out there', but the humility before the awesomeness of the ability and tremendous power of man's ability to create, of YOUR ability to create. Of your ability to reason and recognize and appreciate what man is capable of. Be grateful for what man has created before and what he creates now, and foremost, what YOU have and what YOU are capable of!

8. **Be Proud.** Take pride in being Man. Specifically, be proud in who you are as a man or woman in the full congruence and integrity of the values you hold dear and the virtues you exercise to obtain them. Pride has been defined as moral ambitiousness—always seeking to be Good. "There is no excuse...for a man who resigns himself to the flaws of his character. "Flaws" do not mean errors of knowledge, which involve no evasion; it means breach of morality, which does involve evasion. The moral man may lack a piece of knowledge or reach a mistaken conclusion; but he does not tolerate willful evil, neither in his consciousness nor in his action... He doesn't demand of himself the impossible, but he does demand every

ounce of the possible. He refuses to rest content with a defective soul, shrugging in self-deprecation "That's me." He knows that the "me" was created, and is alterable, by him." -L.P

9. **Be Giving.** Give! Adopt a Giving Mentality...a contribution mentality. Develop the ability and desire to 'give'. Create in yourself the DESIRE to give, the NEED to give. Give without want—as in contribute without want as a primary—as in pursue your passion, your central purpose. Contribution mentality IS abundance mentality. In the same sense that your supply is your demand, your Contribution IS your Abundance. Your reward in terms of emotional high and material wealth is in direct proportion to what you give through the productive genius that resides within you. Do not give as a martyr, but give as a trader.

You have it in your being to give, so GIVE!

AND as your material well-being increases and your wealth grows, consider giving, not out of obligation or guilt but out of mere human compassion, to charities that in fact do help those who are in a bad place to get back on their feet, or take care of the needy and infirm who can no longer take care of themselves and have no one to help them.

A rational man or woman has a well-developed sense

of empathy. Empathize with those who are good, but for whatever reason are struggling and suffering, but yet still try to be better—still try to make their lives better. These, and the truly helpless, should be the target of your generosity.

10. **Live With Integrity and Be Just.** Integrity means living in accordance with one's values, however imperfectly you manage to do so. Justice means judging men's character and conduct objectively and acting accordingly, granting to each man that which he deserves. You have heard the saying "judge not lest ye be judged?" Well, bullshit. You judge and be prepared to be judged. A man calls a spade a spade as he sees it. If you wrong in your estimation of other men, the universe has a way of making you see your error, the severity of which depends upon how harshly you judged in error, whereupon you respectfully nod, admit your mistake, take your lumps, and do better next time. However, that said, the moral man, the rational man, makes few mistakes in this regard; you know almost instinctively if a man is of poor character and values, or good. Know yourself, know your moral worthiness, and do not be afraid to call a spade a spade. Your life and the lives of those you interact with will benefit the more this is practiced.

11. **Happiness, Contentment, and the Brevity of Life.**

a) **Be Happy Now.** Why not? Your opportunity to be happy is NOW. In this moment, right now, while you are reading these words. For crying out loud, THIS is life! Not the next moment and not the one just past. You live in <u>this</u> instant. A major secret to being happy is to be happy now, not five minutes from now. Not a decade from now. Not when you finally achieve "X". Of course things aren't perfect. Everybody has problems. Everybody has pain in their life. And you may even have major challenges going on in your life right now that hinder your happiness. Some of you may be consciously aware of facing your impending death from health issues. But to a rational man, pain "only goes so deep"— even the pain of the prospect of death—and happiness IS the normal expected state of a normal mentally-healthy human being. Truly, for a rational man, that which does not physically kill you can serve to make you stronger. **I suggest that you become a happy warrior for personal fulfillment and happiness.** Through the selfish maintenance, extension and enjoyment of Your life lies the welfare and happiness of not just you, but of anyone you care about. Want an immediate gauge as to how happy you are in the here and now? How easily do you laugh at stuff? Meaning, with respect to pain, setbacks, and upsets...how serious do you take them?

b) **Do Not Be Content.** I don't believe a rational person is ever content. One can be happy but not content. One can be happy with how the journey is going, but not content with the milestones achieved. There is ALWAYS something greater to shoot for whether you're a billionaire CEO of MegaCorp, a cubicle-dweller, a janitor, or a housewife. I believe that a normal healthy person can be happy in the moment in gratitude for what has been accomplished so far, but that he or she also always seeks better. Better in health, better in work and wealth, and better in relationships. In fact, I think that if you are content, something is wrong.

c) **Acknowledge Your Death.** Life is short and you are going to die. Be aware of the brevity of life and your own mortality. Every piece of flesh that has ever lived had its day and then died. There is no escape. Whatever your beliefs regarding an after-life, as far as your time here on this rock? It's limited. It is Finite.

When it's over it's done. Kaput. Finished. No Mas. You will never be here again. You will never have the opportunities to LIVE and be happy and enjoy a life on this planet <u>ever again</u>.

Watch this scene from the Band of Brothers where Lieutenant Speirs is talking to Private Albert Blythe....maybe you'll see what I saw:

<u>Lieutenant Speirs</u>: *"They just don't see how simple it is."*

<u>Private Blythe</u>: *"Simple what is, Sir?"*

<u>Lieutenant Speirs</u>: *"Just do what you have to do."*

<u>Private Blythe</u>: *"Like you did on D-Day, Sir." (regarding rumors that Speirs had killed captured German soldiers)*

<u>Private Blythe</u>: *"Sir when I landed on D-Day I found myself in a ditch all by myself. I fell asleep. I think it was air sickness pills they gave us. When I woke up I didn't really try to find my unit...to fight. I just...just kind of stayed put."*

<u>Lieutenant Speirs</u>: *"What's your name trooper?"*

<u>Blythe</u>: *"I'm Blythe Sir. Albert Blythe."*

<u>Speirs</u>: *"You know why you hid in that ditch Blythe?"*

<u>Blythe</u>: *"I was scared."*

Speirs: *"We're all scared. You hid in that ditch because you think there's still hope. But Blythe, the only hope you have is to accept the fact that you're already dead. And the sooner you accept that, the sooner you'll be able to function as a soldier is supposed to function. Without mercy. Without compassion. Without remorse. All war depends upon it."*

I remember wondering when I first saw that episode why that scene was there. It kind of struck me. Why? There is a powerful message here. Whether this fabricated scene was put in the movie to draw a parallel between acting like a soldier in war and acting like a man in normal civilian life, who knows. But it works for me...maybe it's just my tilt on life that makes me see things.... Do you see my point?

Take all of the military context out and try it this way:

Blythe: *"Sir when 'unfortunate event X" hit me, I found myself in a ditch of life all by myself. I fell asleep. I drifted. I lost focus. I think it was the conditioning they gave us. When I woke up I didn't really try to find my proper place in life...to fight for my life. I just kind of stayed put."*

<u>Speirs</u>: *"You know why you hid in that ditch Blythe?"*

<u>Blythe</u>: *"I was scared."*

<u>Speirs</u>: *"We're all scared. Scared of change, scared of failure, and scared of dying. You hid in that ditch because you think there's hope that good things will just magically come your way, that maybe if you don't try you can't get hurt, and you won't suffer setbacks and disappointments, and that somehow life's going to go on forever, and things will just turn out the way you want. But Blythe, the only hope you have is to accept the fact that you're already dead. And the sooner you accept that, the sooner you'll be able to function as a man is supposed to function. With conviction. With aggressiveness. But with humility, mercy, compassion, gratitude, and without remorse. All good life depends upon it."*

I think the reason that clip has its own dedicated YouTube entry is because most people somehow identify with the hidden message. It gets their attention. It rings true (but judging from the comments below the video, they can't quite put their finger on it.). I think most people identify with Blythe's ambivalence and lack of confidence about life, and it hits home in a way.

I also like this quote:

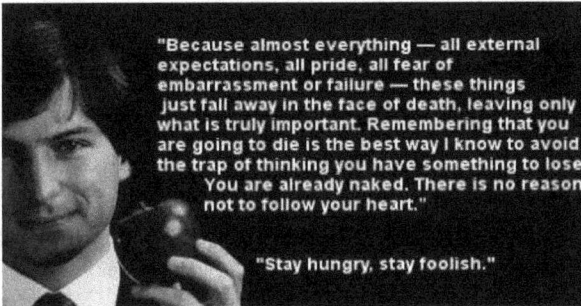

"Because almost everything — all external expectations, all pride, all fear of embarrassment or failure — these things just fall away in the face of death, leaving only what is truly important. Remembering that you are going to die is the best way I know to avoid the trap of thinking you have something to lose. You are already naked. There is no reason not to follow your heart."

"Stay hungry, stay foolish."

You are going to die someday... what are you doing with it?

I retained something my buddy recently passed on to me that goes like this: "Everybody has two lives. The second one starts when you realize you only have one."

Let that sink in for a minute or two.

Have you started your second life yet?

If not what are you waiting for? A heart attack?

Some experience this realization of the brevity of life and quickly approaching death as a mid-life crisis. Maybe others never experience it. I do think most people experience this either as the result of traumatic events or they have lived long enough to gain a certain healthy perspective on the rapid passage of time.

But only a relatively few act on it.

In the words of Thoreau, "Most men lead lives of quiet desperation and go to the grave with the song still in them." Most do go through life living lives of quiet desperation because they don't know how to do otherwise. No one has ever told them that it's ok to get pissed off about it and to do whatever it takes to get their life on a track that they can be happy with. Lives of quiet desperation? What the hell is that? For a mentally healthy man that is totally unacceptable.

d) **Believe!** Belief is nothing more than a feeling of certainty about something. What I am talking about here is not blind faith that, no matter what you do or do not, things will work out for the best. That's for losers. Rather, believe, feel certain, that if you start changing your life today, even in small almost unnoticeable increments, that your life will be in a dramatically different place a year from now, and that all kinds of unseen and unknowable doors of opportunity will open up for you if you just exercise the courage of your convictions and begin and do not quit.

e) **It's The Journey Not the Destination.** ALL of the things above are about the journey. It's all in how you live your life moment to moment. Outlook, values, beliefs, focus, thought, action, results, and most important, the quality of the emotions you feel from moment to moment based on how well you internalize, associate to and practice these things while you live. In the process of living. Through living. For a refresher go here.

12. **Adopt a Personal Code of Conduct** that will set you free—a Freeman's Creed as I call it. In essence, from Ayn Rand: I will never live for the sake of another man, or expect another man to live for mine. In a future edition of this book I will include and Appendix that lays out a proper perspective on life from the point of view of the businessman and from the point of view of the employee and/or non-worker. I am sure you will find this creed very useful in your daily goings-on. In the meanwhile, start with the overarching creed above and see how it can dramatically influence and change how you interact with people on a daily basis.

13. **Find Your Central Purpose.** This is some of the really fun and exciting stuff! You get to decide for yourself what your main passion is! You get to define the

central purpose for your life. Your WHY. You get to soul-search and discover and define what DRIVES you. Yes, yes, you now know that your very life is your primary purpose...the maintenance, extension, and enjoyment of your life. This is very true at the philosophical level. But by doing what? We don't live in order to pursue values; we pursue values in order to LIVE. So maintaining, extending, and enjoying your life by doing WHAT primarily?

Go back and read about productiveness (here and here) being THE cardinal virtue for a healthy person. "A central purpose is the long-range goal that constitutes the primary claimant on a man's time, energy, and resources. ALL of his other goals, no matter how worthwhile, are secondary and must be integrated to his purpose. The others are to be pursued only when such pursuit complements the primary, rather than detracting from it."

And the key to productivity leading to happiness is that you have to be productive at something that is uniquely you. At something that matters to you. At something that burns within YOU.

And again, life ain't about money. A good life is not at all about money. A Good Life is about being productive. It's about discovering what you're supposed to do with your life and then busting your ass in pursuit of THAT. Any money that comes from it is gravy.

We have all heard the saying "do what you love and you'll never work a day in your life." For you to feel fulfilled in the central purpose of your life, you have to produce at something that you absolutely love and cannot imagine your life without. Anything else is a stepping stone. And if you pursue anything else for any great length of time, you are going to become disillusioned.

Happiness is temporary and fleeting if you're doing less than your central purpose.

And by fulfilled, I don't mean kinda-sorta content in a way that you really can't explain...at least until something better comes along—I mean downright utterly joyous and thrilled that you actually get to do THIS for your life!!...whatever THIS is for you.

You see, we all have an innate need to find that central purpose that is unique to us that drives us to get up in the morning, get out there, and slug it out against whatever obstacles come our way in order to realize our dreams.

Fundamentally we all have the one master governing purpose of maintaining, extending and enjoying our lives, but each of us needs to find his central productive purpose that integrates all of our values, dreams, goals and aspirations in the four areas of our life (health, work, relationships and spirituality) as the means, as the vehicle, to maintaining, extending and enjoying our lives.

So part of the producer's mindset that I have been talking about comes from the process of searching for, discovering, and developing within yourself a clear, concise central productive purpose for your life towards which you can devote the vast majority of your time, energy and other resources.

When it comes from within you; once YOU have taken that self-imposed walk in the desert in search of who you are, the resulting unstoppable convictions that you give birth to are the engine that will propel you to do whatever it takes to achieve your purpose, to LIVE your purpose, no matter what trials and tribulations come your way. ...Even though there are no guarantees and even though the world is still a dangerous place.

Ask yourself WHY you are here. Whatever it is you are doing in this moment or the next, get yourself in the habit of asking yourself "Why am I here? Why am I **here** in this particular place doing this particular thing? Does this serve me in the fulfillment of my central purpose?"

If not, then DO not.

We all have about 16 waking hours a day to live our life. Don't waste it on anything that detracts from your central purpose.

And a final word of caution: DO NOT GET IN A HURRY to find or determine your central purpose! If you do not know what it is yet, search for it, yes. Think about it. Ponder it. Take some time off maybe and sit out and gaze alone at the stars some night. Go sit on a beach for a weekend. You have a central purpose. Just give it time to arrive if it hasn't yet. Don't get in a big rush to find out what it is. There are no canned rules here. Just until you DO find it, enjoy life with whatever you are doing currently or change what you are doing so that you are more relaxed, less stressed, and more receptive to your internal messages.

Consciously tell your mind you are looking for it; your mind WILL tell you what it is.

14. **Create your Grand Vision.** I wrote this above regarding vision: We, you and I, as men who desire to live like men, must revive that vision of The Shining City. Not only must we revive it as a vision for the country as a whole...for what the country can represent to all of us and to the world as Reagan states in his Farewell Speech, but **first and foremost we have to create it for**

ourselves, for our own lives, and in that very process create it for the world. We have to create a Grand Vision for ourselves as to what we want our lives to look like five, ten, thirty years into the future....in consonance with that grand vision of the country. In fact, it is the individual Grand Visions that we create for ourselves and our families that will ultimately, in aggregate, manifest themselves in that Shining City.

Can you see this?

Folks, without preconceived ideas of what is or is not possible, you must define for yourself a Grand Vision of what you want your life to be in the future. Include the four key areas of Health, Work, Relationships, and Spirituality.

Begin Your Personal Crusade for Wealth. STRIVE to be wealthy! Understand, embrace, participate, and contribute. You ARE fully capable and deserving if you will allow yourself. Participate in the brotherhood of productive man; **make the betterment of your life your CAUSE**.

You live only once! Why would you not go hell-bent on creating the life of your dreams? And the first step in creating that life of your dreams is to visualize it. To see it clearly in your mind. The ONLY limit is your imagination.

Create!

It's <u>Never</u> Too Late.

15. **Create Your Derivative Values.** There are four main areas of focus in your life: Health, Work, Social (love, friendships, associations), and Spiritual. Whatever your belief in a supreme being, understand that you were created as a certain specific kind of being that requires the integration of health, work, and social values as the manifestation of spirituality. And by spirituality I don't mean going-to-church spirituality. I mean possessing the right harmonious relationship to reality, to the universe—between you, the world around you, and to others. For each of these four main areas of your life, state your values in the form of "I want to gain or keep X because I want to feel Y." YOU MUST DEFINE THE "Y" as clearly as possible. We do things for emotional reasons and if your emotional reason—your emotional payoff—does not mean enough to you...if it isn't <u>burning in your soul</u>, the X simply will not happen.

You may have one or several values for each area, so <u>write them down</u>! Practice this.

Start out with it rough. Fine tune it over time, but DO IT.

16. **Create Your Long Term and Intermediate Goals.** This step works differently for different people. Ideally you

want to define a Really Big Goal (RBG), one that directly aids in manifesting your Grand Vision. For example, if you want to envision a wonderful life on a ranch, you may logically have as your RBG a really big ranch. Some can create the really big long term goal and manage to work toward and achieve it without clearly defining shorter-term intermediate goals that clearly lead to the RBG. Most of us cannot. So I recommend creating at least one RBG that is achievable in 5 to 10 years, and several intermediate goals for each of the four areas of your life (health, work, relationships, spirituality) that span the intervening years and which are clearly necessary stepping stones to the RBG.

And it goes without saying that ALL of these goals have to mean something substantial and serious to you, with your RBGs as the real drivers behind the lesser intermediate goals. Don't fiddle fart around. Don't waste your time unless you are going to create goals that mean something to you... and by that I mean that when you read them back to yourself they shake you up!

And of course it goes without saying that each goal you create has to meet the classic goal-setting criteria of Specific and Simple, Measurable, Attainable, Realistic, and Timely. I am not teaching the details of goal setting here as there are already tons of free resources online if you Google "SMART goal setting".

As a final word on these types of goals, BE FLEXIBLE. Stuff happens and you may not always make your goals when you wanted or in the exact manner that you envisioned. But nevertheless you won't have made any progress without having taken action to get to something.

17. **Remove the Negative Influences in Your Life.** This little message is directed at those who may currently be suffering from tragic events in your life. If you are happy and doing well, please go on to Part 2 below.

But if you are having tough times, please read on.

....

We all have stuff in our life that upsets us, makes us mad or unhappy. We may have felt cheated, or betrayed, or lied to, or in some way that an injustice has been done to us. And these things may all be accurate. Some may not. And of course MOST of this stuff comes from dealing with other people. Divorce, bad blood in business dealings, betrayed friendships, and the list goes on and on and on.

But ALWAYS you have a choice to make. You have to choose whether to hang on to all this crap or to remove yourself from the people and places, things, and events that bring you down, and move on and LIVE YOUR LIFE. I am not saying that you stop being human; each of these kinds of events in our lives requires a certain degree of grieving and sorrow for our loss, and of justified anger and disillusionment at being betrayed, but always it's not what happens, it's what you do. What matters is that you get past the negatives as quickly as possible and get back on the horse.

And having the right mindset about life to begin with makes this process easier, because for the healthy man or woman— the one who is right with the universe—"the pain only goes so deep" and it is relatively easy to regain one's mojo and get on with real living again instead of perpetually wallowing in negative emotions.

Loss is actually the catalyst that drove me to finish this book and pursue my Grand Vision anew with renewed vigor and passion.

I constantly remind myself of the refrain in an old 1978 classic REO Speedwagon song Blazing Your Own Trail Again that goes like this:

Sooner or later you will find a way
To feel like sunshine even on a cloudy day
To feel like morning in the dead of the night
Sooner or later it's gonna be alright.
Now don't be thinking your life's a mess
Rather start thinking in terms of happiness.
And it's gonna happen!
Just decide where you're going.
Get out in the open....
And start blazing your own trail again.
Oh it takes time sometimes to figure out
That there's nothing to worry about
And that there's plenty to be thankful for
Oh it takes time sometimes to know the score
See everybody's got a smile inside
So put it on your face and wear it with pride.
And it's gonna happen!
Just decide where you're going.
Get out in the open....
And start blazing your own trail again!

Listen to it here.

That is a simple but powerful song. You know that it is a healthy person's natural inclination to be this way—to get up from falling down. Maybe onto one elbow at first, and then to one knee, but eventually to stand erect facing the sun saying to yourself "Bring it on dammit." You just get back on the goddamned horse and make your way again. For the healthy man or woman with the right relation to reality, THIS is normal. THIS is how you deal with defeat and upset and obstacles that will certainly come your way and knock you down. And the more conviction you have regarding your path in life before crap hits you—the more conviction you have regarding your Grand Vision—the easier it is for you to recover and get back to blazing your own trail again.

Is it always easy to deal with the crap in life? To get back up?

No, of course not. Sometimes it is extremely difficult. Sometimes the hurt and disappointment goes very deep and it just takes time to deal with it and heal.

But it IS simple.

And for the healthy man or woman, you have no choice. Not if you want to LIVE.

You must have the willingness to deal with pain and see the light at the end of the tunnel. Time heals all wounds it is said. This is certainly true. Doesn't mean you won't have scars but scars in and of themselves cannot hurt you unless you let them.

Go back and re-read Peikoff's take on pain. For the good person, the kind of pain due to spiritual injury only goes down so deep. That pain can only destroy what is truly important to you if you let it.

And as for living into the future, have you not learned this far into your life that 99% of the crap that you worry about NEVER HAPPENS? And if it does happen, it certainly never happens the way that you think it will or be as bad as you think.

It takes as much more energy to focus on the negative as it does on the positive. So choose. And choose again, and again, and again, and again for as often as it takes.

Dump the stuff that does not help you and focus on and pursue the stuff that does. This is an actual SKILL that you have to practice!

Make a commitment NOW to kick the negative crap OUT of your life! Do the proverbial "geographical" and move away and start anew if you have to. Stop associating with those who have hurt you or influence you in unhealthy ways.

This reminds me of a business person I met ten years or so ago during my business management consulting career. This person had a terrible divorce and lost virtually all that he had except what valuables he loaded into a cardboard box, his car, and the clothes on his back. He told me of how he left the city where he had lived in bliss with his ex-wife and family and friends for most of his life and moved to another city far away to start over. He recounted how the extreme mental anguish of the situation literally made him grab what valuables of his he that could, get into his car, and drive away, leaving virtually everything behind. He recalls during the lowest point of his transition that he actually took comfort in the few belongings that he had managed to take with him, and it changed his perspective on life—on what it takes to be happy.

Well, he started a brand new successful and thriving business from nothing. And I still recall him telling me one day while he was recounting the story, with a completely dead-pan expression on his face, gesturing with his hands as if holding a small parcel, saying "You know, there's something to be said for the box."

Some of you can relate to this perspective more than others, but the moral of the story is that there comes a point where the pain and abject stress of dealing with other negative people or situations causes you to mentally break, and all you can think about is getting away and getting free. When your mind screams at you ala Billy Joel, "I am an innocent man" and all that matters to you is your sanity and willingness to start again, no matter what you have to leave behind.

Not money. Not stuff. Just pain-free living, no matter how simple or with how little you have to restart with.

Whatever you do, get FREE. Don't intentionally hurt others in the process. In fact it is possible you may hurt innocent people in this process, but you MUST decide at what point your mental well-being and happiness is worth more than the baggage, and even the innocents who are associated with the baggage. Sometimes it will suck terribly during the break, but you deserve to be happy. Do you not? Find a friend and just get through it. It WILL end if you want it to.

If you are good of heart, you deserve to be happy!

It's not what happens, it's what you do.

Just decide where you're going, get out in the open, and start blazing your own trail again.

This is how you deal with the bullshit in life. You refuse to let it have any power over you.

This is part of the mindset that you take into the breach of the 'big bad world' out there.

Part 2: Changing Your Daily Reality

Anyone can hold the helm when the sea is calm.

Ok. So we have some Mindset tools in place.

The first several steps above are the "Be" in the "Be-Do-Have" context. They are the fuel for the engine that the following steps represent. Those first macro steps above you need to revisit maybe bi-weekly, or whatever works for you.

Now we get into more of the micro-level, external-existential-derivative stuff that will not only guide your daily actions but daily drive you forward and compel you to take those daily actions and remove obstacles and achieve the life that you want. These steps are the practical day to day, hour-by-hour focus and conditioning stuff—the nuts and bolts of your daily work—the footsteps in your journey in support of your Purpose and personal Grand Vision—your place in that Shining City. These last steps represent the DO part of the Be-Do-Have mental process:

1. **Create your Weekly Goals and Plan of Attack.** I find it extremely useful to create and write down what you want accomplish for the week ahead. This is a great exercise for Sundays over your favorite beverage

somewhere in peace and quiet. I do this to identify what I MUST accomplish by the following Saturday evening in each area of health and fitness, work, my social life (including my family, my friends, and a prospective mate), and spirituality. I write it in bullet format with a couple of words for each bullet under each area of what I must get done and anything to remind me of what I need to make it happen. Nothing fancy. Brief and to the point. If it helps you, write down your WHY for each one as well and tie it into your Grand Vision and central purpose. Once you get clear on where you are headed, the WHY becomes ingrained and automatic, and the mere sight of your goal reinforces the WHY without having to write it down. Also, write at the top of your list that these things MUST get done this week in large letters, in whatever terminology works for you.

It is from this general weekly plan of attack that I create my daily plan of action each morning.

2. **Create your Daily Plan of Action.** Create and write down the specific goals and action steps that you MUST accomplish for the next day. Do this the night before. You can do it each morning early while drinking coffee like I do, but you may get an additional boost if your brain has all night to subconsciously cogitate on it. As with your weekly plan, create goals and action

steps for each of the areas of your life that you want to focus on. Write across the top that these things MUST get done TODAY.

Before you start on this list each time, get and stay present. Focus. THIS is your life! There is no more important time you spend with yourself than now.

Now, because we are not robots and do need variety, I recommend adding to your list a separate section called your B List, or fun stuff, or whatever. And on this list you put things that you want to get done that don't directly support your daily goals, but which have to get done sooner or later or are otherwise fun to do. I like to add a few home improvement tasks or fun stuff like tinkering with my motorcycles or fiddling with the sprinkler system. I find this list extremely useful when I have been focusing on intellectual stuff all day, and writing, and editing, and formatting. It is a good way to reward myself for having worked hard and accomplishing my A list or MUST DO goals.

My personal daily plan of action includes the following items:

- Gratitude exercise (I focus on what I am grateful for in my life);

- Wealth affirmations (get online and find one or two that work for you);

- Goals (and action steps if needed): A-List (MUST list) prioritization with time blocks for the areas of health and fitness, work, social life; and

- B List fun or reward items for accomplishing specific daily goals, or for recharging.

- Sometimes if I am under a time-crunch and I want to make progress on all of my goals for the day, I designate certain time periods for each and often set an alarm to remind me to move on to the next.

3. **Take Concrete Action.** Here is where the proverbial rubber meets the road kids. Nothing happens unless you take action, and action is in the moment: it's moment to moment. And the best way to take action is to get up, get your head in the game and JUST START. Sometimes even daily goals are too much to try to get your head around all at once; sometimes you are not quite sure how you're even going to get it done. So just start and the rest will take care of itself. If your head is right: if your vision DRIVES you, you will figure out what to do once you get started; you won't be able to help it. If you are truly not motivated, then you need to re-evaluate your Grand Vision and all of your goals and your WHYs.

I recommend setting aside blocks of time to take action towards specific goals. What works for me is to set aside 2 or 3-hour blocks of time for the more difficult and involved tasks such as writing, and smaller ½-hour or hour blocks for smaller goals. You have to experiment to find what works for you.

Again, just start making progress, even if it is in tiny, tiny steps. Done is better than perfect. Fix it and fine tune it as you go. For example, if your near term goal is to get your credit fixed so you can get closer to your business goals, your very first step might be simply making sure you are current on all of your debt payments: this can be a single goal for a single day for the issue of building personal credit. If you attempt to do all of the things that you might need to do to fix your credit, you are bound to overwhelm yourself and become discouraged.

The journey is happening NOW. Each tiny, tiny step IS the now! BE PRESENT in everything you do and celebrate the wins no matter how small they might be. Being present IS life. Being in the present is where the juice of life IS! Living is in the Present. Taking action is in the present. Living IS taking action in the present!

4. **Observations For Daily Action**

    a. <u>Journey not destination</u>: It's hourly and even moment-to-moment action where lasting change takes place, where goals are achieved and dreams are turned into reality. Footstep by footstep, it's that journey of 1,000 miles that begins with a single step. These are not just nice things to say: you really have no choice except to go minute-by-minute and hour-by-hour. Focus is principally in "placing bricks" in building your Grand Vision. Only occasionally does the house builder look at his plans.... If you find it difficult to take action, redo steps 1 through 17 above.

b. High Personal Standard: Do more than what others would reasonably expect you to do. NEVER QUIT. Practice constantly what you need to get good at, for you will be rewarded in public for what you practice in private.

c. Scale of Vision and Horizon of Focus. Sometimes you don't want to focus on details. Your brain is telling you it's time to step back and see the Grand Vision...to see things along a broader horizon, and to forget for the time being the daily stuff you have to get done. At other times you will feel the need to attack the details of daily activities to get that sense of accomplishment that comes from getting things done...even small things. So in this sense you need to be able to scale your vision from large and broadview to small to large again as needed. Another way to look at this is to change your horizon of focus from what is close-in and requires immediate attention to what lies far in the distant future yet, while crucially important as your vision or Really Big Goal, can only be achieved by dealing with what requires immediate attention.

d. <u>Struggling with Progress</u>: Also known as Bad Day Syndrome: Accept that you are going to have bad days. Everybody has problems. Struggle is a necessary part of life. EVERYBODY falls down....and the bigger your goals and the farther your reach, the bigger you fall down. That's life. That's just the way it is.

We all have bad days, but putting one foot in front of other is like adding bricks to the Grand Vision. Stumbling higher on up the mountain, you are STILL higher and further toward your goal. If you slide back down by losing focus or giving up.....then yes, restart, but harness the pain of having to recover lost ground as incentive to avoid falling so far in the future; you must not permit that pain to prevent you from getting up again.

The hardest lesson to learn is JUST DON'T QUIT. Slow down, take a knee when stuff gets unbearable. Cry some boohoos if you have to. BUT DO NOT GIVE UP. DO NOT QUIT. Recall Will Smith being willing to die on a treadmill? How important are your dreams to you? Again, if you don't quit, a year from now you will be on a whole different planet and all manner of unforeseen doors will open up to you because of the fraction-of-degree changes that you continuous make beginning now, especially when you are down and in a funk.

I realize that I keep repeating this, but it's crucially important to understand: recall what Peikoff said about pain...for the moral man it can only go down so deep and you WILL rebound. If you are right with the universe, you will come back.

e. When it comes, <u>Embrace Alone-ness and Loneliness</u>: My best thoughts and work have come from periods of frustration and self-doubt, at times when I was struggling and I had no one to turn to—at times when I felt most alone. If you are hell-bent on doing something Big for your life...something truly substantial, you will inevitably find yourself depriving yourself of social interaction at some point or other, sometimes for days or weeks on end.

But you won't even notice it while you are working. Oftentimes you notice it when you take a mental break from your enterprise and can sit back and contemplate the effort it has been taking to get to where you want.

But again, if your head is straight and your Mindset, Central Purpose, Grand Vision, and goals are aligned and are truly DRIVING your daily actions, all you need to do is recall Peikoff's words regarding productiveness as the cardinal human virtue: *"There is only one purpose that can serve as the integrating standard of a man's life: productive work. Nothing can replace productive work in this function...neither social relationships or recreational pursuits can replace it. Social relationships are an important value, but only within the appropriate context. First, a man must be committed to the development of his mind and must achieve the right relationship to reality. Then, as a form of reward, he can properly enjoy people (those who also achieve such a relationship and who share his values).* **First he must be pursuing a productive purpose. Only then, as a complement to such pursuit, is he fit for love, parties, or a social life.**

f.   "Stuck": It's funny how when you get stuck, frustrated, doubt yourself, and you push the nuclear button ("I refuse to feel this way dammit!") all of a sudden you find that there is so much to do that you can be engulfed both with a sense of being overwhelmed AND an intense desire to get after it.....do you recall what you learned about the ineradicable shortage of labor? Life has highs and lows, some out there are more blessed, some of us have more challenges, but we are NEVER stuck! Unless you are dead there is always possibility for action.

g.   Enlist the Help of Others: There are ALWAYS people willing to invest in good ideas, in a cause and there are ALWAYS others interested in the same passions as you and eager to help you with your Grand Vision. If you are intent on building a business, the fact that there is competition out there is a great sign that your idea has market viability. All that is left to do is find a way to differentiate yourself in the marketplace and find people to help you do it. In the day of the World Wide Web, there is no excuse not to find whatever resources you need to succeed.

h. <u>Affirmations</u>. Harness the power of your subconscious mind by not only reviewing and reciting your values, Grand Vision, and goals frequently and regularly, but by listening to wealth or success affirmation audio/visuals. Get online and find a few that fits your personality and listen to at least one of these each morning before you get to work, but after associating to your goals.

i. <u>Beware of "The End Is Near"</u>! There are all kinds of prognostications out there about an impending "end of life as we know it" here in the United States. Most of it has to do with the stupendous amount of debt that the governments and central banks of the western world has created and the resulting probable end of the dollar as the world's reserve currency, and all of the tumult and chaos that may likely result. One thing is certain and that is that the current monetary systems cannot be sustained and will eventually have to be replaced. So the only unknowns are 1) when the present monetary system comes to an end, and 2) how bad will it actually be for all of us during the "end" and the creation of a new system. My advice is to read up about it, stay current on events, prepare for it as best you can to protect your family and what wealth you currently have, and then....keep busting your ass with your Central Purpose.

Regardless of such prognostications as to how the current financial crisis will play out, you really have no choice but to plug ahead toward your goals and dreams. If any blowup puts a stop to your plans, you can probably be reasonably certain it won't be a permanent stop...and we will probably be left reasonably free, at least comparable to the semi-free state of today, and enough so to allow us to continue to produce wealth and abundance for ourselves.

5. **Done is Better than Perfect!** This book is good example. I wasted many years waiting for a right opportunity, the right set of circumstances to come along to launch my business! I kept telling myself that when I had enough money I would launch. That once my living situation was just right I could then have enough time to focus. I started and stopped several times because things were not "perfect." STOP! DO NOT DO THIS! Let the courage of your convictions go! **Just get started, let it be imperfect, and Let it rip**!!! You can clean it up as you go. As you begin to act and continue to act, doors will open up, you will

instinctively know what to change and when to change it.

As an example, there are many imperfect speakers and unpolished speakers out there. Have you ever known a speaker who was not perfect, was maybe not too refined in his or her delivery, who was maybe not the best looking of characters, but who was absolutely gripping in his ability to get his message across, regardless of his imperfections? When the message is meaningful and heartfelt and true, NOBODY NOTICES THE MISTAKES! Nobody notices the little stuff...the imperfections in message or of delivery. When what you say or do comes from deep down, from your convictions, what listeners (or clients or customers) are mesmerized by is how you feel about what you are saying! They get the message, but what they are captured by and what makes the message sink in is how YOU feel about it.

"When it's coming from the heart, all the people sing along.

It's the man behind the music. It's the singer not the song.

When there's magic in the music, it's the singer not the song!
"

-Survivor

With respect to so-called "failure," I attest from personal experience that the pain of regret from not sticking with it is a THOUSAND times worse than whatever very temporary pain, discomfort, or inconvenience that you have to go through to start the change process and just keep it going. And if your Grand Vision and goals mean something substantial to you, you won't even consider inconveniences to be of much consequence because there is a reason—a purpose—for them. The pain and suffering along the way is no sacrifice.

And all that fear of failure means is "what if it doesn't work and I wasted all that time when I COULD have been doing X instead." Folks, when your purpose is true. When your central purpose IS who you are, and your Grand Vision grips you, and you know that you cannot be otherwise there is no such thing as fear of failure. You <u>don't</u> fear. All you know is that you have to DO. All you know in your gut is that you have to make it happen and damn the torpedoes.

You have no patience for fear.

To close out this bit, here is another quote that I really like:

"He alone can arouse passion who bears it within himself."

-Adolf Hitler

Please don't let this offend you.

I am a history buff and when I first read that sentence from Mein Kampf, it hit me like a ton of bricks.

Why do I quote such an evil person?

Because there is a tremendous lesson here: As evil as he was and as evil as what he created was, the man could not have accomplished what he did without a maniacal conviction about what he believed was possible and certainty that he could accomplish it.

It is powerfully useful to me because when I read it, I automatically think what can be accomplished out there if only one carries the same degree of intensity and passion for his central purpose of Good.

6.   **Get a Coach!** Coaching is MAJOR LEAGUE important. I will go so far as to say you may be a fool if you do not have a coach. A coach is someone successful who has mentally been where you are, is driven in their own right, and is thus an ideal person for kicking you in the

ass when you need it.

I offer mindset coaching, but if it ain't me that you use, get SOMEBODY!

Folks, the game is ALL mental. Your coach does NOT need to know the details of your enterprise. In fact he or she can be in an entirely different line of work. All they need to know to help you is that you are committed and want desperately to keep your head in the game and making progress—even if you have no clear idea yet on how the heck you are going to make it happen. The mechanics of ANY business, the production, the sales, the accounting, is maybe 5% of the challenge you will face. You can teach a relatively intelligent monkey to do this stuff, right? Its mental presence and voracity of mind that is 95% of the battle and the key to winning at anything. That is why you should plug yourself in to guys like a Mike Dillard, or a Robert Hirsch, or a Fabian Calvo or anyone who motivates you and is a good person.

Do it! YOU HAVE NOTHING TO LOSE! When you're dead, you are so DEAD.

7.   **Be Flexible.** I have mentioned this before above in goal setting. Stuff happens and you may not always make your goals when you wanted or in the exact manner that you envisioned. But nevertheless you

won't have made any progress without having taken action to get to them. And be flexible in doing whatever daily tasks need to get done. Do not compromise on your major goals and the Grand Vision, but only the day-to-day how of making them happen. There are just too many events, interactions and distractions during the course of a day to force yourself into some rigid structure or unrealistic expectations. Stuff happens, so be flexible in working around the stuff in life. You will still get there!

8. **Reward Thyself.** You have to reward yourself for making progress, for doing well towards your goals. And you need to reward yourself for small wins as well as when you achieve big goals. In fact, rewarding yourself for small daily and hourly wins is crucial when you are starting out on your new journey. If you will do this you will find it more rewarding over time as you raise the bar on your wins that are worthy of rewarding yourself for.

For an example in starting out, if you successfully spend a productive 2-hour block of time that you said you were going to devote to a task, then reward yourself with a half hour break of doing something else fun but unrelated to your task. And it is important to set up in advance that when you achieve goal X, then you are going to reward yourself with specific activity

Y. Have list of favorite recreational activities (3-5) and DO them, but LIMIT the reward; if you go overboard, you are destroying the reinforcement process.

The reward must always be commensurate with the magnitude of the win.

Work hard, achieve goals, and only then play as a reward.

I've been a stand-in, a stunt-man
I've taken some falls

Troubles, I've had my share
But one has to learn how to run before walkin'
'Round breathin' that million air

-Jimmy Buffet

9. **Be Alpha.** By this I mean first and foremost take control of who you are and what you are about each and every friggin' morning! Assume control like the captain of your ship and ACT like the captain. The buck stops with you. If your Grand Vision is to become reality, if you're going to reach goals, if things are to get done on a daily basis, YOU are the go-to guy or gal.

There is no one else.

Look at your life as an enterprise and then take control of your enterprise. It is easy to slack off, but you cannot! You be responsible for keeping yourself motivated and alert and focused and effective. Refuse to make excuses! Anyone can hold the helm while the seas are calm! What will distinguish you and your ability to succeed is your ability and willingness the take the bull by the horns, stay focused, continuously take action no matter the setbacks and obstacles, and simply refuse to give up.

The great news is 1) if you've laid the foundations above, and 2) NEVER EVER GIVE UP, never ever quit, then you cannot help but succeed. If your dreams and aspirations <u>burn in your soul</u>, then all of this is almost automatic, and the more you practice, the more you take action in even the tiniest steps, the easier it becomes.

Below are "Alpha Traits" you should develop. These will benefit you immeasurably no matter what you want to do. Add to the list! Post these in your home alongside your goals. PRACTICE them till they become second nature:

- Know What You Want

- Radiate Confidence, Energy, and Positivism

- Maintain a Strong Physical Presence

- Look People In the Eye

- Be Socially Powerful, Outgoing, Humorous and

Fun, Secure

- Speak in Strong Clear Confident Voice

- Keep an Abundance Mentality-Never Come from a Place of Scarcity or Need

- Be Intolerant of Disrespect or Vicious Criticism

- Love Yourself and Be Filled with Self-Esteem and Pride

- Intelligently Articulate Your Opinions

- Live Healthy and Dress with Style

- Uplift and Improve the Lives of Those Around You

10. **Be Good.** All you can do is be Good. All the time. That is the absolute best anyone can do. The absolute best anyone can do is to do life-promoting stuff all day every day, all the time. Don't lie. Don't cheat. Don't steal. And don't tolerate anyone around you who does.

It IS simple!!

Do you want to live well and live happy?

BE good.

DO good.

And the major part of being and doing the Good is being productive at something you love.

11. **Defend Yourself.** Open your mouth in your defense. You may have screwed up in life along the way. We all have. But if you're a good man, then you are also an innocent man. So defend your right to live your life in happiness.

How you do so depends upon the degree to which you find open public discourse important to you. Not all of us are motivated by the power of ideas to change the world and thus willingly jump into the political fray to slug it out against the enemies of individual liberty.

You may be content to fight the battle in the rear by running your own business, by promoting free markets and capitalism in your business interactions, and by voting for pro-capitalist politicians and supporting pro-liberty institutions, campaigns, and legislation. You can do this without hardly raising a confrontational or controversial voice.

Not all of us are cut out to fight on the front lines.

And this is perfectly fine.

Some of us however, cannot resist hunting the bear. Some of us want to hunt down and kill the beast that has been slaying our children's future. We want to stamp out the virus that has been infecting mankind from our earliest history, and western man since at least the early 20th century. For anyone with such a bent, I encourage you to fight on and fight on more aggressively.

And to you warriors out there, I remind you that all politics is local. So you must fight locally. Maybe start at city council or chamber of commerce meetings, and become a regular and well-known voice for freedom and pro-capitalist ideas. You need not be a professional speaker; it may be best if you remain a common man—a common business man—a common free individual.

The path to Freedom is the same for each of us: we must 1) understand things must change and WHY, 2) understand basic economics and the fundamentals of our human nature, 3) consciously state to yourself why you do not agree with bad ideas when presented, 4) voice your opposition in a civil manner and venue, 5) support pro-business, pro-capitalist, free-market leaders, 6) promote pro-business pro-capitalist ideas with employees, and for some of you 7) make the promotion of capitalist pro-individual-liberty ideas your business.

Listen! **There is a terrible dearth of philosophically-sound leadership in the world!**

Fill the void, let it be imperfect, damn the naysayers, just let it rip, and you shall be tremendously rewarded both in wealth and in spirit.

Regardless of your chosen purpose in life, in regards to those who would destroy your liberties, always be vigilant—be HAPPY and earnest about living fully—but be fully vigilant.

Never be silent or inactive.

There will ALWAYS be those who will seek to enslave. As the old drug-war mantra used to go, "just say no."

Epilogue

"Do, or Do Not. There is No Try."

In this work I have said what I have wanted to say for a very, very long time.

I almost wish I could, like most writers, say that writing my book has been difficult, but it has not. Sure, there have been times when I just needed a break from the effort, but for the most part when I have set myself down to write, the words simply began to flow.

I can only attribute this to the fact that I have been cogitating on this stuff since my twenties—since that day in 1982 a young fellow 2nd Lieutenant named Dave Richards handed me a copy of Atlas Shrugged and said to me "Joe, read this. It will change your life."

My book is imperfect and incomplete and there will no doubt be revisions and new editions: There is so much more that I want to say and expand upon, but as it is, it is the core of my message to you.

Until I can revise it, it will just have to be flawed and imperfect because I cannot wait any longer to put it out there and get along on my chosen path to do battle with the statists.

And that is how it should be with everyone in their pursuit of their central purpose in life.

Do it. Fail fast, fix it, and move on.

Early in the book, I said that this book is not about me—that it's actually all about you. But that you could learn more about me at the end of the book, so below is a bit more as to who I am and what I am about.

....

Originally born in Colorado in 1958, and like many families back then, we lived in relative poverty. At least it seems so looking back on it. I grew up in Arizona and Oklahoma, and after high school was blessed with opportunity to attend the U.S. Air Force Academy in 1977. As an adult, I traveled to all over the planet during my 10 years in the Air Force as an eager mountaineer under the guidance and tutelage of a good friend and senior officer. My experiences of seeing how people in other countries lived impacted me deeply and it gnawed at me why there were such huge differences in the well-being and lifestyles of people in other countries compared to the United States.

With this interest and my exposure to Ayn Rand's philosophy of Objectivism, I naturally began to study economics and politics, and it is in this realm that I give great thanks to Professor George Reisman who advanced me a pre-published edition of his then forth-coming book Capitalism, A Treatise on Economics. As a former student of Ludwig Von Mises, his path-breaking ideas on political economy have influenced me profoundly.

Through the Air Force, I earned a master's degree in engineering, and went on to various marketing and business management consulting positions involving large corporations, and most recently, small-medium sized businesses. The focus of my business management consulting career was always the proverbial "People, Product, and Process" lately popularized on the television program The Profit.

I continue my business management focus, only now my focus has shifted principally to the People factor. While I am versed in and enjoy delving into the mechanics of running businesses, I find that I get antsy when buried in the details of production, sales and marketing, accounting, job costing, etc., when there are bigger issues afoot in the arena of ideas, of what people think. How they think. What leads them to do what they do. Why they are here.

I have always held that possessing the right frame of mind is the most important aspect of living, and certainly of working. Get your head straight first and the mechanics are comparably easy.

One of the key lessons that I learned in all that time of advising others—business owners, management team members, and rank and file employees—is that you are meant to be productive, and to be truly happy you have to do what you love. You have to be productive at what you love. You have to provide value in doing what you love. You have to find your central purpose in life—your reason for being—and then pursue it like a man possessed; all else of any real importance will naturally follow, including great relationships and your personal emotional and material well-being.

A corollary lesson of course is that the surest way to find unhappiness is to pursue money. Sure, this is real basic stuff, but it's amazing to me how few people actually heed the wisdom, so it bears repeating.

But I had found through my experiences that promoting "being productive" by itself is catching the human process of living at mid-stream.

I discovered that there is a profound lack of understanding the fundamentals of human nature that precede being productive. Without the right moral compass, a thief and your run-of-the-mill bureaucrat can be considered "productive."

Hence the reason for this book and for all my subsequent efforts related to its topic: the philosophical foundations of proper human values and virtues, of values and behavior that are life-promoting, that underlies real happiness and fulfillment. That underlies productive work as the main claimant on a man or woman's time and energy.

So my focus has shifted to speaking out about Capitalism and its philosophical foundations as the only type of society suited to free men living and working together—if they truly desire to BE happy and fulfilled. And it is in this context that I have revamped my business consulting career to focus on the mindset of business owners and their management teams as those warriors leading troops in the trenches of production so-to-speak, and who are most immediately in the position of influencing others by their words and their actions.

I have also charged myself with the task of reaching and coaching individuals who value freedom...to kick start them on a path of a proper orientation to reality until they can carry on by themselves.

Only by influencing those who are seeking answers to the literal economic insanity that passes for a "free country" can the world be changed. And there are plenty of those who are seeking. There has always been a dearth of values-driven leadership out there and the need has never been greater than it is now.

In this respect I am very encouraged by the entrepreneurial and libertarian spirit of many of our young people. Their refusal to be slaves is highly inspiring to me. To those of you who are cut from this cloth of the yearning to be truly free, I dedicate what I do to you as my heroes.

Is the Shining City possible?

No only yes, but hell yes.

Evil IS powerless if the good are unafraid.

And the evil out there is propagated by paper tigers who cannot win on the battle field of ideas. They win by convincing us that ideas are relative, that ideas and principles based on individual liberty are invalid and useless.

Hear me when I say to you that what they fear in their hearts is the rediscovery by the masses of good men and women that individual liberty IS the means to happiness. That it is the ONLY means to happiness. Not the cultural relativism, self-sacrifice, and literal servitude that they serve up with an ever-expanding web of economic and social policy designed to control us in the name of the common good.

Do not doubt that it is this that they work to prevent.

Thankfully, the human spirit, that yearning to be free and to live a life that matters, still lives in the breasts of most Americans and can easily be awakened, and once awakened, grown to thrive as a self-sustaining engine the compels each of us as individuals to be the best we are capable of being, and then led to become once again the most powerful force in human history.

I look forward to the day when the vast majority of Americans have regained and hold dear the crucial value of individual liberty and actually use those words in the living of their daily lives.

I am always seeking to enlist the energies and intelligence of fellow radicals out there to join my crusade. Those of you who are like me are willing to go down swinging if that is how it must be, but we will be damned if we are to sit another day in silence.

Joseph Miller
Phoenix
August 2015

www.ingramcontent.com/pod-product-compliance
Lightning Source LLC
Chambersburg PA
CBHW050447270326
41927CB00009B/1646